ON

SPECIFIC AMBIGUITY

THROUGH THE IDEA
OF TROPICAL SPACE

OR

THE REASONED
PRACTICE OF
TRANSITIONAL FORMS

ON

SPECIFIC AMBIGUITY

THROUGH THE IDEA
OF TROPICAL SPACE

OR

THE REASONED
PRACTICE OF
TRANSITIONAL FORMS

CAMILO RESTREPO OCHOA
DIRECTOR, AGENdA AGENCIA DE ARQUITECTURA

/.

MEXICO CITY, ARQUINE
2022

Contents

3.
A Tropical Laboratory

Epilogue
Camilo Restrepo Ochoa and Juliana Gallego Martínez

Regionalism in the Expanded Field or: How AGENdA Learned to Stop Worrying about the Critical and Love the Tropical

Mark Lee

From the Universal / Local to the Regional

To situate the work of AGENdA, it is helpful first to review the historical context of Colombian architecture and the international architectural discourse from which this generation of architects emerges. Their unique style engages especially with the dichotomy between the universal and the local in modern architecture; this has long been a subject of debate.

Currently, the universal versus local dichotomy is often framed in terms of critical regionalism, a notion from European critical discourse introduced in the 1980s to reflect on phenomena from the 1950s. This theoretical paradigm posits two opposing cultures whose architectural impulses are intertwined with the political circumstances of colonization and resistance. Yet postcolonial and post-war architectural cultures in the twentieth century already reflected a desire to find national architectural identities by incorporating local and indigenous elements within the International Style of modernism. This impulse represents a notion of regional modernism that is distinct from the colonization versus resistance framework introduced by critical regionalism.

Historically, this regional modernism tried to bridge the difference between the universal and the local with various strategies for integrating the two. From the work of Geoffrey Bawa in Sri Lanka, to Luis Barragán in Mexico, to Laurie Baker in India, regional modernist architecture often starts from the local and gradually approaches the universal. Buildings are often based upon local typologies and construction methods as points of departure, while accommodating the encroachment of modernism. This position is in sharp contrast to the work of Kenzō Tange in Japan or Oscar Niemeyer in Brazil. Their work starts with the precepts of modernism as a predominant baseline and localizes them with regional features.

With the advance of globalism in the twenty-first century, the relation between the universal and the regional has taken a different turn. Rather than seeing the regional as an antidote to the colonization that made everything homogenous, globalism is seen as a form of universality that enables regional specificities to become more visible in their differentiations. Cultural identity is therefore not suppressed by a homogeneity brought on by globalism, but instead exacerbated by the advance of globalism. Regional architecture now takes on another role that is distinct from the resistance associated with critical regionalism. The two poles of the universal and regional are no longer diametrically opposed, but rather can be seen as partners in a dialectic in which each pole actively participates in constructing the other.

Whether constructed as an opposition between the universal and the local, or the global and the regional, the region has been the scale of focus in polemical debates. The regional is often conflated with the local, however: regional emphasis is usually discussed in curiously local terms such as site topography or indigenous building materials. Without an intermediary scale between the expanded universal and the myopic local, the extremity between the universal/

local opposition becomes exaggerated and polarized. This renders invisible the balanced co-existence between the two found in regional modernist work. It also leaves the door open to a clearer vision for regionalism, which is where AGENdA is making a contribution to the ongoing polemic.

The Late Arrival and Early Departure of the Modern

Modernism arrived relatively late to Colombia. Compared to other Latin American countries such as Brazil, Venezuela, or Mexico, where modernism flourished in the early twentieth century, Colombia was late to take up the spare, utilitarian buildings constructed out of expediency and economy, whose architectural culture eventually became dominant around the world.

Lateness, however, can have its benefits. For example, Scandinavia's embrace of Nordic Classicism in the early twentieth century also resulted in a delayed arrival of modernism, so that the modernism that did eventually arrive around midcentury exhibited a more refined and matured form. Scandinavian modernism, relieved of the anxieties and pressures of being role models for the proliferation of early modernism in other parts of Europe, could sidestep the burden of being polemical and could instead develop its own manifestation. The result was a synthesis, an architecture that combines the best of the classical and the modern. Late-arriving modernism hence could become a tool to build bridges to the past rather than one to break away from the past.

In Colombia, similarly, modernism was adopted as the predominant architectural language in the middle of the twentieth century. Propagated through the intellectual presence of European architects Le Corbusier and Josep Lluís Sert, its universalist language was expanded through local influences in the works of Colombian architects such as Rogelio Salmona and Germán Samper. The dichotomy between the universal and the regional was not invoked until the 1980s, when theorists of critical regionalism began to adopt Rogelio Salmona's brick, and the dominant vernacular materials of masonry and concrete, as signs of Colombia's architectural identity. Critical regionalism assigned to this architectural identity the demonstrative role of modeling resistance to the universal by championing regional design languages and construction practices.

Modernism prevailed as a dominant discourse in Colombian architecture until 1990s, when another kind of globalization brought in a new narrative that turned away from critical regionalism and towards architecture as a neoliberal device for societal transformation. After a long period of economic stagnation, a generation of architects from Bogotá and Medellín began to find more abundant opportunities to build. Like architects from many countries who prospered from the globalism of this period, many Colombian architects rushed to embrace new forms of universalism. The early modernist figures of Le Corbusier and Josep Lluís Sert gave way to the generation of Aldo Rossi, Rem Koolhaas, Álvaro Siza, or Eduardo Souto de Moura as diverse models for a globally oriented practice. As a result, the global architecture of the twenty-first century that first emerged in Colombia seems to lack coherence. Brilliance abounds in singular projects, and some shared values can be detected, such as the use of a limited material palette or a predilection for expressed structure. Still, the work seen as a whole eschews a discernible collective identity.

Perhaps this stylistic variation was necessary for a generation that needed to shed the constraints of critical regionalism before a platform for a new identity could emerge. In any case, the globally minded generation of the early twenty-first century opened a pathway for AGENdA, whose participation in the history of lateness-to-modernism meant that they did not have the pressure to be part of a larger international scene or to assert any specifically Colombian characteristics to the rest of the world. Instead, they had the freedom to be inventive. Oscillating between the poles of the universal/local spectrum in each of their projects, they formulated an architecture in a scale they call the Tropical, a terrain between the global and the local. Their founding in 2010 also coincided with a pivotal moment—slightly before the awareness of climate change became ubiquitous—so that their use of international practices of collaboration, art installations, and teaching as part of their architectural practice formed an avant garde aspect of their vision of the Tropical.

From the Regional to the Tropical

Departing from the previous generation without swinging the pendulum back to an earlier critical regionalism, AGENdA developed a hybrid sensibility, combining high-modernist universal convictions with a vernacular sense of scale and form. This is made possible by defining and situating a practice within the notion of Tropical Space—a homogenous existence with an abstract sense of time. It derives its sensibility from the tropical zone, without regard for local and national boundaries, where seasons are indistinguishable from one another. This notion evades the dichotomy between the universal and the local and instead demarcates a geographic scale between the global and the regional which is imagined as the local. Hence for AGENdA, modernism and regionalism no longer need to be at odds (as in critical regionalism), but instead can represent two scales fused into an intermediary, Tropical scale.

The architecture that results from this Tropical conception of space-making is reflected in recurring tropes of design techniques, such as the use of a second skin as a system of climatic control. A preference for lightness, both in temperament and in construction, is often set against the weight and seriousness of archetypal forms. A project such as the **Orchid House**, for instance, occupies a scale between a building and a forest, yet its massive volume is contrasted with a light metal mesh and a delicacy with which the structure encounters the ground. Its pragmatism and thrift resemble Dutch constructions where the circulation is made explicit; the project exudes a lightness both in visual weight and state of mind.

In the **Farallones Community Coffee Wet Mill**, the building comes across as neither stereotomic nor tectonic, but combines a solid and elemental rectangular prism with strategic and precisely detailed excisions. It combines the imposing heaviness of Herzog de Meuron's Ricola Storage building with the airy lightness of Abalos & Herreros' Gordillo Studio, shifting between weights and scales. In a series of houses—**Abanico** and **MAE**, among others—a contrast occurs between the looseness expressed in massing and the rigor expressed in the traditional architectural elements of roofs and columns. Innovative hingings in the plan manifest in the fracture of the façade of one house and in the fractured roofline of another. V-shaped supports, repeating in a staccato rhythm, serve as both the pilotis and the porch.

In circumstances where the site does not appear to offer as much for the generation of the building, AGENdA architecture becomes more self-referential and autonomous. Considering the notion of a building as a collection of individual components, the illusion of an aggregation of towers in **10B Housing** evolved into a vermiform circulation in **5G Housing** reminiscent of John Hejduk's mythical creatures. These vermiform stairs reappear in the **Argos Innovation Center** to unite a series of stacked terrains that form a sedimentary texture on the façade. And in the most Semperian way of distinguishing an architecture of the ground from an architecture of the roof, the **Shrine of our Lord of Tula** expresses the contrast between earth and structure, heaviness and lightness with the most rudimentary, dramatic expansiveness.

Being firmly grounded in the Tropical, AGENdA is able to produce an architecture that appears on the one hand easy and relaxed, and on the other serious and Teutonic. At times, their buildings could do light modernism better than Dutch buildings: they are rugged and worn in. They are deliberate like Belgian buildings but graphic and vibrant like Spanish ones; at the same time they could be sober like English structures and modest like those in Japan. They infuse the scale and form of American architecture with European sensibilities, yet the architectural language it speaks is undoubtedly Latin American. The Tropical approach of AGENdA is able to create an architecture that is truly regional, falling between the universal and local.

From Neoliberalism to a New Global / Vernacular Model

The notion of the Tropical as a new regional scale is in conversation with a globalism defined not as a universalist type of International Style, but rather as a recognition of many worldwide "centers" and scales of production and creativity. This pluralist dialogue has heightened significance in today's historical moment, when the dichotomies between the universal and the local, Colombia and Latin America, and Latin America and the world are being called into question, and at a time when scales are being expanded from the regional to the global, especially in taxonomies such as the Global South.

The architecture affiliated with a neoliberalist globalism could be characterized by tropes such as the adoption of a decipherable diagram in place of a parti, a celebration of an expedient approach to details, or the promotion of disposable materials to reflect a rapid life cycle. The alternative model of the Tropical, as utilized by AGENdA, does not simply resist the recent global and universalizing trends associated with neoliberalism; it is not a return of critical regionalism. Instead, AGENdA's regional approach is closer to that of a Trojan Horse. Starting in the stylistic middle ground of the Tropical, a project can shift its emphasis towards the global or the local during different stages and aspects of its development. The intermediate, regional scale of the Tropical allows the architecture to hone in on precisely indigenous forms as well as to expand towards global, historically modern forms. This Trojan Horse is the wellspring of surprisingly winning design solutions.

The waning of neoliberalist globalism has created a welcoming environment for the intermediate, mutable regionalism that AGENdA offers. In the past few decades, planners have decidedly shifted away from hiring the starchitects who created singular, stand-out buildings, so that design now is focusing more on "everyday architecture" and on the relationship between the "iconic" and the "everyday" within the urban fabric. While some of AGENdA's projects, at first glance, could come across as leaning toward an "iconic" detachment from context, closer scrutiny reviews how much they emerge from their local/textural settings. Often, a vernacular architectural vocabulary is infused with abstract form. Most of their projects emerge from urban and social infrastructures that are woven into the "everyday" fabric of the city, and in turn their architecture responds to this fabric to reinforce it from within. This design strategy has a quieter and deeper effect than what we experience from iconic architecture, or of course from the media.

The evolution of AGENdA, from embracing the global as latecomers to redefining the regional as the Tropical, has presented alternatives both to globalism and to critical regionalism, all without becoming culturally monocentric or hegemonic. By actively engaging Tropical Space as a fresh, environmentally informed iteration of the regional, AGENdA models a new type of architectural practice that is both global and vernacular. The responsiveness and variability inherent in the intermediate, flexible scale gives the architecture of AGENdA the potential for continual innovation.

Foreword

Specific Ambiguity is about ideas and theory, built works and projects that approach architectural space as a cultural practice. Architects whose work is established through practice but who also develop theory, while committing their own work to the ideas of the written text itself, are performing a triple somersault.

This book will strike some experts and readers in the field of pure theory as being too broad-ranging and ambitious, while for others taking the perspective of a purely practice-based, professional approach to architecture and design, it may seem overly theoretical. As a result, we find ourselves halfway between regular publications' two precisely defined extremes: books of texts and books of projects. As such, our work exists within a barren theoretical and critical landscape. It is mainly focused on South America, a region where it is unusual to simultaneously publish and reflect on architectural practice, or to put ideas into practice.

We are aware of the potential danger of tying ideas and perspectives to our own projects and expressing them in writing as a theory. This is particularly true when the desired outcome and objective is to articulate both an analytical theoretical framework and the creation of systems of planning and understanding—essential as a means of creating spaces—to produce an easily accessible theory, and to free the ideas from a purely autobiographical interpretation. We hope others will find a use for our ideas or expand upon these theories and explanations. In our case, the projects do not give rise to theories or positions through a totalitarian approach, nor do the projects set out to be dogmatic or support an absolute theory. Therefore, we firmly believe that the theory set out here resists being unpacked from these projects or being aligned with other similar or familiar practices.

We see this effort as an opportunity to connect practice with reflection and, in this way, construct and occupy a position for exchange and dialogue. The book offers an analysis and observation on the types of territory, city, and working conditions in the tropics. Above all, it presents architecture as a necessary tool in the participation and elaboration of new alternatives for the built environment, social, and cultural challenges of our age, without disregarding the discipline itself.

This text places architecture in a sphere that makes it necessary, without this implying that it should neglect its disciplinary concerns, commitments to history, and ability to construct well-being. From this perspective, architecture is presented as a means of addressing this or that, of being ambiguous without lapsing into ideological formalisms or the extremes of being purely theoretical or exclusively concerned with the practice of architecture. In other words, we are envisaging architecture as a confluence: a gaze onto the contemporary world and onto a historical background with its possible scenarios, explained and analyzed from a purely architectural perspective, without this implying that construction is completely isolated from a more porous world or shut away in a silo that solely relates to, and is guided by, itself. On the contrary, our writing and architecture aims to embrace other areas of knowledge, without ignoring the reverberation of these other disciplines on architectural praxis and theory.

In this text, we shun the idea that our work is a closed system and that by writing this book we can work in isolation from other variables and influences. Here we are interested in positioning ourselves precisely as a type of well-rounded architectural practice in terms of our social, public, and professional role. We can achieve this by limiting the field of theory and action, while using education and pedagogy, reasoned practice, and the transformation of the built space to occupy that space thoroughly.

Above all, this text is a written and committed perspective on what has been published and built. It is a form of understanding and practicing architecture today from a tropical perspective and in tropical locations, revealing hidden narratives that were somehow waiting to be connected.

Many of the projects included here may contradict some of the writings or fail to fit neatly into the various categories. There will also be long-abandoned ideas, which will make some projects less legible within this framework. Nevertheless, they are included here because, at some point, they contributed to the creation of these ideas or acted as bridges that helped us reach them. Many other projects helped us indicate routes that are latent today and that have not yet been post-rationalized or unraveled; routes that indicate ways of working in the near future, and that, today, we see as formal searches and strategies of spatial definition produced through instinct. Similarly, some words, phrases, and ideas are not completely supported by our projects; these are paths we have yet to explore that remain open to interpretations and for use by other architects to open up new options and, above all, employ these ideas in their own way. For some architects it may fill a gap in their academic work or architectural practice.

This book is written for those who enjoy reading and who are patient and receptive enough to read it calmly, comparing the information and ideas with their context. It is aimed at readers, wherever they may be and whatever their particular area of activity, under the umbrella of an open and generous universal architectural narrative.

Readers also need to be open to new ideas and receptive to the complexities of our discipline in a new way, ideally without preconceptions, although without losing sight of some of the narrative conflicts of our time, or of the subjectivity implied by a personal gaze such as our own.

This perspective is not the result of arbitrary ideas or critical whims. On the contrary, it derives from an accumulation of readings, conversations, and reflections about our world and the challenges lying ahead. This is nested within a well-defined position that, of its own accord, has become separated from its own context, which will never be entirely local. As with Alvar Aalto's boat, the decision has been to remain distanced from the immediate surroundings, from the most naïve and clichéd positions, consciously avoiding the deceptive and futile task of searching for a monolithic identity, or pigeon-holing actions in closed and defined compartments.

Specific Ambiguity is an invitation to rekindle a dialogue between different locations on equal terms, through architecture and as an encounter of different architectural cultures, on a shared foundation: the discipline of architecture and its challenges. As a space for many other voices, it is also an invitation to resume, without prejudices or complexes of architecture's universal history, an exchange that does not differentiate in its critical gaze between content and context; hence it is necessary to establish a position that recognizes and presents ideas and projects based on their disciplinary and architectural values, in terms of what they question and propose, and not only on their geographical location. In other words, we aim to avoid the compartmentalization that assigns value to something because it is exotic.

Based on the ideas set out here, *Specific Ambiguity* is primarily a critical gaze opposed to the theory and history that has circulated as the official narrative of this part of the world. Many have been inspired to explain and put into practice this approach, whose exponents claim that architecture on a low budget is somehow heroic, describing it opportunistically as being socially committed. This may hold true for many architects who have indeed enjoyed great success; however, others have self-victimized themselves in an effort to carve out a space in which they receive global acknowledgement and status, directing the gaze of the media and chatrooms in a limited and limiting way; those who opportunistically boil down the narrative to the aforesaid characteristics. Architecture is rarely recognized in this geographical area for its spatial, urban, material, historic qualities, and so on, but solely from a reductionist perspective on its social context and location.

By the same token, architects working in these places have been explained their work with the naivety of a superficial phenomenology: to make space as a reduced poetics of the light's effects on materials. Here we wish to dispel the commonplace notion that architecture in the tropics is interesting for its natural backdrop, and that its only relevance lies in its construction or positioning through its link to modern narratives, critical regionalism, or commitment to society.

The book is divided into three parts. First, it provides a critical survey of tropical architecture in the past and in the present, including its conflicts and instabilities. The argument is built upon a series of perspectives on history and interpretations, territories, and their conditions. Second, it actively defines what we consider to be the essence and content of tropical spatial architecture, with its opportunities and possible components, instruments, and interpretations. And third, a selection of images, plans, and other representative documents create a journey based on experience and practice, detailing the studio's projects over the past twenty years. This final part is accompanied by self-critique to be separate, as far as possible, from the actual authorship of the projects, and suggests considering them with a degree of objectivity accumulated over time.

Although we recommend readers to proceed in a linear fashion for a full understanding, this structure also gives them the option to read the chapters separately as short essays organized into respective subheadings.

Through the built and unbuilt works of architecture described in this book, *Specific Ambiguity* explores projects that have been small-scale research projects and intellectual and material searches for a particular and personal way of creating spaces, in specific and global approaches that are intertwined in a complex and contradictory way based on transitional forms.

In the projects described in these pages, we clearly do not need to work with abundance to make the architecture exist; there is no surplus in terms of the materials chosen, the details, and the proposals. However, the decisions that have shaped these projects have not been taken on the basis of criteria, perceptions, or a mindset of limited budgets. All our projects are made with what was available at the time: creating the best possible architecture with a pragmatic and specific reality.

Although the text has been written from the place where we have developed our work, with all the associated limitations, risks, and opportunities, we have also had a privileged standpoint. We have many connections to foreign education centers, conversations, and friendships with local and foreign architects who have been receptive to our ideas and positions, and who in return have established exchanges and criticism through their own work: to position themselves like us, along that fine line between reflection and praxis, construction and writing.

Finally, we can state that the content belongs more to the world of ideas than of images. And these ideas have come from observing the tangible world, or the physical and material world as an imperfect space that changes and is eroded through use; from those works of architecture that generously offer more than they are asked to give; from an authorship that refuses to look at architecture as the creation of precious objects that close off the possibilities of appropriation and use. The ideas presented here exist in architecture past and present; in architecture that is local and foreign, tropical, northern, and southern: architecture created by all those who, in some way, have worked to build the universal narrative of architecture, regardless of their places of origin or work, without this implying that they no longer belong to them.

In order to verify, doubt, and respond to the ideas and architecture contained in this book, readers should ideally visit the projects. This experience can give a personal and critical perspective on this way of thinking and doing. At a distance from what we have written and done, readers may doubt the objectivity of our gaze. They may then allow us to land on solid ground, arms open, both looking ahead and looking back to the point from which we were able to leap.

Introduction

We will need a new idea of time and society. After the Covid-19 period, we will see time differently, even in productive terms. How do we want to spend our days? What is loneliness and community life, and what does this mean in design terms? What is the connection between public and domestic space when people are prohibited from being outdoors and socializing with others? Undoubtedly, at this juncture we will need to focus in new ways on housing typologies and healthcare.

What does architecture and design need to co-exist with and confront this new reality? What forces have shaped our cities up until today? What will change? Where do we place the role of architecture and design within this new beginning?

Now is the time to free architecture from its self-proclaimed and unnecessary aspiration to make an impact in unconnected areas with too many intentions, yet not enough to ensure high-quality, relevant, and responsible works. This presents an opportunity to refrain from giving inappropriate responses as misunderstood artists, as bogus sociologists making rash judgements on what is good or bad, or as false and self-appointed community leaders. Perhaps we were in the wrong place.

Architecture may play a role that is no more and absolutely no less than a comprehensive, material means to help redefine collective or individual social interactions and relations. Social space is often the term applied to places that give dignity to people's daily lives; it is usually undervalued by politicians and overvalued by dogma, and largely disdainfully ignored by real-estate corporations. Covid-19 may be the first tangible and undeniable event of a new, post-globalized era. The truth is that we have changed, and architecture will have to follow suit or disappear.

Globalization has transformed value into constant waste by reducing things and experiences into exclusively economic terms, turning beauty and potential generosity of globality such as solidarity into a purely transactional exchange. Some politicians and corporations may have distorted the beautiful idea of globality, abetted by the lack of participation by citizens and their absence from political representation. Can we remain politically apathetic while our needs and challenges are being redefined, and continue feeling that we lack representation?

We see an opportunity for a new definition of globalization emerging from the idea of globality. For Bruno Latour in his book *Down to Earth,*[1] "global" means shifting away from a univocal and uniform approach and toward a broader perspective that comprises phenomena and organisms, a variety of living creatures and, therefore, a richer world made up of differences rather than homogeneity.

Globality could mean a new global awareness, a new attitude: globalization as understanding and solidarity; globalization as acceptance and an awareness of globality. Globality is cooperation instead of competition.

We will need a new, shared horizon to redefine globalization; a good starting point would be to establish a fresh ethos that values difference and, with it, a wider range of perspectives to offer a better understanding of reality, a shared global reality. Could this lead to a new ethics of solidarity, over and above moralism and nostalgia? Do we have the right politicians? Are they true leaders? Are we being represented?

We feel it is our duty to think about what kind of world we want to live in after this crisis, and also about the role of architects. Our

1 Bruno Latour, *Down to Earth: Politics in the New Climatic Regime* (Cambridge: Polity, 2019).

idea of space will never be the same again. The implications of Covid-19, apart from on public health and political issues, also affect space. It is highly likely that disciplines related to space may be partially or totally remodeled by a new raft of codes and conditions, offering new areas of understanding to confront a new reality, which make it possible to handle and shape a new global order, not only politically but also—and above all—spatially.

It can be useful to place architecture and design at the heart of social demands that have recently emerged, and to question our relationship with others and with the world, at an individual level and as social agents.

Architecture is a useful material indicator of how we look after others. But it also reveals how the state views us, what we expect of it, and how it offers us a specific type and quality of healthcare and social welfare: infrastructure expressed as architecture or public space.

Domestic space has been redefined as public or private community space. This new condition affects both sides of our doors, and even the door itself. A new materiality may also take shape.

Perhaps we could leverage these times as a unique opportunity to establish an architecture that occupies an ambiguous position of converging and diverging from reality and utopia or, in any case, as a discipline concerned about others, independently of economic growth. **Perhaps architecture could be a confluence for knowledge and the understanding of territory and geography, technology and available resources, the new globality—and the new globalization, as mentioned above—and local needs and expectations.**

Perhaps it is time for nodes instead of extremes, to create new networks between real needs and disciplinary issues, between imagination and opportunities, accepting and committing ourselves to be performative social accelerators of change and amplifiers of new organizations of space as a built, ethical, relevant, and responsible form.

Perhaps we should be connecting top-flight architecture schools with other, less prestigious education centers to exchange experiences and ideas about what it means to be global from different perspectives. Perhaps it is time to re-engage and re-commit to the city, the territory, and rural areas, not through separate disciplines such as landscape design, urban design, and architecture, but by taking a single, strong, and more integrated approach. Perhaps spatial disciplines might be able to create a bypass to build a new globality and globalization, using the qualities of the space itself as a meeting place and a biological barrier when necessary; a space able to exchange experiences and reflections, material developments and their applications. Architecture as research of social interactions and their possible results.

History will tell us if we adopted globality as a new, more generous, and more collaborative globalization. Our cities, territories, and private spaces will soon adapt post-lockdown thoughts and limitations as a new vector for reports and commissions—remodeling architecture's social and spatial order, and we, as architects, will soon react to them in disciplinary terms.

The challenge is clear: as architects and global citizens, how can we make ourselves necessary? As our profession's values evolve, how can we rise to the latest global, social, and environmental challenges while we participate in creating a new set of more collaborative and caring human beings.

One challenge facing architecture in these complex times may be the same one that faces contemporary society as a whole: finding room—and there is plenty—to find ways of making us relevant as people and social agents. And we will undoubtedly need to ask how much in our life is about abundance and how much about actual need.

This overall situation is possibly a call for us to come together to engage, and gauge the extent of, our own personal and collective limits, a suggestion of our times to change. This moment undoubtedly calls on us to relocate architecture and the role of the architect, and forces us to reconsider our position, to relocate our pieces on a new local and global playing board, and to occupy the spaces that we need to occupy, not only with great generosity, but also based on the very foundations of our profession, in order to focus on the challenges whose magnitude remains unknown.

Possibly, or thanks to exceptional situations, this is where we feel genuinely useful and provide a tangible benefit to society. Certainly, history is based on exceptional events and our discipline and experience find and acquire echoes of action. Therefore, we can construct the idea of prioritizing collaboration over competition in order to make us necessary in the here and now. This should not be a one-off situation but something permanent. Each catastrophe or unusual situation that upsets our daily lives alters the course of our expectations by breaking certainties and it is undoubtedly a call to action.

Taking the right steps undoubtedly requires a confluence of actors and factors. First: leadership. Someone needs a broad and broadening vision, perhaps something romantic and utopian such as transforming society, with a sufficiently clear cause in an opaque world influenced by appearances.

We need cohesive teams strongly linked by friendship and understanding, working together with constructive criticism. Above all, we need to fulfil promise with unusual responses, and be equal to the consequences. These perfect storms require actors to be suitably committed and qualified to deal with these consequences, not only in terms of results but also in the creativity required by the emergency in order to create new models of operating, managing, and administering the private and public space.

Unusual situations that are particularly unexpected require ingenuity and boldness; their outcome is a measure of human capacity, political traction, and the performance of a collective. They also measure ideals and factors that bring societies together, assess, and renegotiate their social and environmental pacts. It would be fascinating, and even satisfactory, to be able to state that this was not exceptional but described our regular daily life—surrounded by exceptional leaders, collaborators, committed partners, and fantastic results through simple processes.

Possibly this book's sole aim, by constructing this critical position, is to discover a new opening for architecture to generate conversations on both sides of the Atlantic and along the tropical belt. In this way, it might be capable of turning exterior into interior, not only comfortably, aesthetically, and appropriately, but also responsibly. We are convinced that this represents the challenge of the next century.

1.

A Manifesto of Missing Evidence

How to write a manifesto about producing and understanding the tropical space at a time when images generally take precedence over ideas; results over processes; flashy displays over calm reflection?

Manifestos' inherent lack of evidence offers a wonderful opportunity because their originators are allowed to build them out of a world of ideas.

Paradoxically, **architecture in the tropics is riddled with missing pieces of evidence, with manifesto-less ideas, unwritten conversations, unrecorded experiences.** It is plagued by an obsession over identity that, despite its ubiquity, is persistently and willfully ignored.

This text is born of the contradiction and ambiguity of these two observations:

1) Tropical architecture has been the result of built facts rather than ideas or manifestos.
2) Tropical reflections on architecture remains without a manifesto, and still await a narrative and documentation.

The idea of tropical space, the subject of this text, is understood through architecture's geographical location. When we discuss architecture, we do not want only to refer to the built fact or the set of actions and relations that this implies, but also to tropical architecture as a particular approach to considering and building spaces.

This idea of space is a confluence of conditions and forms anchored in the territory and produced in a unique way, as a long threshold of spatial experiences presented as an intermittent series of interior and exterior layers that, without being committed to structuring an idea and absolute experience of space, also refuse to belong completely to the outside. This intermittent succession of layers is supported by the power of the built fact and based on the forms of transition, its articulations, and linkages.

Geography is a confluence of physical, climatic, and ecological conditions coinciding in a specific location with a culture and its material intentions. We could add that geography is also determined by the actions that culture creates within it, with the aim of making it inhabitable and comprehensible.[1]

This definition of geography forces us to ask ourselves how specific groups or cultures attempt to carve out a place in the world, based on how they shape their architecture, particularly in terms of how they locate themselves based on constructions in relation to their traditions and territory. It is not about completely assuming a position linked to geographical determinism, the one that considers that architecture is, simultaneously, a response to—and an expression of—the climate. We also accept and embrace the possibilities offered by architecture arbitrarily and strategically, such as inserting new vectors on the places where it is established, fostering other ways of relating to what was previously established as behaviors, situations, references.

1 For more information about this idea and its spatial and geographical structures, see Lewis Dartnell, *Origins* (Barcelona: Penguin Random House, 2019).

This relation casts doubt on whether architecture is precisely that conscious and aesthetic endeavor, beyond solving problems related to dwelling, designs relations in space thank to the conscious manipulation of the forms inherent to a culture in a specific place. Or if, on the contrary, architecture is a universal way of considering and shaping space with aesthetic intentions, positioned as a material and energy-filled exchange between situations negotiated by geography and culture over time.

Architecture as something inscribed in a geographical area happens in a particular way in a specific place, but through its operation, it links and relates to other places and other times; it connects history and brings different phenomena, behaviors, needs, and gazes together in the built space. This dichotomy of focusing on the details and on general aspects, on the discipline and on the context, may be precisely what allows architecture to work as both place and thought, to join the dots, to give meaning to the occupation of space and to build a system of order; not only operating according to its own rules and conditions but also receptively, openly, and with sensitivity to its location.

Specific ambiguity accepts and embraces an indeterminate quality and objectivity in architecture. But it avoids the absolutist and objectual quality of iconic and arrogant architecture resulting from reductionist, over-simplifying, and mute certainties that are self-referential and opaque. Instead, architecture emerging from tropical, spatial ideas speaks of an architecture that is ambivalent, complex and contradictory, imprecise, mestizo, multi-referential, but above all necessary and generous.

The tropics have been the unofficial laboratory of science, anthropology, art, and architecture. But the tropical narrative has been limited solely to its festive utopia, a clichéd exoticism, a vacation destination, a socioeconomic caricature, a treasure trove of natural resources observed through the spyglass of extractivist economies.

Enlightenment and modernity chose the tropics as a mythical and almost abstract setting upon which to roll out and develop its spatial model and archetype. A place of scientific, anthropological, artistic, and architectural discoveries, experiments, and adventures. Both the historical representations of the primitive ideal and the enlightened narratives about the origins of architecture itself have been located in a seasonless location to the tropics that appear to exist in permanent spring or summer, where the climate is a non-issue and where the making of space is resolved simply by erecting an archaic and primitive canopy, a simple shelter.

From a distance, outside the centers of Western thinking, even from the perspective of the Enlightenment and Modernity, tropical architecture has been characterized as being composed of specific architectural elements but with ambiguous spaces. In this depiction, its component parts are recognizable and legible, and create an idea of space that constantly escapes a definition of the interior as somewhere closed or absolute. Mainly this obeys its permeability and elastic boundaries rooted in spatial transitions linked together by the visitor's movement, or in the instability of the uses supported by the type, regularly an interior void that is unplanned, flexible, adaptive, and generous.

An architecture made of tropical spatial ideas is an intellectual position that tolerates both doubt and certainty, the model and the interpretation, the system and the exception, the relative and the concrete, simultaneously giving precedence to the ambiguous and the specific over the objectual and the absolute.

Avoiding the Commonplace

To understand and define architecture that contains the tropical spatial idea of specific ambiguity, it is necessary to unlock the ideas of commonplace tropical architecture, those that arbitrary and facile narratives have reduced to naïve regionalism or sentenced to endless modernity.

First, we need to understand—beyond its media conflicts and critical consequences—that the tropics invert everything. We need to confront the fact that appearances can be deceiving: space simulates one thing, but it is actually something else, because it constantly plays with misunderstandings and interpretations. Therefore, the complex and undifferentiated mixture of built facts and missing evidence in the tropics means we can only undertake the journey of interpretation of narratives in circulation, those in which we have blind faith but have not been presented as something coherent.

This manifesto is the sum of different interpretations of the past that are linked to a diffuse present when it becomes compulsory to give shape to an idea about how to describe tropical space and its possible pre-history, origins, and consequences. In this way, we can then produce a definition, a restructured gaze on what we assume to be tropical architecture.

This requires us to establish that an architecture that contains tropical ideas builds a third order, one that establishes intermediate conditions, without focusing on a dichotomy or dualisms and simply assuming that it is able to coexist and act simultaneously, preventing the black-and-white extremes in order to become essentially a wide gamut of grays. This is a set of ideas that accepts contradictions and ambiguity as a space and as an attitude.

Therefore, we take the stance of presenting actions, sayings, or events—instruments—that can be understood in different ways to personally conceive, order, or express a way of producing architecture based on tropical ideas about space.

We must claim tropical architecture's right to its place in the narrative of universal architecture, no longer as a material and spatial event notable for its formal clarity as an object-figure on an exotic, green-hued background, nor for the reactionary ideology of naïve regionalism, let alone for its excessive fondness for the use of materials or the simplistic phenomenological narrative. After crossing this threshold, it is essential to shine a light on its generous and public spatial aspect that creates exchanges, on what has become necessary and relevant today because it was never truly a model but simply a fragile ideal that waxes and wanes over the eras and between cultures and geographical regions.

After making this claim and displaying these ideas, we must be generous and inclusive by allowing them to join forces with other spatial ideas already formed in other places and at other times; architectural ideas are borderless and have the power to belong to a broader, location-less narrative that exists outside and above nationalist discourses and unconnected to cultural appropriations.

Specific ambiguity must be understood essentially at face value, as a dual approach to reflection and action: thinking about what has already been built, and building ideas.

Visitors can interpret specific ambiguity in many ways: it is generous and pragmatically optimistic by making connections and being readily available to citizens; hard to control but feasible to build; necessary and autonomous; open to a wide variety of readings, structured around history and the discipline of architecture, without seeking a hermetic style. Above all, it constructs freedoms, not only for architects in their work, but also for how constructions and spaces have an openness, even by inverting the closed character of the private realm and making it public.

But the architects' freedom can only be described and defined by their relation to the most immediate reality and how they can negotiate with their ideas and ambitions. In other words, **freedom is built insofar as that there is knowledge and acceptance of the rules, but also a permanent and decisive effort to change them**, if possible, with the living example of their positions, in other words, their buildings and proposals.

Positioning

We must acknowledge that architects are instruments or actors within a political structure that have a public impact, without this presupposing that architecture is inherently political.

As a mediating discipline to bind society together, architecture needs to take a responsible, broad-ranging, and properly documented approach to its context, the environment, local inhabitants and their history. Although it may not express it literally, the fact that architecture makes connections through projects in various contexts automatically turns it into an instrument of politics and capital, either to shape space according to the ideas of both, or to create market value.

But architects do not need to become prisoners of this situation, even though they may struggle to free themselves from it. On the one hand, architecture with clients or projects is free from obligations and restrictions; on the other, when architects are not forced to negotiate with the many agents and factors involved in a project, architecture becomes an ideology, often self-referential, mute, and limited.

But it is precisely due to this intermediary role, of having to inhabit and understand reality and to respond to a series of requests and desires that makes it necessary for architects to become detached from the illusions of the misunderstood artist and paradoxically forces them to pay attention to professional issues, to be aware of what they can do within their specific reality.

If architects set out to take a purely political approach or hope to enter realms where they cannot display their instruments, such as shaping space, and they decide to immerse themselves in the discursive rhetoric deployed by those seeking to create architecture from other disciplines, their scope for action disappears and instead they move into others' space, making them not only useless but also unnecessary. But if architects are able to detach themselves from all these self-imposed responsibilities, mainly of believing that their role is to be political and engage in politics, they are freed from their delusions and simply become aware of how to become necessary in their work as architects through architecture itself.

By shaking off their delusions, architects can visualize their field of work pragmatically by identifying the small cracks in the system; they can then become genuinely political agents through their skills rather than their disguises.

But it is also by appropriating their role that generates doubts, and accordingly our attempts to try to define their position accurately: How can we place architecture as a discipline and a practice that creates architectural problems for itself, or that resolves problems that go beyond its professional remit? And how can we connect both of these ideas to create a dynamic, unforeseen, and shifting reality?

Questions for Architecture

To find answers we must swim, sometimes against the current, into parallel worlds that permanently define and deny themselves by contrast. It is important to go against the flow with the firm intention of clarifying where architects can move more freely, using the architect's ability to join the dots, as well as to understand and crystalize different analyses on the territory as space, and their projections into something tangible: architecture.

In specific ambiguity, it is important to position ourselves in-between conditions: on the one hand, in the discipline of architecture as a question that is asked and that raises issues inherent to it, and that have the ability to become connected to the tradition of history, culture, and geography in a particular and a universal reality; and on the other hand, in a practice that, once it has incorporated its ideas and gaze, is skilfully related to a context that is never neutral, that tends to be decidedly market-driven and at the mercy of capital. The room for maneuver in a particular context, moment, time, and society is found in this oscillation and evolution, of exchanging the profession's reasons and issues.

It is not necessarily about building novelties or renewing ourselves out of the desire to be fashionable. It is a question of carrying out and expanding our work without abandoning our instruments, pushing the envelope of the discipline by defining the idea of space for our specific situation, time, and space in order to find the best ways in which we can inter-relate as citizens to induce them through architecture.

Pushing the boundaries of architecture is essential for an inquiry into the kind of space we want to create. Therefore, we need to give priority simultaneously both to the construction of architectural ideas and to spatial experience.

Architectural ideas have survived over time by making themselves an essential part of history, but redefining themselves in line with the eras, with their implications for the present, their approaches to space and its inherent contradictions. Moreover, spatial experience is that which is often impossible to visualize completely before the day a building is used and occupied. Constructing correspondences between the conceived space and the occupied space produces a new layer, so that we can learn and expand our notion of architecture, space, the city, and society. Hence, the most interesting architecture is the architecture that not only convinces us what we believe or what we want to do, but one that asks us what we have done.

Professional Realities

To consider architecture from the other side, from the professional perspective, would basically require a focus on aspects related to the working environment, something much closer to what we could call architecture as a production system. Professional issues are much more closely connected to architecture as an activity carried out during specific working hours and in line with working conditions where challenges and demands are much more closely related to the world of capital.

Concentrating solely on professional aspects would inevitably lead us to detach ourselves even from optimism, utopia, and illusion, because we would be entering a world ruled solely by the market and competition. But to renounce participation in professional activities would to some extent mean rejecting the means to participate in the reality of the built work; that which is inhabitable, verifiable; that materialization which transcends the world of ideas and allows us to be there, occupying considered architecture, being there as individuals and as society.

Architecture as practice and discipline is necessarily paradoxical. Although it derives from a confluence of knowledge, disciplines, and ultimately it can only respond to itself as architecture, as material definitions of space and its systems of accessibility and movement. Therefore, if we fail to recognize that architects inhabit both worlds—the world of ideas and professional commitments—we will remain a work in progress. Therefore, a project of specifically ambiguous architecture needs to be open and optimistic, because architecture implies change, inserts something that did not exist previously, or brings to life something that was dislocated. This sometimes happens because it can read something that already existed in order to empower it. Or else simply because architects have a particular and acute capacity for observation of these places; they can transfer those thoughts to the built environment along with idealistic, project-and-material-based baggage. This approach also provides a way of documenting technique and social negotiation as a tangible project, susceptible to questioning the boundaries at the same time as defining and transforming them.

This duality between profession and discipline, ideas and the marketplace, undoubtedly forces us to look at the history of architecture in order to review what we are capable of extracting, reading, and building based on experiences and prior proposals. History is full of examples and situations in which dynamism and the codependency of the disciplinary and professional realms has helped us move the needle and benchmark values. History may not be a linear narrative and unlike mille-feuille, with legible layers overlapping one another without much in the way of resistance between them. It is more a constant flow of geological strata that rub against one another dynamically and constantly redefine themselves: something more akin to the clashing of tectonic plates that upset the balance of the present and in the future, the visible and the invisible. Each time history is rewritten, the present and the future are rewritten too. What tools are useful to tie a culturally valuable practice to a specific geographical area, such as the tropics, where local history is fragmented, ephemerous, and perhaps architecturally and materially insufficient?

Confluences

Specific ambiguity locates and positions projects between conditions, halfway between contradictions and illusions, possibilities and restrictions, turning it into an objective and instrumental action that produces and enables the built fact to possess and generate cultural value. It must also be beautiful.

This confluence is based on the form's strategic capacity as the only way in which we are capable of making connections to places through architecture itself. It is the way of articulating confluences between ways of thinking, observations, working methods and building techniques. Only form is able to show us that in the use of space, other behaviors or relations exist within our proposals.

Furthermore, from a self-critical perspective and with the space already in service, we may be able to discover other ways of inhabiting and living that we had overlooked when conceiving the project.

Guaranteeing that our ideas, forms, and methods—despite a limited and restrictive context—are aligned and backed up by a technically viable process or work force, is what gives the built fact its relevance. The installed capacity of labor and the material and technical availability existing within a tropical context informs us what is viable there: in other words, the conceived forms versus what we can build. Creating architecture that we are unable to actually build is perverse, because the incoherent relationship between the control over forms and their existence as tangible space would only cast suspicion on our mediating capacity, which is between the world of ideas and occupied reality.

This questioning forces us to opt for some architectural elements instead of others. For many, this may seem to limit the architectural potential, but in the tropics this is the available reality, the one that obliges us to support one or two ideas, one material or another, a situation that encourages us to strategically position ideas/forms so that architecture can reveal the multiplicity, its adaptability, and its performance in order to become necessary and have a positive effect on reality. In many cases, this is limited to a cantilever and short span, while the structure is highlighted as a conceptual principle of space and an emphasis is placed on its repetition in organizing space, so that it is porous and permeable and consists of walls of columns, planes of beams.

At the same time there is a clear effort to give a public dimension to what is normally private, usually with a focus on the section, so that the boundaries are negotiated and negotiable for users to come and to fluctuate, to move, to nest in successive pockets of exteriority: in many occasions turning the private space into a public realm without necessarily enclosing and excluding.

Given the economic and social structure in tropical contexts, the processes of material decisions, production, manufacturing, and structures are always connected to informal work or tools of economic survival, to craftsmanship, to industrialization, as technology looms into view as a mechanical or digital instrument. This linkage takes place unevenly, imbuing a material quality and formalization largely free from archaic factors and perhaps subject to serendipity. In other words, it is not architecture exclusively dominated by the machine, by standardized industrial processes or cutting-edge material manufacturing. Architecture that produces specific ambiguity occurs where materialization processes are constantly shifting. Therefore, building instructions in the form of plans, drawings, and specifications are temporary documents that, given the technical pragmatism of this profession, obliges constant negotiations with contractors, meaning that they are never closed documents. Therefore, we must accept the bittersweet truth that everything is temporary and blurred. Hence projects become living assemblages or mestizo creations, able to combine areas of knowledge between elements and lessons that mainly respond to a need, never as a luxury. As a result, it rarely appears surplus to requirement.

The construction process therefore takes place through a process of accumulation and saturation, of trial-and-error, which often takes place in real time as building work progresses. It does not necessarily happen during the editing or the summarizing stage since these conditions do not rule out or preconceive ideas. The sum of ideas, discussions, of placing elements on the board, guides discussions in order to create a confluence between many ideas, times, places, and reflections, based on the history of the ordinary and the vernacular or echoing the universal history of architecture, one without borders and that encourages its unrestricted use according to the pressing requirements of the present.

A Critique of Naïve Regionalism

Therefore, how can we build a coherent narrative to describe a past in order to position the present in a new light, in order to opportunely refocus a critical gaze that previously only made useless observations and categorizations into purely binary compartments consisting solely of opposites?

The way we look at things needs to be based precisely on the ambivalence and possibility of constructing a third space, not based on machinery or cultural nostalgia, optimistic but not positivistic, unlike the ideas of those who believe that the world is organized into complementary opposites, or else who consider that time and decisions are taken at a given moment are so decisive that they completely rule out chance. Arbitrariness and the unexpected also forms a part of architectural assemblages, their forms, effects, and physical realities.

To understand this approach, we need to move away from the widespread belief that cultural erosion accelerated by processes of interconnectivity and globalization only causes the decay of knowledge and traditions. The past is not pristine, either. We need to distance ourselves from the mistaken belief that the past contains the pure ideals of architectural culture and was invariably better and held all the true answers. But equally, we must be wary of those who consider that the undefined and slippery future is an accidental consequence of the present.

In some way, positioning oneself as an architect midway between past, present, and future entails a risk that some would say is necessary given the speed of the present and its capacity to devour all in its path, whether this be as an image, a post, or expressing an irresponsible or reckless opinion. We should distance ourselves from the contemporary forces of communication that indiscriminately seek to cancel out the passing of time, reducing it only to the present, future, and oneiric desires. In other words, we need to stand against the purist past of demagogues and populists.

To avoid nostalgic impulses, we consciously scrutinize our immediate surroundings in order to link them to a broader world, for the sake of contrast and in order to doubt and therefore contradict the realm of the homogenous and absolute space, the one that is objectified and feeds off itself.

Our intention is to build a territory of confluences from which to operate, elaborate, and establish from the present spatial experiences through built facts. Only from this standpoint can we accept something as fundamentally visible, specific, and particular to the tropics as geography and culture in which the references and configurations are constantly ambiguous and exist in many different temporalities, since that is the intersection of cultural, social, and political processes that are never closed. There it is possible to be simultaneously baroque and modern, avant-garde and conservative, regionalist and historicist, postmodern and classic, thus producing a layer of permanent instability; a liquid, incomplete status to establish a dialogue with culture before the purely contemporary sphere.

Fighting the Cliché

To accept a liquid condition, we need to find deviations from the common narrative that has compartmentalized tropical architecture within a framework of values based on its most superficial aspects, presenting it as a white beach with endlessly exotic and lush surroundings, praising its ingenuity to make up for a lack of resources, mixing up such shortages with the poverty that it naïvely celebrates. Or something that is exalted for being, or appearing to be, part of a social struggle in response to local inequalities.

Without wishing to completely reject the above we should accept that perhaps these aspects are the easiest ones to recognize for the untrained eye, for those wanting to grab attention.

This compartmentalization entails conflicts, both within the architectural profession in these tropical surroundings as well as in the centers of discussion from where circulating information is valued and given space.

Along with some other architects working in tropical locations, we consider this characterization to be a heavy load to bear. Indeed, in an act of personal silent decency, far from the opportunism of this age, many do not display these qualities as a promotional slogan despite the fact that their architecture silently assumes transformative, socially aware, and environmentally responsible qualities.

Limiting the characteristics of tropical architecture to these simplifications and commonplaces hides and makes opaque many other possibilities tied to broader and universal discourses that are architecturally relevant for today's world, which imply greater complexity and depth, over and above the image already deposited and weighed down by that cliché of the tropics and its architecture.

The Place, the Non-Place, Every Place

For years, the word has been preached in many ways, sometimes even ethereally and divergently, that architecture must belong to its location. Sometimes, projects are criticized for not belonging to their geographical surroundings. But only a few of those who level such criticisms are able to go deeper and describe, argue, and establish how a project should belong to a specific place. Very few indeed dare to go beyond the comfortable and superficial view proposed by geographical determinism, the kind that dilutes everything and assigns it to "pre-existing" elements as an escape route from committing to a particular position of their own.

A building's idea and/or its relation to a location depends on the times, needs, or demands of cultures and societies. It is not a position or a set of immutable criteria. But such commentaries have regularly been based on shared languages, repeated in academic contexts or by critics and automatically accepted as true. Despite being mere opinions and commentaries, these sediments—accumulated over the decades—impede the conversation. At the same time, they have been accelerated by the speed of operations of architectural platforms, social networks, and the empowerment given to malicious voices that spread like wildfire.

Any conversation about architecture's relation to place is a very abstract expression that requires a deeper explanation for a fuller understanding.

Although modernity proposed the same forms for different places, and postmodernity different forms for different places, today we are being led to question not only the meaning of today's architecture but also—at the risk of entering the rabbit-hole of local versus global—the meaning of existing architecture. In other words, our current understanding of place, and what we can do there. From an insider perspective, it is unsurprising that architectural identity in the Latin American tropics may be an unresolved obsession and that, flowing like an eternal present, may circulate unstoppably among groups and media cling tightly to this conviction and purpose.

Part of that obsession emerged in the late 1960s when cracks began to appear in modernizing structures; once their poor functionality triggered an identity-related chaos. That juncture coincided with a series of phenomena that developed from the 1950s and continued for a further thirty years. We will address these issues in the chapter relating to the pre-history of tropical spaces. But before we leap ahead, we should pause and delve deeper into the effects of Kenneth Frampton's *Critical Regionalism*,[2] a category that appeared in 1983 in *Perspecta* magazine. This is undoubtedly one of the hobbyhorses of

2 Kenneth Frampton, *Towards a Critical Regionalism: Six Points for an Architecture of Resistance* in *Anti-Aesthetic: Essays on Postmodern Culture* (Seattle: Bay Press, 1983).

all those armchair critics who have preached the message of naïve regionalism far and wide, making moral judgements infused with social nostalgia and political activism.

Frampton's *Towards a Critical Regionalism* fell on fertile soil and was fertilized some nineteen years earlier with Bernard Rudofsky's MoMA exhibition catalogue, *Architecture Without Architects*,[3] and grew even more strongly with the publication of Christian Norberg-Schulz's *Genius Loci*.[4] The situation was ripe. By that time, there was a critical inertia and a practice that implicitly and explicitly supported a new approach to places and their types of architecture. Or, viewed differently, at the time of Frampton's publication, the shift toward romantic, phenomenological, and pseudo-poetical regionalism had already taken place. Frampton not only put a title on something that already existed in many architecture firms, but gave them theoretical fuel, emboldening them with a broader base of ideas that were more skillfully connected with a European narrative that was paradoxically even more Eurocentric.

Frampton's text falls apart completely in its political naivety. Despite its well-intentioned theories for architecture, in its social and political romanticism the text fails as an alternative construction both as theory and as critical fodder. At the same time, the text proved immensely successful by giving a voice to, and describing, for the first time, many who previously lacked a presence or were ignored due to the fact they lived their lives outside the media's gaze and far removed from the intellectual centers of the time. Frampton's perspective gave many academics and architects access to new systems of exchange which, without the author's views, would have remained virtually invisible. To this day, some of them

3 Bernard Rudofsky, *Architecture Without Architects* (New York: Museum of Modern Art, 1964).

4 Christian Norberg-Schulz, *Genius Loci: Towards a Phenomenology of Architecture* (Milan: Academy Editions Ltd, 1979).

remain architects who occupy an important place in history and architectural practice.[5]

This initiative inspired a plethora of devotees all around the tropical belt, putting into practice a naïve discourse, and consequently downsizing their potential to a tainted and condescending rearguard.

Resistence and Marginalization

Towards a Critical Regionalism appeared as a text that put up resistance, no longer to the threat modernism but to the homogenizing influence of globalization. Frampton argues for an original architecture that emphasizes the handmade/craft or the idea of a "tradition" that uses certain strategies to become rooted to places in its own way, "resonating" with the locations it hopes to interpret and transform. Topography, climatology, site conditions in relation to a broader geographical framework, tectonic conditions in the construction, and tactile sensibility are all some of the key characteristics highlighted by Frampton in his text, not only through his arguments but also, and mainly, through the projects built far away from the centers of debate (United States, Western Europe) to emphasize those building on the peripheries (in the rest of the world), or alternatively those who had somehow avoided the centers of corporate modernity or the most vulgar trickeries of postmodernism.

5 Álvaro Siza, one of the most interesting, unusual, and avant-garde living architects, was initially classified as an architect of Critical Regionalism. However, any attempt to classify the Portuguese architect's prolific, complex, encyclopedic work—which perhaps defies categorization entirely—is clearly difficult. His continued relevance over the years reinforces the idea that there is not necessarily a rearguard as described by Frampton. Instead, some architecture may need time and the cultural development of humanity to find its moment and show its values openly, without being forced into a pigeon-hole.

For Frampton, an alternative attitude to increasing historicism and decadent modernity was possible through careful observation of places that had resisted the globalizing forces with austere and humble, almost DIY architecture. Architecture that to some extent was capable of extending the traditions of their places of origin at the same time as being contemporary, albeit discreet, without the semantic nightmare or the decorated surface of postmodernism. By taking this approach, Frampton acknowledges and selects projects that were more tactile than visual, and that prioritized tectonics over scenography, the hybrid over the homogenous, as described by Szacka and Patteeuw in their text "Critical Regionalism for our Time" published in *Architectural Review* (AR).[6] Based on Frampton's text itself and the indications highlighted by the authors in AR, we could say and acknowledge that, up until now, everything was progressing smoothly and in the right direction. This could even be described as a necessary position, taking into account the contexts of the time and the outcome of events. However, as we show below, words and deeds do not always match. Words lead to actions, attitudes, and positions which, despite our efforts to give them and create for them other meanings, contain ideologies that are always floating and which, although we try to tether them, tend to return with their own cultural values and meanings.

Following Patteeuw and Szacka's work, we began to see the erosion and weakening of Frampton's position as one of *resistance*.

Frampton is not interested in occupying the center ground: he takes a rather naïve, reactionary moralistic position. Paradoxically, Frampton starts out by sidelining himself from the anti-global discussion. But why does he define his position as being about resistance? What is he resisting?

6 Léa-Catherine Szacka and Véronique Patteeuw, "Critical Regionalism for our time," *Architectural Review*, 22 November 2019. The authors of this essay critically reposition Frampton's text in today's world in an insightful and precise analysis. https://www.architectural-review.com/essays/critical-regionalism-for-our-time

Oddly, he positioned himself in a weak and fragile position by adopting the same privileged Eurocentrism to which he objects. In his text, he excludes himself. Yet Frampton successfully champions the marginal voice. Not only did he make a significant impact on criticism of the time, but he also created an audience by discovering new seams of work for many architects. And his discourse is well adapted to the mentality of some practicing architects and molds to the discourse of some tropical academies that tend toward self-victimization.

But let us look back to pinpoint the true failure of his position today. Frampton's text was originally positioned as apolitical and acritical, sidestepping the reality and conditions of the places he wrote about. He is unaware of these locations' underlying fabrics, social structures, poverty, inequality, injustices, and even genuine traditions and narratives. In fact, he generalizes phenomena that, seen from a distance, might appear to fit but which, upon closer inspection, function as narrative adjustments that connect forms, references, and improbable genealogies between architectures, histories, and contemporary manifestations that never really coincided but that, to make history more believable, occur irresponsibly, generating various confusions and misunderstandings.[7]

In some way, the side-effects of Frampton's text create a canon of beauty for the peripheries that sadly continues to exist to this day as the accepted and shared understanding of tropical architecture: low-budget but ingenious architecture that works wonders with scant resources; tactile in its materials and phenomenology;

7 Colombian architecture receives a curious mention in *Modern Architecture: A Critical History*, republished in 2020. Rogelio Salmona provides the basis for references to pyramidal and pre-Hispanic architecture, with a particular focus on the Fundación Cristiana para la Vivienda of 1966, whereas in reality the country did not have any such pyramids, and not enough remains of dwellings from those periods exist in order to provide a reference that could be defined as being close to local architects. See *Kenneth Frampton, Modern Architecture: A Critical History* (London: Thames and Hudson, 2020), p. 402.

generous with its immediate context, as well as austere and localist; and, above all, critically incomparable to first-world architecture. In other words, Frampton promotes a condescending view of the tropics and the architecture of developing countries as something celebrated, followed, accepted, and assumed to be true even today, both by local populations and by foreigners. Frampton creates a two-tier approach, holding first-world architecture to a higher critical standard than that of developing countries.

Frampton also skillfully acknowledges a series of important values, perhaps even worthy of the current moment, which appear and reappear in this text, redescribed and reinterpreted, no longer impermeable to an underlying reality but even resulting from it; in other words, recalibrated.

The author's perspective on rearguard architecture is undoubtedly where he finds most success, because unfortunately he manages to construct an image that assigns a totalizing identity to many divergent forces, which also acts as a straitjacket for local populations and a cliché for outsiders, unwittingly inventing a tradition. Frampton presents and validates an architecture uninterested in finding novelty or inventiveness in typologies or in the form of the space that is built there. Instead, Frampton is content with covering and wrapping them up in this sense of lateness, an alternative for the periphery as a new vanguard. And this is precisely where naïve, well-intentioned acts only have regrettable consequences. On the one hand, for local populations it opens and empowers the idea of superficially expressing architecture in poetical, ethereal, and diffuse terms; an unsophisticated and limited phenomenology that describes highly subjective sensations that lack foundations and are dressed up in an exaggeratedly poetical language. This method is used to describe locations and architecture lacking both solidity and substance.

We need to highlight the fact that Frampton's new narrative has been fully accepted not only because it has endured over the years, to the point of becoming accepted wisdom, as a shared identity for many developing countries and cultures. Its ideas have even evolved. Is this not the same architecture celebrated in the Venice Biennale in 2016, Reporting from the Front? Is this the same "Front" that Frampton proposes as being about "resistance and the rear-guard"? Is this not the continuation of the same discourse, almost thirty-five years on?

This is no more than the incontrovertible proof of how the discourse of *Resistance* and the *Front* refer to a confrontation that is not only unresolved but also accepted and self-owned, as a clash in which marginality and the acceptance of poverty as an aesthetic and disciplinary resource are suggested as positive, critically valuable systems. According to these precepts, doing more with less is not about the clever use of resources: it is about normalizing poverty, accepting and feeling comfortable with the stylization of inequality.

The most iconic example of such cases is Torre David,[8] winner of the Golden Lion in 2012 at the Venice Biennale. Opportunistically and superficially, the architects pointed to a squat in a high-rise building in Caracas, Venezuela, as an example of imagination and creativity, leaving to one side the harsh reality of its inhabitants in order to show the exoticism of their solution to a housing problem.

At the same time, this kind of positioning places architecture in a position of absolute fragility in relation to itself and to the world. We can also simply cite the aims of the 2016 edition of the Biennale:

> REPORTING FROM THE FRONT will be about sharing with a broader audience, the work of people who are scrutinizing the horizon looking for new fields of action, facing issues like segregation, inequalities, peripheries, access to sanitation, natural disasters, housing shortage, migration, informality, crime, traffic, waste, pollution and the participation of communities. And simultaneously it will be about presenting examples where different dimensions

8 Torre David: https://torredavid.com

> are synthesized, integrating the pragmatic with the existential, pertinence and boldness, creativity and common sense.[9]

Can architecture truly shoulder the burden of the world and solve the problems of segregation, inequality, periphery, access to sanitation services, natural disasters, housing shortages, migration, informal economies, crime, traffic, waste, pollution, and community participation. Is this not a populist statement that distances us from what architecture can genuinely achieve? Architecture—like any other professional discipline—is not equipped to save the world. However, it was to be expected that, in-between the vanguard and the rearguard, the confrontation would be mediated by impossible objectives to measure and define. It is impossible to establish criteria of quality. Ultimately, good intentions would weigh more than realities in order to escape from the position of architecture amid conditions that are more rational and even more instrumental for a complex world in which it is difficult to intervene.

None of this is Frampton's fault, but rather the error of his followers who assumed that his idea should be established as a moral principle that could only be carried out by a select few with a manifest destiny. As a result, the story of many of the chosen ones has been rewritten to shoehorn it into the framework created by Frampton, hiding relations, influences, correspondences; it encouraged the publication of biographies to fall into line with the pre-existing narrative. Co-evolution and exchanges were compromised on both sides of the Atlantic, engendering an obsession with seeking the hard-to-define identity of architecture beyond the shared modernity in these countries, and which have been established as a common fabric to a vast number of cultures that are impossible to exist under a single label.

9 Extract from a Venice Biennale press release (16th International Architecture Exhibition, 2016): https://www.labiennale.org/en/architecture/2016/biennale-architettura-2016-reporting-front

Searching for a single architectural identity in Latin America is patently absurd. The territory has so many different cultures and in so many different territories that any such attempt would be irresponsible. We believe that the determined, obsessive phenomenon of seeking an identity in each tropical place or nation is basically a response to the fact that, after modernity has burned to the ground, its ashes fell onto a prior fabric that had already been demolished with the aim of making it modern—that same fabric imposed by colonial forces and that, in turn, was placed on the ruins of some ancestral cultures abused and reprogrammed by religious or "civilizing" forces.

The phenomenon continues relentlessly because of the violent rejection of what arises after each period of rupture. The result has been a mestizo identity that, many, or even the majority, find it hard to accept, since it is a question of being in the middle, not being either one or the other but both things at the same time and place. To be mestizo is to be ambiguous and specific.

A Web of Doubts

How can we escape from the trap of identity, assuming that tropical architecture produces tropical spaces, and that this follows a spatial logic other than what is displayed strictly and exclusively in the tropics? Due to its spatial and relational values, how can we understand tropical architecture as being a different design approach, one that surpasses its place of origin?

In other words, can we identify—through a kind of tropical archeology, if you will—systems, ideas, strategic frameworks, and typologies that have been drawn up in the tropical laboratory, permeating the discipline and practice of architecture throughout history. Also, does tropical architecture have its own history, traditions, and lineages? If so, how is that local history linked to the universal history of architecture?

How much is based on the modern European idea of space in the experience of the tropics, its landscapes and architectures. And how many examples of modern tropical architecture emerged from modern European ideals? Are we capable of establishing or acknowledging historical links between both conditions?

Why has the universal history of architecture not yet emphasized in its narrative the influence of tropical space, when ideas about tropical space have been constant and tangible in its most iconic projects and images?

A Prehistory for Tropical Space

The prehistory of tropical space consists of events taking place beyond the actual tropical belt and following successive exchanges between North and South. Over the course of history, cultures and influences began to intermix, in addition to ambitions and ruptures on both sides of the Atlantic and across the tropical belt.

This prehistory consists of two conceptual frameworks that are also two kinds of architecture or intellectual constructions that, over time, began to interweave in order to end up coinciding in modernity.

The first enquired into the myth of the primitive hut and its derivations, through a series of elements for the construction of a kind of space mediated by the strategic succession of filters, elements that watch over space and administer relations with the exterior. The second tradition navigates through the origins of modern architecture and its heterotopia, mainly those of transparency, contemplating its effects.

Here the two conceptual frameworks are interweaved to explain the genealogies that originate both a notion of tropical space as well as the conditions that create links to a broad narrative, not only in time but also in geographical space, beyond the tropical realm. To some extent, by defining genealogy as an involuntary mixture of missing and existing evidence we can pinpoint where the history of tropical space was broken or interrupted. That moment came with the dispute of Team 10 with the first moderns and founders of International Congresses of Modern Architecture (CIAM), and identifying it helps us recapitulate and review, looking ahead and projecting a narrative that can be reconciled with history in order to guide us consciously and, in this way, allow ourselves to occupy spaces that were innocently ceded to naïve regionalism.

The Primitive Filter

To begin this journey, we need to define a special moment in the search for existing evidence. We have picked the year 1755—the year of publication of the second edition of Marc-Antoine Laugier's *Primitive Hut*, with a frontispiece illustration by Charles-Dominique-Joseph Eisen. This publication sustains a myth of Western architecture that enquires into humankind's initial spatial organization, a theme already addressed by Vitruvius. It also establishes and proposes a new archetype, a model to follow, an ideal. [1]

Eisen's frontispiece is not only interesting for its pictorial composition and the architectural aspects in his illustrations. It is also interesting for the inaccuracy of its natural background. The trees are leafy; there is no indication that the setting has seasonal variations. Perhaps a dark cloud is a portent of rainfall. Otherwise, the image reinforces the idea that the enigmatic construction is located in somewhere with a good climate, possibly in spring or summer.

The engraving shows a young woman sitting on the ruins of a classical work of architecture made of stone; in front of her is a hut depicted as part of nature, a work of living architecture. Today we would call it a hybrid. Its columns—its structure—are living trees whose branches are formally treated to create a sufficiently ambiguous image that calls into doubt whether we are looking at house-shaped

[1]

trees or a tree-shaped house. Its gabled roof merges into the branches that support the beams, with a canopy above: a faint mark that proposes a diffuse boundary, a shadow, a shelter without an interior and far from being an absolute space. Does this mean architecture is nature, or vice versa? This creates a simple spatial gesture that defines an ambiguous limit to provide protection from the sun, the origin of a strategy that will be maintained throughout this search for existing evidence, such as interjecting a filter between interior and exterior in order to control light and to regulate the heat and prevent rain from getting in, by administering the airflow. The result is an architecture conceived and developed as the space of intermittent successions based on voids and discontinuous elements; an architecture of filters and layers in an eternal spring climate.

Machinic Transparency

Almost a hundred years later, specifically in 1851 in London, the Great Exhibition opened in a revolutionary new glass-and-metal building: the Crystal Palace, designed by the gardener and landscaper [2]
Joseph Paxton. The construction celebrated glass as a metaphysical and functional material, heralding the arrival of the premodern man to achieve the age-old dream of communing with exterior space, sheltered by glass since, in the greenhouse typology, its own interior exists. This gave the feeling of being outside when inside, sheltered from the rain but with complete visual contact with the outdoors while protected from the elements. If pleasant weather enabled the primitive hut to erase this boundary thanks to clement weather, the Crystal Palace turned man into lord and master of his dwelling in accordance with the age, not only ruled by Chronos but also Kairos.

Not content with this achievement alone, the Crystal Palace introduced something never seen before by the masses: the ability to introduce local or foreign (tropical) plants into a new interior where

[2]

light penetrated but no-one got wet, an impermeable yet transparent space, thermally and visually regulated by the wonders of the steel structure and the transparency of glass. The interior was an eternal spring, with its own controllable climate that could deny the existence of seasons, shut them out, defeat them.

Unfinished Genealogies

New models and ideals emerged from these two conditions and from their various confluences for modern space and, therefore, the ideals of tropical space. Identified in the transparency of glass was the social, material, and atmospheric vehicle to build a new world. For its part, the primitive and specific would be the instrument to expand history and reformulate the primitive acts of producing space. It is necessary to point out how, in its early stages, modernity evolved out of a series of purely expressionist gestures. As the 1920s progressed, the tendency toward machinery informed the production of transparent, clear, and rational architecture made of glass which in turn, from the Second World War onward, adopted Le Corbusier's heliomorphism, which was supported by exposed concrete, resumed by Brazilian progressive architects of the 1930s.

The most representative set of spatial ideas of Western European tradition prior to the Second World War were Le Corbusier's Domino system (1914) and Mies van der Rohe's Barcelona Pavilion (1929), which became spatial systems that would not only move in a tropical direction but also in terms of its most characteristic iconography. These projects are a permanent invitation to question the limits, perimeters, and membrane that manages the transition between being inside and outside.

On the one hand, the Domino system freed architecture from the wall-structure-roof enclosure, opening the possibility for every element to be autonomous, and independent of the structure. This made the enclosure much freer and more open. Moreover, the Barcelona Pavilion reflected the kind of space proposed by the primitive hut, as a simple canopy, which would powerfully communicate the idea of specific ambiguity, spaces made on the basis of their element's specific qualities, with flexible boundaries and intermediate spaces.

It is not enough solely to work on the basis of the most representative ideals of pre-war modernity, ambiguously interpreted and perhaps excessively theorized as the Domino system; or the theoretical hermeticism surrounding the Barcelona Pavilion. Therefore, it is worthwhile building on this approach, taking it a little further, so that we can distance ourselves from the ideals, constructed or otherwise, and search in post-war events for other facts with their respective intellectual constructs, so that they can expand different seams of the genealogy of tropical space, and create a broad platform to revise our beliefs and reposition ourselves, mainly in terms of Le Corbusier's new relationship with sunlight, not only for his connection to Brazilian architects but also following the impact of New York's 1943 MoMA exhibition, Brazil Builds.

Fire and Sun

In *Fire and Memory,*[10] Luis Fernández-Galiano argues that primitive models of spatial organization are based on the handling and relation of energy as a thermal instrument, making a good case for revisiting and broadening these ideas.

On the one hand, architecture organized around fire is igneous, built around the hearth, protected, arranged into sheltered areas, compartmentalized, and with a notable volumetric hierarchy. The parts are organized and expressed in line with their thermal

10 Luis Fernández-Galiano, *Fire and Memory* (Cambridge, Mass.: MIT Press, 2000).

performance to the same extent as they are defined organizationally in plan, with chimneys clearly playing a compositional role as articulators and centers of space. This is clearly Frank Lloyd Wright's architecture: the energy-based, igneous model.

Finally, we have heliomorphism, where the sun defines spatial organization and structure. An extra piece exists between interior and exterior space, a system of passive temperature regulation that not only administers light, heat, and air, but also acquires a fundamental position in the structuring of tropical space: an intermediate space found inside and outside; an indefinite space that is elastic, democratic, and generous, which becomes a tangible experience of shadows and multi-directionality. This was the architecture proposed by Le Corbusier and the Brazilians.

In the tropical laboratory, these models can only coincide, fuse, and be simultaneously rejected in order to be redefined; this is the site of an architectural production that can, at the same time, incorporate glass, brise-soleils, latticework, chimneys, eaves, patios, balconies, pergolas, canopies, and zaguans, all elements that can be usable 24 hours a day, 365 days a year. As opposed to the exclusively three-monthly shifts in northern or southern countries, in tropical regions seasons can change in a single day.

Due to these conditions, in the tropics we can construct a different idea of the interior that questions where the shelter begins and ends, the limit and the threshold. There, the enclosure is transparent but can exist without glass, adding thickness and depth to the architecture, not so much by adding mass and volume but by creating transitions. This repositions architecture's relationship to the sun, the rain, and the air. It creates a space that is organized through layers, denying the experience of space as an absolute, univocal, and self-referential space.

Tropical space stimulates movement or rather is conceived from movement itself, both by the physical effort of what/who occupies it, as well as by the role of the air and the sun. It can also construct a dynamic space to absorb and respond to various social needs and their shifting ways of occupying the exterior. In short, it provides experiences in liminal spaces.

The genealogy of tropical space reveals traits and characteristics that confirm, without any doubt in our minds, that tropical space is anathema to the absolute. Its porosity and elasticity—its kinetic quality—can be used to build an idea of space that refers to the relations created by space, before even trying to shape the void in a self-referential manner.

The Tropical Laboratory

To fully understand the genealogy of tropical space we need to locate, in our catalogue of existing evidence, how two scientific excursions in the tropics made an impact on the perception of nature, religion, humans, society, and beauty.

[3] The first incursion was made with Alexander von Humboldt's explorations of the American tropics between 1799 and 1804. These journeys ushered in a new way of understanding and defining sciences, introducing a new romantic and naturalist perspective on culture and art that became cornerstones of premodern, heroic, and positivist culture.

The Prussian scientist's travel journals opened a new chapter of adventures for the young and artistically inclined, a sort of initiatory Grand Tour that inspired many to follow in his footsteps, draw his landscapes, and narrate through dioramas, paintings, engravings, and even photographs. These documents gave broad access to a new aesthetic culture that became imprinted on retinas far and wide. The unofficial idea took root that the tropics contained a living laboratory which subsequently would be reproduced in the nineteenth century in textiles, gardens, decorative features, and further scientific expeditions. In other words, a climatic and spatial ideal was replaced by the "noble savage" and the "enlightened paradise."

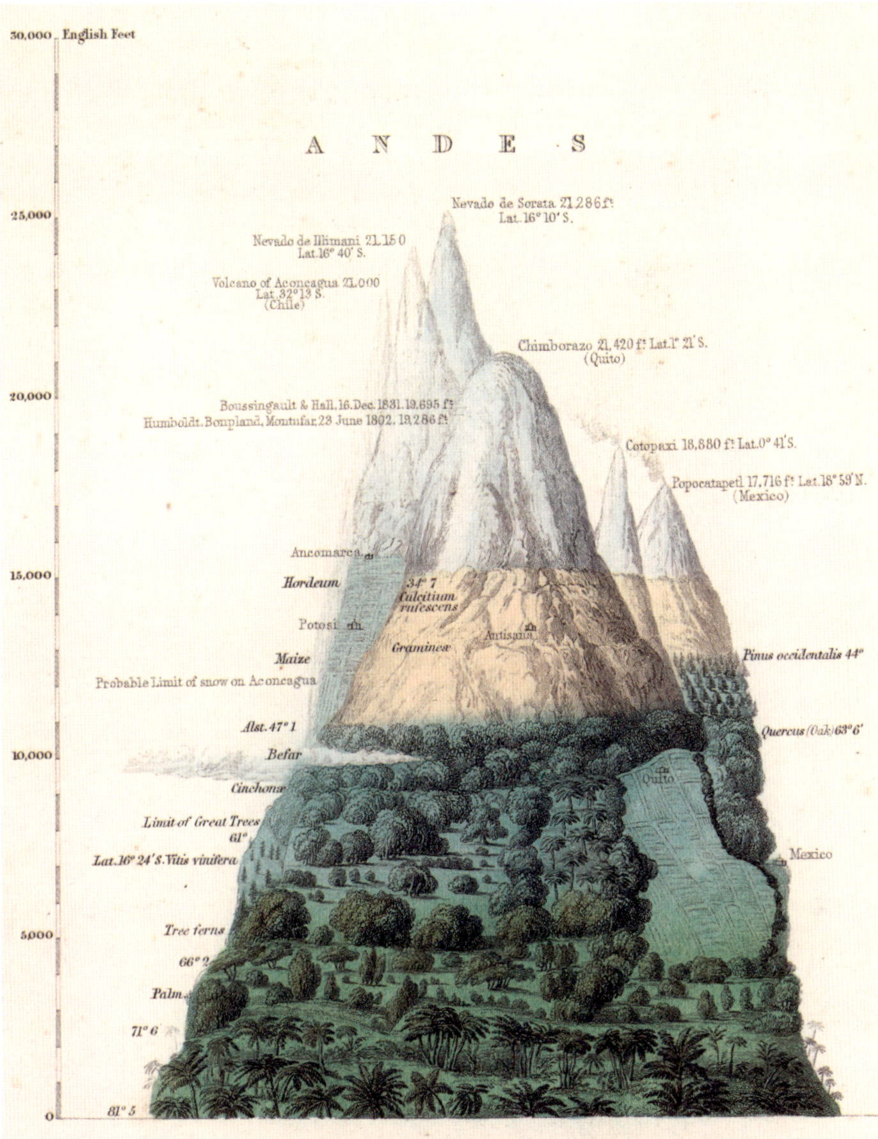

TORRID ZONE, LAT. 0°–10°

(Humboldt, Bonpland, Pentland.)

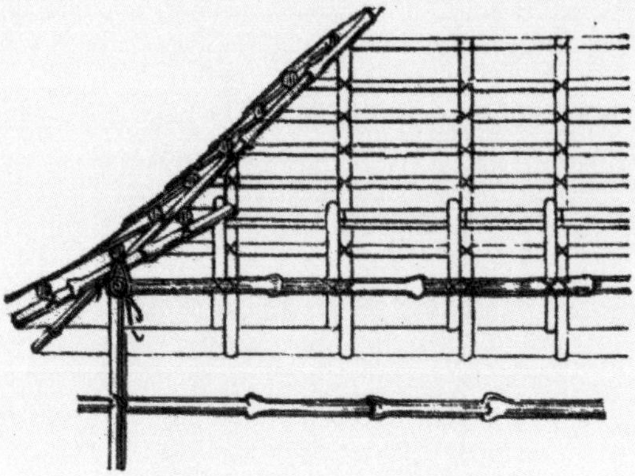

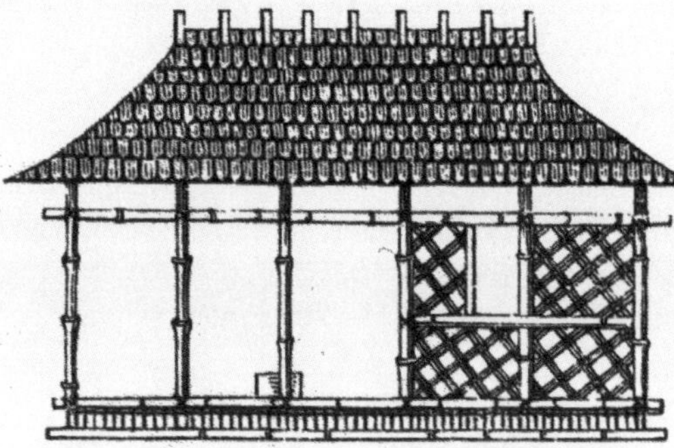

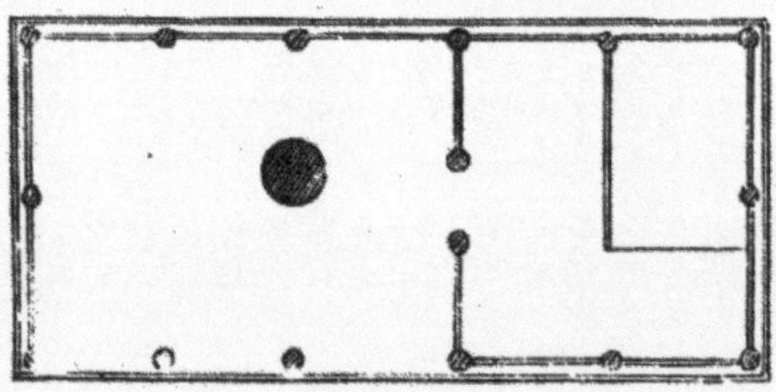

The second scientific treatise on the tropics arrived on 24 November 1859 with the publication in London of Charles Darwin's *On the Origin of Species by Means of Natural Selection, or the Preservation of Favoured Races in the Struggle for Life*. This title, modified after the sixth edition (1872) became a fixed point of reference ever since as *The Origin of Species*. This book—written mainly during Darwin's journey through the Americas between 1831 and 1836—introduced the concept of nature, science, and the role of the human under the concept of evolution, forming a completely new narrative.

From a scientific perspective, both approaches to the tropics encouraged many others to visit, explore, and represent them. As mentioned previously, this created a sense of a laboratory, exoticism, freedom, and mystery that survives to this today. Both narratives were also a powerful influence on how people considered architecture. For example, Darwin influenced the formation of the gaze created by Semper[11] on the idea of type, which connected evolution [4]
to the development of typology in time. For his part, the engraving of Humboldt's *Geography of Plants* helped give a different understanding to the states and variations of nature in relation to the climate and temperature, providing a new perspective on geography and nature, and a fresh understanding of landscape.

Before moving onto the specific aspects of architecture in the tropics, we should recall one of the essential phenomena of modern architecture that did not take place in the tropical American laboratory but in Asia, specifically India. We need to transport ourselves back to India during the British occupation between the late-nineteenth and the early-twentieth centuries. We refer to the fight against malaria.

11 Gottfried Semper, *The Four Elements of Architecture and Other Writings* (Cambridge: Cambridge University Press, 1989). Originally published in 1851.

Bad Air

The discourse of hygiene and its modernizing policies can only be understood through the lens of the British colonists in India. Cholera, malaria, typhoid, and yellow fever were not only diseases and health problems in a hostile territory. They were public health issues that went beyond the human body, since they involved health infrastructure and places of inhabitation, coexistence, and domination. Therefore, a new perspective was needed to sanitize places where people could gather, one based on the latest progress and protocols of tropical medicine and how these places should be transformed.

Green belt, sanitary zone, differentiated housing from the rest of the city, painting things white all combined to give new ideas about air indoors (we should recall that the word malaria derived from *mal aria* in medieval Latin, bad air in English) and a new relationship with the sun and light that would produce a modern code derived from hygienist policies, initially developed in the tropical laboratory and later transported to Great Britain and Europe, which coincided with a new aesthetic and an entire movement that continues to cast a shadow over all of us to this day, as an eternal present. The fear of "bad air" inaugurates, like today, a new kind of space and aesthetic that sheltered the world in the shape of modern architecture.

Existing Evidence

Marion von Osten[12] and Jorge Francisco Liernur clearly elucidate the journey taken by tropical space, taking into account both sides of the Atlantic, from CIAM to Team 10, as well as its origins, consequences, and pending narratives.

12 Marion von Osten, *A Hot Topic: Tropical Architecture and its Aftermath* (2014) in https://static1.squarespace.com/static/56ec53dc9f7266dd86057f72/t/581f40224402439b560ff56e/1478443043626/BookletMVO-online.pdf

Both texts are based on political, technical, and propagandistic decisions developed over the course of the twentieth century, specifically from the late 1940s up until the 1970s. The personal ambitions deposited in the CIAM (from Le Corbusier and Sert to Van Eyck and the Smithsons) were no mystery either for Liernur and von Oosten nor for anyone else. The development of this arc of events after the 1947 CIAM in Bridgewater marked a flourishing and the decline of structural ideas of tropical space and, therefore, defined future works of architecture. These decisions and events conditioned our current perception of tropical space and, directly, at the same time they paved the way toward an almost-religious appropriation of two tendencies that, although they were European reactions to Americanism, found fertile soil in the Latin American tropical territory: regionalism and historicism, ideological pillars of the Seminars of Latin American Architecture (SAL).

Before detailing the Seminars, which belong to the realm of the missing evidence, we need to briefly analyze the narrative created by Liernur and von Osten to discover the key to what was to come, the reactions and consequences.

Fleeing the War, Maintaining the Modern Spirit

Some years before the start of the Second World War and after it had begun, many European members of the CIAM—including Josep Lluís Sert, Walter Gropius, Marcel Breuer, Mies van der Rohe and many others—fled to the United States. Many established themselves in various powerful positions where they could exercise new influence: Gropius and Sert in Harvard, Mies in Chicago IIT, and Breuer in Yale.[13] In these positions they made political contacts to build on

13 Walter Gropius held the post of chairman of Harvard University's Architecture Department (1938–1952). He was succeeded by Josep Lluís Sert (1953–1969). Mies van der Rohe was director of Illinois Institute of Technology (IIT) College of Architecture from 1937 to 1958. Marcel Breuer was a professor at Yale.

CIAM discussions, readapting them to the reconstruction of Europe. Similarly, they could have an influence in Latin America through the United States' newfound dominance.

After consolidating their influence, cracks began to appear within the organization. On the one hand, some tried to redefine themselves. No longer revolutionary artists but reliable experts, they became bureaucrats, as Liernur's text clearly shows.[14] The hardcore CIAM members, consisting of those who migrated to the United States, began to present themselves as officials keen to bureaucratize and professionalize urban planning, with the aim of expanding the ideals of the prewar CIAM into other geographical regions. The US government and international cooperation agencies helped them make contacts and garner support for projects in Latin America and with architects from that region. To implement their plans, Latin America was a territory ripe for intervention due to the need for urban planning, and because new financial packages were available to modernize the region. Wiener and Sert found projects in Colombia and Peru, Richard Neutra in Puerto Rico, Le Corbusier in Bogotá, and so on. Before the Second World War, these architects saw themselves as modern, independently of their place of origin. This changed after the war. Suddenly they were no longer modern architects: some belonged to developed countries and others to developing ones. This slight distinction permanently changed between both fronts and how the different narratives were divided, those linked to architecture centers and those that speak of peripheral architecture.

Brazilians, who already had a place on the world stage, not only in Europe but also in the United States, thanks to the MoMA exhibition (Brazil Builds) were reluctant to participate in the new initiatives. They were already stars in their own right: they had close ties to Le

14 Jorge Francisco Liernur, *Vanguardistas vs. Expertos* in *Block* # 6. Buenos Aires, 2004.

Corbusier, one of CIAM's most influential member many of whose projects and ideals had already been displayed constantly and in a consolidated fashion.[15] Furthermore, Brazil took center stage in Giedion's 1951 publication, *A Decade of New Architecture*.[16] The book included various Latin American projects with large-scale tropical spaces.

As Liernur writes, Brazil stands out as the example of a creative and unprejudiced use of the language of modern architecture without the need for cutting-edge technologies. This situation created a new international audience in Africa and Asia, establishing a tropicalist movement that soon spread across the whole world thanks to Hollywood, many of the casinos in Cuba, and the tourism boom in Miami. This movement expanded and represented a new idea and new values based on post-war sentiment: freedom, sensuality, a new hedonism.

The climate inspired the creation of the skin-filter, as an element separate from the modernist glass curtain wall. This second skin gave depth to space, prioritizing transitions rather than solid, floating planes or walls. The modern paradigm was recreated with the advent of intermediate spaces between exterior and interior: a completely open architecture, of eternal spring, primitive and transparent. This second skin dislocated the interior from the façade and created indeterminate shapes through the interior character. It also provided a new means of handling elements of scale and its elements of reference that, freed from horizontal and vertical partitions, opened the possibility for a new monumentality.

This new approach spread all across the world as a style that over time would become emptied of meaning. However, it introduced a new language to structure space along with a series of elements that would no longer belong exclusively to these geographical

15 *Brazil Builds*, Museum of Modern Art, New York, 1943.

16 Sigfried Giedion, *A Decade of New Architecture* (Zurich: Girsberger, 1951).

regions. Tropicalism is not exclusive to the tropics. Mediterranean-
[5] style houses exist in Cambridge, Massachusetts, such as the house Josep Lluís Sert built as his own private residence, structured around
[6] courtyards. Even Mies's Neue National Galerie, a readaptation of his Bacardi Office Building in Santiago de Cuba in Cuba, did not lose its projected roof/canopy once in Berlin ("for objective reasons") as he would say himself a few years later. If we look at this decision technically, we need to ask ourselves: Why do we need to bring a projected roof/canopy from (tropical) Cuba to Berlin?

While this was happening around the world, CIAM failed to gain traction in North America because its professional and technological structure was unreceptive to ideas and aims that were particular to Europe. Many American architects failed to join CIAM. At the same time, Lewis Mumford and Frank Lloyd Wright were both influential figures for students and the specialized media in the United States, and their ideas were clearly at odds with those championed by the CIAM.

Simultaneously, young moderns such as Peter and Alison Smithson, Jaap Bakema, Aldo van Eyck, Josic, Candilis and Woods, who later came to be known as Team 10, reacted against this tropicalist wave, mainly because it was supported by bureaucratic architects based in the United States whose status as officials betrayed the vanguard. In protest, Team 10 presented itself as the new postwar vanguard. They sought an authentic architecture and art, one to be found on the streets and in popular preferences in a consumer society. They worked to restore architecture as an intellectual practice free from contradictions and more interested in questions related to the discipline itself than professional matters that had nothing at all to do with bureaucracy. Temporarily, this positioning enabled them to recreate a vanguard that was at the center of Europe, leading to the departure from the universalist character of the old moderns and a disassembly of their plans with the Latin American luminaries, thus truncating the tropicalist experience.

[5]

[6]

Returning to the words and history narrated by Liernur, we can describe Pevsner's position in 1954 when he surfed the anti-tropicalist wave in *Architectural Review*, criticizing Brazil's tropicalist architecture for its disinterest in the latest construction technologies and for its formal autonomy. Peter Smithson himself, who kept his faith in machines, believed that tropicalism was the product of primitive societies and should be confined to warmer climates. Smithson rejected the principle of working on the basis of climate and physical environment: "A glass box and a mass-concrete cave can produce the same comfort conditions if one can afford the right mechanical equipment."[17]

Americanization triggered other reactions in Europe's architectural culture, particularly regionalism and historicism, which became established in Latin America with the same intensity and speed as tropicalism was forgotten. As we saw above, these European influences successfully introduced a new identity in these cultures obsessed with discovering their own identities.

Team 10 worked to revive the modernist essence and principles through a return to a pure and sincere world after its pioneers had cast a pall over it by permitting frivolity and bureaucratization to creep in and cause the downfall of more noble ideals. It was necessary to find new types of transparency and technological authenticity. Therefore, it became essential to rediscover paradigms of those purities in societies uncontaminated by modernity: that was where the new primitive was found; basic but sophisticated, child-like and primary; those languages that were pure of heart and spirit and that had remained within the realm of the exotic, un-intellectualized in a modern way, combined with some manifestations brought over from

17 Peter and Alison Smithson, *Ordinariness and Light: Urban theories 1952–1960 and their application in a building project 1963–1970* (Cambridge, Mass.: MIT Press, 1970).

North Africa, such as masks, sculptures, and the occasional drawing of the twentieth-century vanguards. This interest would lead Team 10 to discard tropicalism as an option since it was also too close to the United States, making it essential to find the primitive among its "own": the colonies.

This search would inspire the young modernist members of Team 10 to explore different aspects of new ideas, such as those explored by groups of artists and architects such as the Independent Group, who developed their "as found" positions in their quest for new meanings, whether in the streets, in newspapers, or in daily situations and events. This was the location of new representations of the primitive, the archaic, the Oriental, and the African.

Following Liernur, the second option that arises from this search are historiographical technicisms, Russian Constructivism, and Dutch Pragmatism, which would reconnect to the scene of a new vanguard movement.

Finally, another seam led to a series of new approaches to the primitive. The emphasis was no longer placed on tropicalism but on the paths of the former tropical colonies that would be presented as authentic. For them, the primitive and the archaic were visible in primitive societies or belonged to the infantile universe. These manifestations would also be integrated into the new working discourses of the new CoBrA (Copenhagen, Brussels, Amsterdam) art movement that produced alternative civilizing lucubrations and art works such as Constant Nieuwenhuys's *New Babylon*. Other examples include the work of Asger Jorn and Dubuffet with its primitivist tone that would be one of the great influences on Aldo van Eyck's observative perspective.

This movement inspired many journeys and approaches to Africa, in particular those undertaken by Team 10—by Josic, Candilis, Woods, the Smithsons, and van Eyck, who supported popular ways of life in the outskirts of London and the new Mat-Building model[18] at their meetings and gatherings after CIAM. Their idea was to blur the boundaries between architecture, city, enclosure, intimacy, spreading across the territory as a system to dominate everything. The model, clearly inspired by North Africa and the Mediterranean, references the Casbah model, its vernacular point of reference. With its open organization, it would originate and give substance to the Berlin Free University and other works never built. But this model would be the basis for new systems of spatial organization more firmly established in "peripheral" cultures than in Western and European art. The result would be a pause in the tropical interest, which has lasted to the present day. Many of its consequences, already explained above, have created a fertile soil to abandon new searches for tropical space.

To close the circle, we need to look at missing evidence. Despite a lack of complete documentation in historical and critical texts, these are particularly relevant because they have been experienced. They can be presented from experience. It is worth clarifying that this is an attempt to organize events, comments, references, and reflections in uneven, episodic, and often contradictory situations, which refers the narrative of these facts to events that appear disconnected and intermittent within a context where the pieces do not all fit together.

Missing Evidence

In the Latin American tropics, it would be sufficient to mention a political event, an exhibition, an association of architects, and the influence of two texts, all of which took place between the 1950s and

18 Alison Smithson, *How to Recognise and Read Mat-Building* in *Architectural Design*, N°74 (London, 1974).

1970s. The history and evidence can be disconnected from each other by the ambitious hope to find an identity. As in Poe's short story, *The Purloined Letter* (identified by Lacan as the unconscious) is on public display yet ignored by many.

The Cuban Revolution and independence and decolonialization processes in Africa and Asia in the 1950s and 1960s; Bernard Rudofsky's *Architecture without Architects* MoMA exhibition catalogue (1964); Christian Norberg-Schulz's *Genius Loci* (1979); and Kenneth Frampton's *Toward a Critical Regionalism* (1983) all undermined the relationship of exchange and co-evolution taking place between the tropical belt and more southern and northern parts of the world. Suddenly there came a requirement to belong to a local tradition that could build with pre-existing elements and refer to the local and only the local; or else as an extension of assumed or imposed modernities to simply slot into a complex system of spatial and critical values created through interlocking texts, social concepts, and political utopia. This situation and these ideas gave birth to the Seminars of Latin American Architecture (SAL), which began in 1985 and continued to be held periodically thereafter.

Thanks to its strategic connections across the continent, the SAL —through camaraderie and academic peer pressure—managed to ensure the rejection of any project or text that failed to toe the line of critical regionalism or established historicism, as well as social ideals such as austerity or a modern tradition that could be connected to the political ideology or vernacular material spirit. In other words, emphasis was placed on architecture that could be attributed to a local identity isolated from "external" conversations or influences: a new canon of "particular" architecture. These judgements suspended more than two centuries of global exchange. The approved, surviving global references were in fact few in number, mainly heirs of Le Corbusier and his collaborators were to return to their countries of origin and continue with his ideas, either through imitation or rejection. Above all, any architect mentioned in Frampton's text was considered, like an Aldo Rossi reinterpreted at will to push the agenda of the new "tradition." Any architecture that came from abroad and failed to pass this filter was immediately written off and kept at a distance.

The shadow of the high-rise power of the SAL[19] still falls on the Latin American territory and continues to write off values that were built over time between north and south. These qualities were reduced to the narrow set of critical values that are still recognized for these works of architecture and that minimize conversation and exchange. These characteristics are ingenuity in the face of limited resources and the appearance of being socially combative given the inequalities of the context. With this heritage, practicing architects opportunistically saw that their architecture was recognized in these categories. Therefore, for the most part, they have not wanted to abandon this definition, which is still visible in the contemporary narrative established by architects and curators who expose "truly" representative Latin American and tropical architecture.

Today, global centers of critical authority look down on tropical architecture since these became self-victimized in a fit of opportunism. The few examples of architecture in these geographical regions that do not fit within this critical characterization or classification are hard to understand and relocated. Mainly because there is little theoretical material to delve into their work other than clichés and associated nostalgia. Furthermore, in practice it is harder to sidestep the obvious and the information spread by the media.

19 Since 1985, architects from Latin America and some from Spain have met regularly at the Seminars of Latin American Architecture, mainly gathering around the Argentine Ramón Gutiérrez. This ideological and academic bloc established the official version of most Latin American countries' history and narrative. In their radicalism and arrogance, the Seminars established power structures in a critical posture that accepted or rejected architecture in black and white. The outcome has been fragmented and often arbitrary narratives. The SAL's resistance continues to be felt in its rejection of contemporary architecture.

Therefore, what questions should we be asking ourselves and which paths do we need to take to identify, recognize, and locate all these qualities, characteristics, and experiences that have been ignored for decades? How can we define other values for tropical space and its architectures that can also connect to peers and institutions, as well as locate and exchange experiences and positions that can be useful when addressing urban, rural, and territorial challenges?

2.

Describing the Territory, Implementing Ideas

Describing the Territory

The world may currently be heading toward a megaculture. Compared to some fifteen years ago, it is now more common for places to share objects and behaviors than to have dissimilar and distant ones. Paradoxically, this planetary acceleration toward cultural homogenization—partly mediated by the connectivity and proliferation of social networks—is coinciding with a notable resistance to globality. This tendency is a reaction to a reckless use of capital and its relentless pursuit of returns, no matter how detrimental to the wellbeing of society at large. Some cultures have been displaced as a result.

We now face a still-unresolved dilemma: **How can we be sufficiently local for things in a specific place to be meaningful and to connect with what was already there, but also for them to spark discussions and to acquire universal relevance over and above this hyper-localization?** Through this global connectivity, we can develop ways to protect the weakest, including the most fragile territories.

Describing the territory is essential for us to understand our localization and situation. It enables us to prepare ourselves technically and culturally for the built fact to connect to the specific aspects of the place, in harmony with the broader possibility of crossing national borders and creating universal values, without ignoring architecture's capacity to respond independently.

When referring to region and territory, we do not imply that both consist of isomorphic conditions; their slight interior variations make it possible to construct small differences: some shared, others unique, but in any case, a reactive input in the architectural project. We even contemplate those differences that mediate between the architects' observations—their discoveries and instincts—and what the different social and cultural organizations in those locations expect from them.

We will refer to territory as the time and place of confluence for a culture and its ways of inhabiting a geographical and environmental space. Interestingly, tropical areas consist of a the wide variety of territories: urban, agricultural, rural, jungle, or wildernesses. Which tools can architecture use to intervene in these territories, and how can we construct the narratives of these territories through architecture?

We could speculate by suggesting that the tropics constitute a heterogeneous territory made up of homogenous components. This condition inevitably raises the question: How do we relate to the elements and differentiate them in order to construct a narrative and an approach that can work on the homogenous front, where the gaze is confused and everything appears the same, and therefore complicating work in similar or undifferentiated spaces? How can the sum of homogenous objects construct a heterogeneous territory? We may find answers in the tropical condition. Everything is inverted and multiplied in the tropics: time is not necessarily marked by the variations in foliage, nor the climate and temperature by equinoxes and solstices. Instead, it is regulated by a climatic tedium, with the exception of torrential rainfall and swelteringly hot days. Observation becomes essential. An oscillation between differentiation and continuity may appear the only probable action in a context clad in the appearances of similarities or likenesses, where everything seems to be the same but is in fact different.

Only through careful observation can we appreciate that differences consist of small variations that must be managed and incorporated into the project as architecture, never as a translation from another discipline. Otherwise, we would be excluding them from the architectural experience and turning the tools of architecture into something generic, which would in turn falsify our knowledge and become fraudulent.

Describing the territory is an essential prerequisite for building. We can use various documents, ideas, and observations; a system of tools and mechanisms to help us understand and explore the components of geographical areas. This is where we can provide built facts that are an integral component of specific ambiguity, expanding the reduced and problematic notion of context.

Art as an Instrument

Inhabiting a natural context of sharp contrasts and dissimilar conditions requires us to find new ways, instruments, and tools to describe the territory. And by describing it, we can discover useful elements to help define tropical space and its characteristics: to make it graspable. For example, the gaze of artists helps us broaden the spectrum. Their actions show us ideas and knowledge to help us construct our methods and thus give meaning to copious amounts of information that is disperse and divergent, hidden and veiled.

We do not understand art as the artist makes it. We view art as a critical and public manifestation of the world that does not only exist to describe it ethically or aesthetically, but to transform it. The idea is use art to research ways of conceiving the space that may temporarily help us appropriate other gazes. Perhaps architecture is the reflection that takes place in the world before and after art, as a precise framework for considering spatial relations. Architecture cannot be something other than itself, but it can avail itself of other disciplines to understand and find ways of operating and becoming necessary.

However, architecture is sufficiently distant from art for it to be autonomous, yet close enough to forge links of codependency and coevolution; in other words, it absorbs and connects to information coming from art, its social responsibilities and freedoms, although in no way does it seek to create art.

From this perspective, art for architecture is an instrument of observation and critical reflection that helps shed light on issues relating to landscape and society, similarly to describing surroundings that point out ways forward and how to develop ideas. Art is a tool to define tropical space and its specific ambiguity.

We use the work of various artists with this aim in mind. Some work within the landscape tradition, from Edwin Church to Abel Rodríguez, Camilo Echavarría to Thomas Struth. Others focus more on the world of ideas and their artistic experiences, reflecting on space more directly. From this perspective, the latter propose a different type of spatial experience, one that is ambivalent and powerful, and which questions the boundaries of sculpture and painting, of space and time. In particular, we refer to the work of Jesús Rafael Soto. His many ways of looking at space can be revealing and instrumental to establish the characteristics of tropical space.

The appreciations of artists are made through architecture. In no way do they seek to be art criticism. Above all, they are interpretations to broaden our gaze on the tropical space.

Jungles, Exoticism, and the Enlightened Landscape

The tropics had a strong influence on nineteenth-century spatial and pictorial representations. They formed part of the building blocks of a new ideal that, over time, came to define modern architecture and, consequently, they constructed our definition of tropical space.

One of the best ways to immerse ourselves in this subject may be an analysis of some works of Frederic Edwin Church[1] and his paintings made during his journeys along the same routes taken by Humboldt in South America, particularly *The Heart of the Andes* (1859).

Let us briefly explore the spatial experience that Church offers us in *The Heart of the Andes*. The painting depicts spectacular scenery, possibly at dusk or in the cool of the early morning. A broad vista stretches out, composed of smaller scenes that combine to create a complete image, articulated by elements of the landscape itself, of mountain ranges where the light and atmosphere complement the pictorial tone and create a markedly romantic feel.

The climate is depicted ambiguously in the image's upper corners: at the top left, the day promises summer's weather with a blue sky and few clouds, as opposed to the storm brewing on the top right, where dark gray clouds threaten a downpour, as the clouds gradually accumulate the water that will fall on the valley. Mist, sun, shade, and shadows are just some of the most distinctive atmospheric aspects of the changing and unpredictable climate of the Andean tropics.

It is important to note the radical contrast between the paintings' various component parts, which are highlighted and marked by their differing scales of relation as individual and combined elements. Monumental trees and mountains are next to small settlements. Small roots and intricately depicted vegetation in the foreground contrast with the more homogenous mass of the mountains behind, a superimposed contrast between the hyper-detailed and the general. Seen as a whole, the painting constructs a spatial experience, with its temperature, atmosphere, and natural geographical monumentality.

1 An American artist (1826–1900). A founder of the Hudson River School.

Church was aware of this performative quality, so he decided to enrich this perception as a spatial experience. For his 1858 exhibition, held in what would become the first building used as a studio for painters, New York's Tenth Street Studio Building, Church displayed the painting on specially constructed stage, strategically designed to amplify his own impression of the tropics' spatial and environmental sensation. Therefore, he erected an almost theatrical set-up for people to view the painting.

He put up a cordon to ensure that visitors remained at a considerable distance, so that the painting could only be seen from "a distance." He also rigged up a lighting system of candles and oil lamps. To intensify the theatrical effect, he framed the painting within black curtains, thus removing any spatial reference of the place from the outside and from the location of the exhibit. Opera-glasses were available for visitors standing behind the cordon to appreciate the level of detail in some tiny parts of the painting; they could switch between viewing the detail as well as the entire composition. Everything ranged from the level of detail up to a panoramic sweep, from the particular to the general, constantly oscillating and questioning scales, not only the ones referred to in the painting itself, but also in relation to the room where the painting was put on display.

This painting provides some reference points for the tropical space. First, the contrast of gradients between elements and that idea of temporarily confusing the spatial perception based on contrary scales or the subtle clash of elements. We can also refer to how the parts are assembled and the entirety, not through additions but by the impulse contrary to perception, enabling different experiences within the whole: a system of relations mediated by the scales and experience of the roving gaze. The system creates links and scenes through addition, never by subtraction.

The second case is that of the indigenous Colombian artist, Abel Rodríguez, who questions the representation of the boundaries of the jungle.[2] His paintings and drawings efface the interior. The ambiguity of representation helps clearly define an interior or exterior. Rodríguez does not portray the jungle as a unit of specific bodies (trees), but represents the differentiated whole (trees, jungle, foliage) through the apparent homogeneity of minute details. The jungle space is the accretion of tiny details of almost undifferentiated foliage, which simultaneously constructs the entirety and the particular through small shifts in the use of color or textures in something that appears similar and homogenous, appearance and reality subverted at the same time as being veiled by the use of the green, a color that prevents us from any absolute or immediate differentiation of the elements.

His paintings require patience. Although the depiction seems naïve, slight differences emerge once we pause and patiently observe the images, in the same way that we place ourselves in a forest and feel the uncanny sense of the falsely homogenous. The accumulation of intricate details creates a whole where this spatial condition is revealed and unveiled, at times lacking a background in the sense of a figure-ground. In this case, the space consists of small layers that need to be crossed and experienced by the gaze, not necessarily observed through the tradition of a Renaissance perspective where there is a vanishing point, a foreground and a background. In order to understand the superimpositions, each one independently,

2 Abel Rodríguez is an elder from the Nonuya indigenous group with knowledge of traditional medicinal plants and ecological systems of the Amazon basin. In the 1990s, during the armed conflict in Colombia, his family left their native lands of Chorrera. Rodríguez found a way of preserving their legacy by drawing his knowledge. Now, thanks to the work of contemporary artists, curators, and scientists, his work is highly valued for its artistic qualities and the unique understanding that it conveys not only about the jungle but also the human condition. By registering and describing the Nonuyas' botannical and religious environmental knowledge, passed down through the generations and retaining a strict lineage through diets and severe restrictions, Abel Rodríguez's work is an ancestral treasure, a gift from the jungle for this globalized, totalizing, and homogenized world. Information from https://institutodevision.com/visionarios/abel-rodriguez/

adjacencies are blurred. This is the way to discover that tropical space. Similar to the interior of a wood, which activates its liminal condition.

Thomas Struth's series of photographs of the jungle ("Paradise") constitutes another way of recording and describing the territory.[3] This is not the gaze of the jungle's native inhabitant but that of the intruder who creates the Western and European image through the structure of contemporary photography, almost turning it into an object that even sets the time with the exact hour, climate, and coordinates, as if pinpointing a moment full of data.

In his photographs, Struth frames every possible species of plants that fit within the frame. The climatic conditions and the light give the sense that everything is happening on a single plane, halfway between Romanticism and Impressionist painting. The idea is for each figure to work by suppressing its autonomy in the image to make way for the atmosphere, for a space covered by a kaleidoscope of light and backlighting. The leaves and foliage stand out more than the trees or plants. In the image, everything means the same. There are no hierarchies of size, although paradoxically this questions the European canon of the observer—that European notion that nature is something that can be spread out scientifically on the table to be catalogued, classified, and understood. Struth proposes a complex, possibly over-texturized space but one that above all appears before us as a thermal flow with a heavy presence of air. The weight or volume may appear not to be influenced by gravity or by the tiny gaps between the different elements: by the air that holds up the various components and relates them by using a dense system of spatial filters.

3 Thomas Struth is a German photographer, born in 1954 in Geldern. One of his most representative works is the "Pictures from Paradise" series that records various kinds of jungle landscapes in different parts of the world; in this series the jungle poses, as if sitting for a portrait, far removed from the idea of the still life.

Camilo Echavarría,[4] a contemporary photographer from Medellín, Colombia, bases his work on the history of nineteenth-century travelers and on the enlightened landscape, building on the foundations of Church's work and the travelogues written about exotic, Romantic locations. In various parts of the tropics, Echavarría creates landscapes with photographs of those journeys, based on digital assemblages of photographs. By digitally superimposing and transforming images, he proposes new ones, citing the ideas of representing the pictorial Romantic landscape.

In his images, nature is all-powerful. It is far stronger than man or any mark of civilization, creating a unitary and episodic setting uses exaggerations and suppressions to superimpose exaggerated lighting and scales of existing elements, to express and represent the character of such places as if they really existed in such a way, and with such a dramatic quality.

Echavarría's photographs can be defined as something lodged in the memory after a journey through the tropics; the sediment of experience of someone affected by close contact with an incomprehensible nature. In no way do these images seek to represent something actually observed. They retrace the steps of memory, the recollection of having wandered through densely vegetated spaces and with an impressive and contradictory multiplicity of geologies, climate, and atmospheres.

This artist's work is instrumental because it reveals to us what it means to have within reach, like a catalogue raisonné, many of the tropical places with their thermal and spatial qualities. His work establishes a graphic and pictorial atlas—a landscape manual—to understand, develop, and select various architectural elements that must be used according to the rules of the game that the tropics impose as territory and living culture.

4 For more information about Camilo Echavarría's work, see "Atlas of the Andes": http://www.camiloechavarria.com

Multireferential and Dynamic

We need to distance ourselves from the various representations of the territory from the purely photographic, artistic perspective to find another type of idea about tropical space. Other sources are required to broaden our gaze and resources in order to define, perhaps more abstractly and immersively—through the non-architectural experience—what constitutes the space of a tropical mindset. From an artistic standpoint, no better example exists than Jesús Rafael Soto's *Penetrables*.

In the 1950s, his Venezuelan artist created these works, which offer a total experience of the tropical space, mediated by art. The *Penetrables* open a door into an atmosphere through an ambiguous media that combines a pictorial object and performance; the contained and multi-referential space; the abstract and the figurative; a material experience that simultaneously breaks down into dynamic and unstable elements which are activated through the act of entering —penetrating and moving—not within a space consisting of an excavated voice but one made of multiple filaments and interstitial spaces. Like a cascade of vertical elements separated one from the other by millimeters, compressing the experience of a wood into a few square meters, but possibly exaggerated by the playfulness and element of surprise. This work makes it possible to combine the story of sculpture, as Jean Clay mentions in his text *Los Penetrables de Soto* and, also, to construct a new sense of space, to which Sigfried Giedion refers but does not completely develop in his text *Space, Time, and Architecture*. Clay says:

> The history of sculpture will be based on these early ideas: Transparent (Gabo, Archipenko), Hollow (Pevsner), Mobile (Calder), integrating more and more space to the point at which energy systematically enters the static masses, and where the sculpture of undulation with light begins (Moholy-Nagy, Vantongerloo), the

> Magnetic Forces (Takis), etc. Hereafter, with Soto's work, the external and internal cannot be told apart, as they merge into a generalized de-materialization.[5]

Clay's quote is important for the multicultural dimension of the ideas and accumulation of experiences over time, based on sculpture. Also, but above all, its relevance lies in the construction of a spatial ideal that despite finding an expression in art, has its foundations and repercussions in architecture.

Entering into a *Penetrable* is the artistic and Western rationalization of the experience of being in a tropical space, translated through codes, elements, pictorial, and spatial traditions of the twentieth century and a direct participant in the avant-garde. Clay adds:

> Here, the spectator always needs to participate: first, because it is the spectator's movement that visually dematerializes the volume; second, since the very act of entering the work of art generates a whole new perception of it: both tactile (we apprehend the object with our entire body) and psychological (we experience a piece of art that completely enfolds us in an immaterial layer that inspires and perturbs our perception of the physical universe.)[6]

Is this not a way of understanding and describing what happens to us when we enter and perceive tropical space?

If modern space for Giedion was clearly structured around the relation introduced by the time factor, in Soto's work it is where that spatial multi-referentiality is produced and experienced thanks to the time/movement factor that implies passing through a *Penetrable*.

When we go into one of these works of sound or pictorial art by Soto, we enter a work of specific ambiguity. Although this space

5 Jean Clay, "Los penetrables de Soto," in *Imagen*, No. 34, 1–5 (October 1968).

6 Ibid.

is absolutely autonomous, it is impossible not to acknowledge or ignore its proposed ambivalence. We leave the "outside" world behind and enter its jaws, in the repetition and sequence of its elements, but we never stop being in a long threshold, one that constantly shows us its intrinsic and particular characteristics and that, at the same time, connects us in multiple directions with a present and inescapable exterior.

Clay necessarily refers us to the ambiguous sensation of entering a tropical garden, filled more with a material quality than plantlife or vegetation. Clay writes:

> Soto's ambience is radical. His first role is to knock down the walls surrounding us. He pulverizes them optically. The room, invaded by the *Penetrable,* no longer has describable proportions. The volume is elastic, fluid. Sometimes the eye wanders in a boundless jungle, or else fastens on a vibration two centimeters from the retina. The basis of our vision—and even our thinking habits—are lost in this universe of perpetual metamorphosis where all systems of possible perspectives are linked. We no longer know where to look, where to reset the customary dimensions of space that we are used to inhabiting. As we struggle with signs that are forever becoming knotted and unknotted, of forming tirelessly before our very eyes, we experience a proportionless world, whose center is everywhere and circumference nowhere, a shapeless world without barriers, where there are no longer plastic relations, where the old rules of artistic appreciation (interplay of colors, balanced volumes) disappear under the influence of an all-encompassing, totalizing size, which is a universe in itself, at the same time as returning to certain essential laws of matter.[7]

7 Ibid.

This sensation and spatial experience of being between conditions and that question our senses is the most relevant aspect of the idea of tropical space: that which is inherent to tropical architecture, but which is hard to explain, describe, and apprehend.

The Territory's Forms

In the tropics, the territory's various forms could lead us to experiment with alternative spatial conditions. In its variations and transitions, in its intermediate status, we see that common threads exist between the urban areas and the wilderness that strengthen the idea of inhabitation based on relations in space, though their origins may seem uncertain. However, clearly defining our movement through these spaces is complex. We are even unaware of it. We can only see and understand our ideas about space, and therefore how to occupy it, when architecture shows us "intermediate" transitions.

How does this idea of tropical space unfold at the territory's distinct levels? How does it organize and define the city, the countryside, rurality, the wilderness? How does architecture operate under these conditions? How can an architecture of specific ambiguity participate under these conditions?

Codependency is the unifying thread that weaves together our territory, sometimes opaquely, or else directly and transparently. Those relations of codependence have subtleties that establish connections based on several factors, some of them deeply marked by the possible relation between what is built and what is around us. The small variables that exist in the way of producing architecture in line with the territory, as well as with the cultures and societies settled in each one of these variations, call into question what kind of architecture can exist there. Similarly, it becomes essential to try to describe and construct a framework of understanding for these territories, so that architecture does not become an automatic response of the know-how of the architect with an urbanizing instinct.

These differences in the territory are variable. Although they may appear the same, they have underlying rationales and dynamics that elude a superficial and descriptive perspective.

In the tropics, the territory is regularly characterized by four types of condition.

If we imagine a horizontal line with the "City" on the left, and the "Wilderness" on the right, we will see that the "Countryside" is located immediately to the right of the "City" and to the left of the "Wilderness" we find "Rurality."

This relation of codependencies would undoubtedly be better expressed as a network interconnecting all the elements together. However, for practical purposes—to identify the instruments demanded by each of these territories and to express more clearly how each one of them consumes the energy and resources of the other—we have left the representation as a horizontal line that suggests the City and the Wilderness touch each other in their contrast. Inevitably, the City as the center of decision-making, influences the state of, or the pressure exerted on, the Wilderness. Although they do not necessarily connect physically, the fate of each one depends on decisions taken in the rest.

The City of Invisible Frontiers

The tropical city consists of contrasts and marked social boundaries, imposed by the relentless flow of capital and often by topography and its implications for infrastructure. Tropical societies are also unable to create and adhere to social and political pacts to share targets and aspirations. In the tropical city, different moments and models are recognizable, even those that have responded very briefly to public policies that consider the public realm as a common weave of accessible and democratic spaces, independently of its inhabitants' incomes, race, or social status.

Another factor is the lack of planning and a culture of social equality. This also undermines the capabilities of local leaders, who lack innovative urban, political, or social ideas of the caliber required today in order to manage land and to give equal access to public services and to provide collective spaces where people can gather. Within this panorama, there exists an enormous mass of settlements and constructions surrounding everything and that respond to the dynamic and basic instinct of carving out a place in the world: constructions without architects, the result of informal economies, of hardscrabble lives; economies that exist beyond the basic standards of quality-of life-indicators. The tropical city is an unequal, rough, and unsustainable one.

This type of urban area has been organized around interior boundaries and this is where the architecture of a tropical mindset is a constant presence. Architecture seldomly operates directly, as specific ambiguity, on collective public housing; it has only sporadically been able to influence or act upon the public realm given the possibility of blurring or at least diluting the boundaries, and enabling exchanges between different inhabitants of social classes, beliefs, or racial backgrounds.

The city of interior boundaries is surrounded by, or exists within, rich and exotic natural settings; filled with landscaped instruments that are paradoxically also a drawback since in some cases they separate rather than connect. The landscape may be the only useful way to create communal fabrics that build places for collective living, except when obstructed by geographical features and road infrastructure.

Inspired by constant internal migrations, the city of interior boundaries treats neighborhoods like old toys: once they no longer give pleasure they are discarded, expanding an increasingly disconnected urban sprawl devoid of life, separating social classes. This process applies almost constant pressure and has caused the disappearance of historical and heritage centers that are hard to maintain (or so the argument goes), leading to mass demolitions for real-estate developments or in return for compensation. In parallel, the rich and powerful claim for themselves plots of Rurality to turn them into the Countryside for leisure activities or to expand the periphery with private urban developments.

Tropical cities' urban centers are almost invariably residential deserts functioning as sprawling, open air shopping malls dominated by informal traders and occupied temporarily as nodes for different transport systems. Thousands of people pass through them during the day, but they are very seldom residential. This creates an archipelago city where everything that physically binds it together as an urban fabric is also what separates it socially.

In the world of architecture there are currently two contrasting tendencies for interventions in such tropical urban fabrics. At one extreme, some argue that interventions should be based on bottom-up community processes, where projects are co-designed and co-authored. This well-meaning approach tries to fill the void left by the state. In collaboration with others, architects become self-proclaimed community leaders or facilitators of processes given the lack of committed and targeted public measures and policies that are inclusive and democratic. They get involved, prioritizing solutions over ideas, leverage artisanal knowledge and in processes in time. To some extent, this model scorns architectural reflection, which it considers aestheticist, domineering, sophisticated, elitist, and, in some cases, invasive and patriarchal. Albeit well-intentioned, this approach is certainly unequal to the challenges facing today's societies, in situations that constantly call into question the architect's capacity, education, and tools.

At the other end of the spectrum, another operating model advocates top-down public policy interventions: grandiloquent plans with ambitions over time and space, closer to the modern ideals of the masterplan. In such cases, projects are the result of vertical policies and involve bureaucrats, specialists, advisors, and any number of public officials, who try in vain to connect the reality on the ground and the mirages they see from the comfort of their desks.

Those who apply this methodology remain closely attached to current trends, whether this means urban acupuncture, tactical urbanism, smart cities, or new urbanism. Before developing their own models they try desperately to import success stories from elsewhere, without showing any interest in building or creating their own instruments or ideas. According to this way of thinking and acting, solutions are interchangeable. If an urban cable car has worked in one place, urban cable cars will become the go-to solution everywhere. If it has proved successful turning centers into technological parks in one city, the same idea will be repeated. Proponents of this approach increasingly believe in the use of technology as an instrument of action but, given their lack of ideas and support for technocratic tools—and with the terms of office prescribed by law—technology is increasingly seen as a "transformative" resource. However, technology is simply a vacuous pretension of bringing about social transformation; a mediocre, short-termist response.

Digital technology as an urban tool hardly resolves the problems in tropical cities. It rarely becomes a truly practical instrument. The system needs to be constantly fed with data, with the corresponding interpretations and applications, rather than as a simple technological device that turns on streetlights, measures the temperature or, in the most disturbing and widespread example, monitors citizens, promising them security or expanding a new border through digital means.

This model eschews management systems that allow architectural knowledge to have a public impact. In a facile way, it rules out the option of opening up architecture competitions, since these require slightly more management; instead, the authorities prefer strengthening their architecture and planning offices within their institutions, at the cost of lowering the quality of life in the city and its public infrastructure. With their policies of austerity, most architects and project directors have meager experience to tackle complex projects. Such decisions lead to repetitive, almost identical interventions. Solutions commonly consist of a mediocre modularity or systematization to produce the same responses for different places, sacrificing valuable opportunities not only for the city but also for the development of architecture itself, where new aspects of knowledge and spatial diversity can be created.

This model only brings architecture into the picture when it decides it wants an icon to give identity, a media profile, and as a participant in the society of the spectacle. In both cases, there is clearly an inability to use both the form and historical precedents, and even previous experiences, as a source of ideas. This does not mean that big ideas call for big projects. Before projects, we need architectural ideas, as well as an analysis of their possible outcomes and opportunities. Urban ideas position projects in an intermediary position to reconcile different groups' interests and the most common corresponding methods of their practice. Projects articulate top-down decisions with bottom-up requirements.

To some extent, this situation is absurd: architects working at a grassroots level with the most vulnerable populations as well as their colleagues issuing prescriptions and general guidance from up on high, unfortunately share the same tendency to dispense with architectural ideas and experiences existing in the space between disciplinary issues and the professional realities through the project. This phenomenon is partly due to architects' inability to make themselves demonstrably necessary.

But a certain type of architect exists who can play an essential intermediary role. Architects who understand and apply a tropical spatial mindset can articulate spatial disciplines. By strategically blurring the boundaries between them, they can introduce a common fabric that can incorporate landscaping, urban design, and architecture through an integral and integrating project capable of blurring invisible boundaries. This gives a common fabric to those who are settled there and brings into play new factors, making room for agents of transformation and other social dynamics through specific projects.

Their architecture is an exception in the system that usually depends on public competitions, or else is linked to a handful of political and economic leaders with a different understanding of the public realm, perhaps with the necessary naivety of believing that people will want to appropriate and care for something beautiful and of high quality. This approach requires processes and is slower, but we live in a world of impatient capital, which makes such a response or solution less likely.

This architecture is socially ambitious. It gives priority to beauty or positions it differently in regard to necessity, ignoring the excessive pragmatism of believing that resolving the problem is enough on its own. Architecture of specific ambiguity is highly idealistic. In its aim of ensuring quality, it understands that simplifications are merely short-term solutions. Therefore, it often loses its legibility in the spheres of power or in the urge to resolve immediate problems, hence the politician of the day usually rules it out.

We may now have an opportunity **to let the architecture of tropical ideas and specific ambiguity occupy the spaces where it can reveal its capacities, where it has constructed its experience and proved its results:** in intermediate spaces facing social pressures and undergoing transitions. The architecture of specific ambiguity operates in the cities of interior borders, in more complex places that do not easily respond to the community dynamics of resolving the most pressing needs and that at the same time pose a problem for the authorities who are trying out top-down solutions. These are places that, as an initial step, require special ideas and for architecture inserted in them to have, paradoxically, enough flexibility and adaptability without losing their identity or crossing a thin and indistinct line that can easily turn them into iconic architecture that belongs to the society of the spectacle.[8]

Under these conditions, architecture of the tropical spatial mindset rejects control. It seeks to be difficult to close. It aims to be usable both day and night, as 24-hour architecture. And like a sponge, it absorbs and captures as many activities as possible and copes simultaneously with its surrounding forces in order to build a point of confluence, to deliver a solution that neither the city, nor the authority, nor the community of the place in question has been able to resolve outside the realm of consumption. The programs' distribution is located strategically, diluting the city and its elements in architecture and in landscape, so that the space is adaptable to many ways of life.

In relation to the places of invisible frontiers, this architecture is never about simplification. On the contrary, it derives from an increasing range of activities without classifying its users or segmenting them by economic status. This architecture assumes that its primordial condition is to insert a new system of spatial order, welcoming any architectural element that admits this conclusion, thus avoiding professional or social discrimination by stimulating, in particular, new behaviors in the space.

The Countryside: Transition and Instability

The architecture of tropical ideas focuses on transitional territories, namely those trapped between different social, economic, and political conditions. This situation currently affects the whole world...

8 I refer here to the idea of the society of the spectacle as understood by Guy Debord: "The spectacle is capital accumulated to the point that it becomes images." Guy Debord, *The Society of the Spectacle* (Valencia: Last Word Press, 2016).

We are undoubtedly living in a time of change. The order and instruments that offered stability and confidence are now in crisis, keeping us in a state of permanent doubt. Political populists are capitalizing on this state of affairs for their own benefit with fake news, nostalgic discourses, and distorted ideologies to glorify bygone eras, stimulating oppression and abuses under the pretense of reviving national glory.

They look for the right enemy to attack while defending their cause, or simply let the ignorance of those around them flourish, arguing that they are responding to the wishes of the people, in order to manipulate a reality unaligned with their interests. They undermine and endanger the construction of more democratic and free societies that have greater solidarity.

This uncertainty, accelerated by transitional processes that are still misunderstood, are also tangible in the territory. Many areas, especially in city outskirts, feel the pressure to transform in order to join the urban space, morph into the countryside, or expand the agricultural frontier of the rural space. The reason, directly linked to the change in the global order and the modification of existing paradigms, unavoidably puts pressure on energy resources, food, water, and the geographical configuration of powers, materialized in the urban and built environment. Although architecture is entirely restricted to establishing relations or to infer in a sphere such as this one, it can still articulate small-scale processes or agreements, as well as small cooperatives with better access to education infrastructure or improved healthcare. It can also mix together all these programs in order to address different realities based on new typologies.

Architecture can create territorial links between different conditions. Smart readings anticipate programmatic or spatial responses that are yet to occur but address current needs. Such architecture can also create spaces for other disciplines to participate without them losing their most essential qualities. This architecture becomes essential when we think about intervening in the Countryside.

The Countryside is inherently uncertain. Although it retains agricultural potential, and its natural reserves are still tangible within the landscape, its population and its organization in the space do not yet conform to purely urban criteria; its population still lacks a completely urban culture.

Oftentimes, the Countryside is a recreational space for city dwellers; it attracts tourism and is particularly busy at weekends, facing spatial and environmental pressures that often overwhelm the local road and service infrastructure.

Local populations inhabit a productive limbo and social dilemma. Although their nearby towns, particularly the larger ones, cannot be considered cities due to their characteristics or their demographic profiles, they do offer some services similar to those of a city, but lack first—or even second—rate healthcare, movie theaters, or institutions offering professional education. The Countryside's inhabitants should not be confused with large rural populations, and especially not with small cities. They are precisely an incomplete process: they are no longer towns but are not yet cities either.

This limbo calls into question the tools of architecture: How can we intervene somewhere without an urban layout but with scattered social services; where public space exists but lacks efficient mass public transport infrastructure; where there is still direct contact with the landscape and the relationship with the exterior?

The architecture of specific ambiguity in the Countryside organizes space with the development of plans that are less spatially prescriptive, supported by the typology's ambiguity by functioning as social catalysts. The regular partitions that classify visitors according to their activities are dispensed with. Spatial boundaries are defined in relation to a largely diffuse exterior, for increased capacity for activities at weekends when the population swells, but which are not unmanageably large during the weekdays. The objective is to create elastic spaces that expand and contract according to the particular day and time of year.

The section becomes more important since it provides shelter from the elements. This is also to make the space sufficiently flexible to handle social changes and different uses over time; it also needs to be easy to build and maintain. Its impact can also extend by increasing the shaded area around it to attract and provide somewhere comfortable for visitors. In the Countryside, spaces seek a multiple and possibly modular layout that must grow or shrink depending on the rhythms of development or the transformation of the territory. Typologically, it is best represented by the canopy.

Rurality: Neglected Territory

Rurality marks the beginning of the neglected territory. This area is used for agriculture and food production that is still worked largely without machinery but instead with intense manual labor; workers toiling in the wind and rain. These tropical lands are areas that, on the political radar and in the public consciousness, lie beyond the urban frontier but are also vital for the sustainability and operation of the cities, both for their capacity to produce food and as places with plentiful reserves of water, gas, energy, and oxygen.

This land is tied to the fate of the city, and vice versa. Decisions about Rurality and the Countryside are taken in Urban areas, while Rurality is still the city's pantry. Ultimately, the reality is that none of the tropical territories have the capacity for autonomy; their destinies and opportunities are interwoven.

These places consist of small and scattered settlements, usually with poor infrastructure, little internet access, poor-quality education, and above all, limited opportunities for the young. It is difficult to lead a full life or grow old in these areas.

Paradoxically, many populations retain traditional typologies or even small-scale industrial or pre-industrial complexes and infrastructure for the production and processing of food or natural derivatives that, in their typology and materiality, still teach significant technical, typological, and climate lessons. Some well-preserved towns have maintained their built heritage: historical landmarks on their well-defined city blocks, in their constructions, in their typologies and in the morphology of how they live. Processing plants for coffee, cacao, tobacco, and sugarcane remain standing and provide valuable information that can connect to contemporary architectural practice. In most cases, they are simple projects whose architectural features are immediately recognizable because they lack material masks or phenomenological tricks. Built in remote areas, at the time of their construction they required an extremely high level of technical and formal competence. In general terms, they operate similarly to the most basic canopies that, supported by a structural grid, carry a lightweight roof. In a planned fashion, this extends their eaves far enough to keep out the rain blown by the wind, and shelter the interior from the fierce afternoon sun, enabling the construction of a space that is more dim than shaded. These spaces provide the historic proof of the sum of knowledge contained in occupying the geography through architecture consisting of specific elements and an ambiguous spatial experience.

The Wilderness: the Final Frontier

The Wilderness is the most endangered territory in the tropics. Its areas and populations are pressured by globalizing forces. Mining and oil are common extractivist forces. If they have not already staked their claim for many years, then these forces are circling around places with predatory intent. Other obscure and illegal powers also destroy the vegetation to expand the frontier of agriculture. The Wilderness is a territory where architecture lacks experience; design is largely absent. Scientific knowledge and the humanities are more present than architecture. Those who have dared to build have met with spectacular failure, as in the case of Fordlandia in Brazil.

Along with Rurality, the Wilderness is rich in natural resources: thick and impenetrable. It also contains abundant energy and biological reserves, threatened by exploitation.

The explosion of global tourism, accelerated by the culture of social networks—which consume the unconsumable in exchange for an image, a post, a like—has caused these areas to begin to feel the pressure of outside visitors seeking out special and unique experiences, hence the need and dilemma posed by opening them to the public. Finding a solution to this problem will not be easy. On the one hand, in most cases these tropical locations are completely beyond the government's control. The precariousness of many nearby settlements, due to the state's absence, has led to deforestation for the sale of timber, livestock, and plantations of soya among other crops. This lays bare the authorities' inability to respond properly. Drugs are also usually produced and transported in this kind of territory. At the same time, humans have never permanently occupied these places, one reason why they have remained intact. Armed criminal organizations prohibit logging and exploitation of the jungle's resources in order to go about their businesses away from prying eyes. How can we manage the Wilderness so that its current inhabitants can earn an income without the need to destroy and consume the forests and jungles, or else leave the future of these lands at the mercy of illegal or large extractivist organizations? How can we protect ancestral cultures living there, without making them vulnerable?

Although these are relevant questions to help the planet's sustainability by protecting and conserving the most fragile ecosystems, architecture can do nothing to help answer them. Architecture is a material act that constructs replacements to make somewhere inhabitable. Temporarily or permanently, it replaces biologically and energetically coordinated areas with new dynamics that are not necessarily closed-circuit or in line with pre-existing elements. This dilemma, while not exclusive to architecture in the Wilderness, is one of the important existential questions for architecture: it lets us question the range of actions in its commitment to sustainability, not as a construction system of half measures or moralistic ideas but for its relevance. Is everything we build and allow ourselves to make actually necessary? Can the commissions we receive be resolved in a different way that perhaps does not necessarily call for a construction?

However, we should not ignore the ideological conflict implied by these questions for architecture. In the coming years, there will certainly be a more frequent, almost inevitable, need to insert projects in the Wilderness. It will also possibly become necessary to attract certain kinds of tourism and turn its attractiveness into a kind of environmental monitor, placing eyes no longer on the streets but in the wilderness, to build a culture of collective consciousness that may seem distant but involves the planet's very survival.

Considering the appropriate architecture for these areas leads us to consider modular architecture that can be quickly assembled and disassembled, small self-supplying laboratories without needing energy infrastructure, which can even be repeated and inserted in the city. Architecture that can use material knowledge of low-energy consumption and zero-carbon emissions; that can manage its waste, use land responsibly, and even revive it.

Typology as History and Geography

Art offers us new perspectives on something that seemed normal and, in that way, convert it into an important input to organize, understand the territory, and conceive tropical space. Without describing the territory, we cannot comprehend it, and without a comprehension of it, architecture lacks meaning, since its raison d'être has no handle on its spatial structures, hence it would be a purely technical and material operation disconnected from its geographical and cultural condition.

It becomes necessary to scrutinize architecture's role in relation to the territory and the possible descriptions about it that are generated from an artistic perspective. Architecture could operate on a broader and more specific level. Which architecture emerges from that relation with the territory? What kind of space is produced by a geographical relation with the territory?

Architecture created by these gazes is a double agent capable of altering our perception about a specific place, and of transforming it responsibly. Architecture based on these criteria offers an understanding of the landscape and produces emotional bonds between the built space and the cultures based there. This architecture indicates to us relations that were unthinkable before it existed in those places. The mark that defines the limit of the space is the one that allows the confluence of factors and layers; that mark is what architecture constructs on the territory. These elements promise a unique link to the location's pre-existing elements that, seemingly scattered, did not have any meaning. Architecture weaves them together as a whole, constructs a new relation, and presents them with a coherence existing between them and the site.

If geography somehow establishes relations and indicates co-dependencies between the culture, climate, temperature, and altitude, then it also orients our perception in space. Typology, meanwhile, allows the confluence of the aforesaid factors and conditions in a spatial and material experience anchored to a site, which regulates the territory and extracts its architectural qualities.

Geography is a raw material because it creates overlaps between ways of life in relation to the surroundings in conjunction with history (typologies) as well as built and cultural facts taking place beyond the close connection to the territory. As such, architecture expands its interest and performance on a supra-regional scale, becoming closer to ecosystems of life. Assuming and accepting this confluence in architecture not only inserts it more broadly into reality but also builds up myriad relations in daily life.

Given the precariousness of traditional constructions throughout the tropics, few documents are available to us to trace the multiple typologies of the past or to catalogue yesterday's ways of life from a purely architectural perspective. Given this lack of material, colonizing societies imposed their typologies. Over the years, these were absorbed and silently modified. The tropics loathe writing their history, perhaps because all their days appear to be the same, due to a lack of any marked change of climate, as in the seasons. Documenting and establishing timelines also would appear to be fruitless. It is difficult to apprehend and extract information that feeds into the present.

Therefore, what is history in a place where the passing of time is not marked by starkly differentiated cycles in terms of temperature, foliage, and animal lives? What historical tools can establish a narrative and a connection with the material world when the very notion of history is practically non-existent?

Thinking about historical remains or ruins as accessible and narrative documents is occasionally almost impossible. Nature takes back control over its own territory, reclaiming flimsy constructions to leave us only with pictorial historical records that, from an Enlightened or Renaissance perspective, lack the objectivity to reveal to us the original ways of living. We are left with the impression given by the European gaze by experiencing an almost magical encounter with unknown people and customs of other lands, without any prior references regarding how they lived.

Due to this situation, these typologies are as true as if they were the living vestige of original ways of inhabiting space. As the sole document that has traveled in time, we refer to it as if it were the original, opening up Western and universal architecture to new references and annotations; this would allow and support an expanded and historical tradition of multicultural and simultaneously degenerated tropics, enabling and empowering the construction of a new discourse that enjoys greater liberties based on a problematic interpretation.

A wooden canopy with a roof to provide protection from the sun and rain—referring to the primitive hut—romantically refers not only to the myth of Adam's house in Paradise, but also to the possibility of a humanistic and enlightened construction whose foundation is the new world. From there, we can link the history of Western architecture with other architecture without a rigorously material documentation. That relationship with materials and with history obliges us to consider and observe which elements of the discipline of architecture are understandable for our aim of drawing up a narrative for tropical architecture born in such contexts while also making links to the wider world.

How can we make room in architecture for the tropical space and specific ambiguity when faced with this kind of situation? Which narratives apply to make the history of universal architecture genuinely universal, unlike the history of a nation for which the only important thing is its own experience?

In some way, the dilemma in which the narrative of tropical space and specific ambiguity is trapped is deciding how to involve local architectural practice by making connections to a possibly European-centered, Western approach. Accepting arbitrarinesses, the loss of facts and, undoubtedly, with the firm intention of also reclaiming that space as its own, the history of Western architecture is mainly the history of architecture conceived and written about from Europe. And as architects, we also form a part of this situation. If we fail to understand and explore this condition, the narrative of the tropical space is likely to remain an exotic anecdote relegated to a mere footnote.

If architects today are incapable of establishing and inserting a new link with that narrative, we cannot engage in a conversation with the world, let alone claim a more prominent position. We would continue with processes of distancing and isolation. Culturally, this would be a loss for the needs of contemporary liberal thinking, and, similarly, it would prevent architecture from being a necessary instrument for culture and politics. By ignoring this condition, we would be forever installing a binary model whereby the tropical space is judged by prevailing ideas, which have pigeon-holed tropical architecture according to certain traits. Such characteristics may be the most distinctive but are also the most superficial, for example in the ingenious use of scant resources or representing a social struggle against the inequalities of its context. We would lose the possibility of inserting ourselves in a more dense, complex, rich, and controversy-filled narrative that, in any case, makes it possible to open the spectrum and upset the playing board to give new value to differences and give them priority over the idea of diversity.

The result is far poorer and more limited when we analyze prevailing narratives. Therefore, we must once again refer to the most basic discussions and those that may even appear anachronistic. These lead us to think and appropriate two models of architecture and sources of universal information that need to be reconsidered: the hut and the cave, tectonics and stereotomy. These two cornerstones, that some consider old-fashioned or forgotten, lead us to suggest and understand that an architecture made in the tropics and through specific ambiguity is in fact an interpretive extension of an enlightened myth, a product of the arbitrariness of an incomplete and misunderstood history. Thanks to history as an open document, we can reformulate the past and glimpse other future options. As Giedion points out in *Space, Time, and Architecture*,[9] "History cannot be touched without changing it." Therefore, let's now touch it to make it our own.

9 Sigfried Giedion, *Space, Time, and Architecture* (Cambridge, Mass.: Harvard University Press, 1941).

Mountain, Terrace, and Layer = Volume, Platform, Wall

Thanks to a good climate and environmental conditions, in many parts of the tropics only some typologies have recorded residential features that have spread to other regions, establishing themselves in dissimilar, abrupt, and temporary locations for centuries. Even now, inhabiting means lightly accommodating some basic materials to give shape to the space for shelter from the rain or intense sun; a basic spatial arrangement that, even to this day, has left no traces as in the case of traditional constructions that are still in use. Some technical knowledge has been preserved and still gives shape to those vernacular forms of inhabitation. However, we cannot ignore exceptional examples of pre-Colombian architecture such as ceremonial churches and other sacred sites in Asia and South America.

Mitla, Teotihuacan, and Uxmal in Mexico; the sacred site of Purruchuco; or the Temples of the Sun and the Moon in Peru provide fantastic historical backgrounds of various ways of living in the American tropics. Since they are not inserted with the Western annals of architecture, we lack sufficient critical instruments to develop our arguments about these works. Although enough archeological material exists about such works of architecture, we are confronted with a disciplinary, sentimental, and aesthetic void in the sense of how they have been appropriated by architects from these regions.

At various points in twentieth-century history, and also in recent times, some attempts have been made to explore these pre-Hispanic works of architecture in high-quality projects and texts.[10] To absorb such references more deeply within the discipline is less important than establishing a broader panorama that might add new material

10 Rafael Moneo wrote eloquently about the wall as an element used by the Incas to structure space and as a building system. See "En los Andes," included in Rafael Moneo, *Escritos y conversaciones en el Perú* (Lima: Pontificia Universidad Católica del Perú, 2009).

to the established traditions to the Europe-centered visions and to the modernity deposited in the Americas.

While acknowledging our limited understanding of pre-Hispanic architecture, we should not ignore some interpretations and comments about some of its characteristics, which help clearly define the ideas of tropical space developed thus far. Similarly, these help thread narratives that have no reason to remain separate. Moreover, with these ideas we can search for ways of putting ideas into practice: we can enrich disciplinary questions.

Therefore, we will limit comments to a series of elements that are notable when visiting some of Peru's and Mexico's archeological sites. These notes are to be read as a travelogue, not as expert archeological opinions. This information has not been reviewed or corroborated, but simply inspired by visits and conversations in Purruchuco, Huaca del Sol y La Luna, Huaca Pucllana, Machu Picchu, Valle Sagrado and Cuzco, all in Peru. We also include our visits to the ruins in Tulum, Chichen Itzá, and Teotihuacan, in Mexico.

At these sites, the first thing that always becomes apparent is the clear intention to broaden architecture's scope to emulate geographical features with volumes, terraces, and walls, echoing the mountains and plateaus around these constructions.

These aesthetic and architectural ideas had already been referenced and registered through *Platforms and Plateaus*,[11] a text by Jørn
[1] Utzon which, along with Josef Albers' photographs and drawings made during his travels through Mexico, becomes an important document to reconcile and weave together European, pre-Hispanic, and tropical narratives.

The experience of visiting many of these sites clearly reveals how geography dictates their spatial, material, and volumetric codes.

11 Published in: https://proyectandoleyendo.files.wordpress.com/2011/01/plataformas-y-mesetas-jorn-utzon.pdf

What is remarkable about these spatial devices is their intention to dominate and tame geography at the same time as emulating and worshipping it.

From this dual condition, the platforms and terraces become [2]
the common thread running through the architecture. The ambivalence of excavating and piling up—terracing/cutting away to create a plane; and infilling/stacking to create height—constitute strategies to place human action in contact with the landscape's transformation through architectural ideas, to make it inhabitable. This foundational element, of preparing the earth, becomes the primordial action so that architecture not only exists but also echoes in the landscape as the dynamic geography that it is.

Flattening surfaces allows volumes to rise up in a partially abstract and literal way. Through imitation, the definition of the mass creates a visual and material link to the landscape. Today, this action reaffirms the cultural need to connect architecture to geography. From the pyramids of Teotihuacan to the silhouette of Huaca Pucllana, the arrangement of the mass becomes a geographical feature by acting as a silhouette, volume, and space.

Our perception of architecture in Teotihuacan is shaped by its [3]
large volumes and bulk. There the mass consists of—and is made with—blocks, both in its material configuration and in the reading produced by the whole. Careful examination reveals those volumes to be composed of tiny stones affixed to the large mass, creating a strange effect of scale that makes us wonder whether something so voluminous and large is truly made of such small elements: a spatial sensation of doubt and wonder. This can be appreciated in the lower
part of the archeological complex, where the condition of mass and [4]
volume changes. Part of its monumentality is emphasized and built by the volumes' relationship with the platforms that connect and receive a geography that manipulates the effect of perspective based on a topographical slope. We walk in a valley of pyramids that dilutes nature and the artifice.

[1]

If we turn our thoughts to the experience of exploring Purruchu- [5]
co, we feel that the space is defined by planes—not by volumes—of walls that are slightly offset from one to the next, obliging us to move and wander through the space; to pass through layers; to seek out the openings that never completely face the axis of the circulation, preventing the possibility of viewing the space profoundly and requiring an understanding of the spaces one by one before we transit toward the next. By inserting various empty spatial enclosures as courtyards with platforms inside, we can look out at the surrounding walls and, in this way, discover a new exterior reference built within complex. In a similar fashion, Huaca Pucllana shows us that the geography, its terraces, and platforms consist of small adobe elements that accrete to form a mass. They rise up above the flat terrain and form a new mountain: mountains on the plains, observatories of the world.

Through careful, comparative observation, we can see a fundamental difference in how space is organized in each of these works of architecture. Today, a possibly arbitrary confluence exists between these spatial conditions in what we call tropical space, with which we define the boundary of the architecture and its volumes. In any case, although the procedure is divergent in the use of elements to structure the space—volumes versus planes—the effects in the spatial experience find coincidences, such as the wonder of scale, the search for monumentality through filters in the passage from the exterior to the interior and in the relationship with geography through thermal regulators, since many exterior and nearby references are inserted to shift from the absolute toward a porous space.

These conditions and qualities do not seem far removed from the aforesaid modern tropicalism. Possibly, the natural and spontaneous reflection on these places and on their forms leads to a conclusion that there is a coincidence, albeit from different perspectives, in how these societies, separated in time and space, have been able to define characteristics and instruments, material and spatial layouts and effects, which maintain similarities in their principles and responses to create their space in the American tropics.

[2]

[3]

[4]

Greenhouses and Canopies

We need to contrast the previous gaze and focus on models of spatial organization that are closer to typological forms that have traveled in time, inhabiting the long history of the discipline of architecture and accepting revisions, new directions, and transformations.

Greenhouse and canopy typologies may provide us the means of understanding space in the tropics, and its most propitious forms. Despite apparent similarities in their model of organization in plan, differences can be found in their sections and operation: while the greenhouse is a spatial system with defined perimeters, in order to concentrate temperature inside, the canopy is the opposite: it provides a roof while allowing air to flow through beneath.

These models of spatial organization help define two ways of understanding and extracting elements to define specific ambiguity. The greenhouse is designed to be filled with the "exterior" thanks to its ability to contain plants and vegetation. Mirroring the tropics themselves, it recreates the tropical effect and operating logic. The canopy, meanwhile, offers continuity to the spatial experience of being beneath vegetation, of extending it. The contention and extension of the exterior constitutes two constant alternatives that create, as an initial impulse, a porous construction: to establish layers, select elements to organize the space. It is interesting to note that both typologies are present in the vernacular architecture for the production of tropical foodstuffs or flower-growing, when they are fabricated with remarkably simple materials and using low-tech construction systems: plastic, glass, wood, iron, straw, and dried leaves are some of the chosen materials.

These typologies contain a series of essential principles and opportunities to respond to the characteristics of tropical space. These constructions establish an order based on the plan, particularly on the structure's homogenous and continuous repetition. This attribute leads to a defined and an undefined scope of action, developed

[5]

from decisions arising during the project's evolution and the needs of the program to be adjusted. The structure operates as a system that is both attentive and unconcerned. The space regulated by the structure tolerates being filled or emptied depending on the moment. Due to that adaptability, it is constructed as an open system. The structural grid creates the possibility for the architecture to operate as a system of undefined adaptive growth that plays with the passing of days or years and adapts to varying topographies, mediating between the ground and the sky without losing its spatial identity.

These open-plan systems construct defined enclosures or exchange the system of partitions for flexible, dynamic, or mixed elements, thus constantly disconnecting the spaces from the structural logic. This gives freedom to programs and ensures multiplicities.

This situation is symmetrical to the spatial idea of the Mezquita
[6] in Córdoba (Spain), whose spatial order and ambiguous elements has led to mutations and adaptations over the years depending on the culture and historical juncture, as described brilliantly by Rafael Moneo in *La vida de los edificios*.[12]

Although the structural system dominates the plan, and the elements that define space are subjected to this rhythm and module, the section is still vital and mainly prioritizes managing the "outdoors," like temperature or air, operating as a landscaping or geographical connection. The section forms relations of scale and spatial ambiance, hence it not only becomes detached from the idea of an absolute interior but, particularly, from the need for the façade to be a compositional element. By becoming free, it can usually be treated with systems of filters and be supported by built facts.

12 Rafael Moneo, *La vida de los edificios* (Barcelona: El acantilado 360, 2017).

The Built Fact

The built fact is not exclusive to the tropics, but it must be given a new meaning in these parts of the world in order to counteract the sediments deposited by naïve regionalism that labeled and limited tropical architecture to the cliché of revolving around its use of resources. Naïve regionalism inopportunely judges and believes that the architecture of the tropical spatial mindset is interesting due to its lack of resources, visible on account of its poor and austere materials. This overlooks or even completely effaces its spatial or architectural qualities. The material condition appears to function as a way of valuing, classifying, and predisposing critical values to analyze and judge such architecture. But in the same way that it is fair to reposition the meaning of the built fact and its cultural construction, it is also necessary to determine that not all materials and technical assemblies are operational in the tropics or in the formation and creation of the space of tropical thought.

Built facts are universal technical models that help understand the spatial understanding of buildings and their structural materialization. Furthermore, they constitute those decisions, instructions, and technical possibilities appropriated by tropical cultures in the construction of spaces for their architecture to breathe freely and to resonate as a primitive and local action: to create a space with undefined yet also impermeable and shaded boundaries. In the tropics, the built fact is an objective, technical, and material decision; it is not a direct consequence of the limitations or possibilities of the context, or of the architect's academic heritage.

In no way is it a random outcome or response of the resource factor given the supposed lack of means. It is not a surplus of capital or the inevitable state of aesthetic and formal ambitions built around a set of limitations. Nor is it a question of just building something that lasts. On the contrary, it is a question of ensuring that the mindset behind tropical architecture be inextricably linked to its material condition and become possible as an experimentable space on the margins of the solutions of habitational problems.

In other words, the built fact is intrinsic to the understanding of tropical spaces; it materializes ideas based on the construction process, so that these notions can become a spatial experience.

Therefore, we argue that the built fact takes into account materials and their technical aspects as well as the coherent continuity of spatial ideas. As such, we can insert interpretations into their physical aspects that explain the type of space built on the basis of material resources, and in this way evaluate its coherence. The built fact is not only a technical or material problem in a context with its possible effects and consequences on architectural thought but also represents an action that defines and conditions the type or form of the space.

Spatial ideas in the tropics imply limited forms and consequently limited building technologies and models. If we work on the basis that indicates to us that material restrictions in the tropics are an opportunity to establish a technical link to craftmanship and to be positioned at a halfway point toward material industrialization, we can assume that the physical aspect of the built fact is a way of constructing freedoms.

One way of finding freedoms can be achieved by exploring Moneo's text, *La arbitrariedad en la arquitectura*, and by recognizing a new condition of common stereotomy and tectonics in tropical architecture. No longer based on traditional definitions but as a constant inversion of its effects on space and its technical and material assemblages to construct spaces that are permeable and ambiguous, porous and undefined.

Arbitrary Facts, Material Instruments

When Moneo explains the background to the Corinthian canon following Vitruvius' *Ten Books on Architecture*, he not only explains and

[6]

describes how the Corinthian capital was formed and invented. He also discusses the dilemma of understanding architecture as imitation or invention. The value of the built fact lies at this intersection, to find freedom—the liberty for architecture to pass through the membrane of the discipline and become verifiable as a spatial experience—which returns to the discipline as a new reference point, and in that way is assumed as its own material. This freedom is rooted in the possibility of constantly verifying the impact of built ideas for a specific place and social group to see and define its successes, to learn from the unexpected, and finally, to be reinformed.

Moneo tells the following story, along the lines of Vitrivius:

> A Corinthian girl, from a good family, already ready for marriage, fell ill one day and died. After the funeral, her servant put in a basket the girl's beloved vessels and cups and placed them on her tomb. He covered the basket with a tile to preserve her belongings longer than if the basket had been left open. He happened to place the basket on top of an acanthus root which, despite being weighed down by the basket, flowered in springtime with a profusion of stalks and flowers. The tile on the basket caused the leaves to curl around them as scrolls. Callimachus, known to the Athenians as Katatechnos for the elegance and refinement of his work, passed by the tomb and noticed the offering and its tender leaves. Attracted by the composition and novelty of this shape, this model gave him inspiration for the columns he carved for the Corinthians, fixing the proportions for this order.[13]

Looking beyond from the arbitrariness of assigning meaning to the shape or constructing a cultural rationale based on a random event—for example, the role of a nature that reclaims everything

13 Rafael Moneo, "La arbitrariedad en arquitectura," in *Escritos y conversaciones en el Perú* (Lima: Pontificia Universidad Católica del Perú, 2009).

for itself—this same arbitrariness allows us to assume a limit for language and for instruments; in other words, it forces us to choose and select. And in this determination and decision, a position is taken. A triple confluence in the above story almost goes undetected yet is remarkable and unique: the technical organization, the construction of a context, and the material constitution in such a simple and significant story. It is worth noting the particular amount of information produced by a simple arrangement: basket, tile, acanthus.

First, we have the circular, handmade basket as a handcraft, bearer of an ancestral knowledge passed down through the generations. This tells us about a transferred cultural knowledge based on a specific use of a technique and a material, such as weaving a fiber. Furthermore, the basket is a receptacle that can contain something inside, defining a perimeter between an interior and an exterior, but thanks to being woven, allows air and light to pass through it, operating firstly as a filter and a membrane that administers the exchange between the two media before forming an absolute shape and limit. Moreover, it insinuated a structure in how the fibers are woven, supporting the weight of the tile and, in the same way, it mediates between the nature that grows and supports the acanthus. The fiber is filter, form, and structure.

The use of the tile as a material is notable. It appears to be an orthogonal and rational shape, impermeable, and prevents rainwater from entering. The tile works by weighing down and covering the basket. Interestingly, the tile is square—in other words, standardized. It has already been processed in a production system that is repeatable to produce the same object. It can be manufactured in exactly the same way for multiple purposes: to cover or to stack. The brick is solid and continuous.

Finally, we should also explore the effect of the unexpected, the exchange between nature and architecture that allows nature and the built form to swap information, so that it becomes impossible to imagine nature (place) without the existence of the built fact (basket and brick) and, similarly, for architecture to be seen absolutely incomplete without the atmospheric and environmental dynamic provided by nature.

Moneo's text interestingly contains a recurring confluence of the idea that architects "are capable of transforming an image, a figure, a form, into an architectural element and, in the final instance, into a building." He adds that "the arbitrariness introduced in the past appeals against oblivion, and all architectural theory justifies the form through a rational approach."[14]

Therefore, we can assume the confluence of the three models of material, technical, and architectural production to be instrumental in the mythical origin of the Corinthian capital: the basket, the tile, and the acanthus. This union leads us to believe not only in the form of things and in the space produced by each material, but also in the idea of an assemblage in response to a specific situation, based on the built fact. Therefore, the built fact is understood as the technical exchange between knowledge and materials being probably more enduring by using the available resources to shape ideas in a specific spatial system.

Inverting the Meaning of Tectonics and Stereotomy

Material and technical confluence has been defined over time within the known criteria of stereotomy and tectonics. Built facts in the tropics notably invert the meaning of these aspects. Both stereotomic tectonics and tectonic stereotomies are buildable thanks to the material, normative, and technical resources. At a midway point between industrialization and craftmanship, it makes it possible to resolve assemblages between these two things spontaneously,

14 Ibid.

offering expressive freedom to the materials and to the great whole in an ambiguous and contradictory way.

Once again, it is worth revisiting the ideas and definitions of stereotomy and tectonics so that, once we have charted our course we can then take a detour. With this in mind, let us be guided by Alberto Campo Baeza's definition, published on his website in a text called *Cajas, cajitas y cajones*.[15]

Stereotomic architecture is that in which gravity operates continuously, uninterruptedly, and unswervingly in a structural system. The spatial and structural continuity is absolute. Such architecture has a massive, monolithic, and even cave-like appearance. Its expressive manifestation is ambiguous. We doubt whether it rests on the ground or in fact emerges from it. This is an architecture with a constant shelter that does not necessarily distinguish between wall and roof. The structure can be hidden within the materials themselves and in the form, but its spatial continuity exists because of its almost uniform substance. With its dim ambiance, this model is derived from the cave.

In the case of tectonic architecture, gravity is not transmitted continuously but mediated by the integration of component elements, creating an expression of divergent multiplicity that nevertheless has confluences: knots where the construction is regulated by articulations that express differences while also integrating them. This is the architecture of bones; it occupies the territory and geography by rising up from the land, constructing a new surface or parallel existence to permit life around it to continue its course. This is architecture designed to create shade as protection from the heat.

For this reason, it is a regulating architecture that controls its perforations and surfaces to control and filter light, in order to decide where to enter and how to move. This model refers to the hut.

15 Alberto Campo Beza, *Cajas, cajitas y cajones* in: https://www.campobaeza.com/wp-content/uploads/2016/12/1996_LA-IDEA-CONSTRUIDA_09_Cajas-cajitas-cajones.pdf (in Spanish).

To describe and understand the built fact based on the traditional principles of stereotomy and tectonics, we need to reposition the meaning of space and the way of creating, defining, and valuing it. We need to understand that its material condition is where the transitional forms make it possible to redescribe the hut and the tomb, the cave and the archetype according to a different set of rules that transform the instrumental into something pragmatic and escape the strictly regionalist or ambitiously modern narratives. These rules allow the flow of the contradictory as material positioning, and of the ambiguous as a spatial condition.

Whereas stereotomy inserts material continuity into the space defining the surface, tectonics has a regulatory and administrative function. By coinciding in a territory where architecture can be free from the technical need for thermal insulation, spaces can be undefined with and interiors arranged as if there were outdoors, ruling out the possibility of an absolute interior as a clearly defined place.

In this way, they become vulnerable in the way that these aspects of regulation/administration and giving continuity to the surface contribute to the whole, which can be distributed and reorganized in the built fact based on criteria to regulate the temperature and on the availability of artisanal rather than industrial processes, which creates an exchange of information models to give shape and become materially and technically located between both environmental and spatial conditions. A cave made of sticks, a monolithic hut.

This opportunity mainly emerges from a pragmatic idea that, apart from enabling, technically questions the instruments and their results. Similarly, it suggests shifting the perspective on how things appear to be in order settle on what they are like actually; in other words, it inverts what seems obvious. In its dislocation, architecture acquires new meanings, constructing novelty on a sense of liberty.

This way of understanding construction as means of shaping space makes a building materially possible at a specific moment and according to a particular set of rules. It also requires understanding and a positioning at the time of putting ideas into practice.

Details, imperfections, accidents; arbitrariness, structures, and anti-details; these factors are essential to prevent the built fact from becoming a deceptive maneuver that conceals how things work. On the contrary, it encourages processes to become clear, objective, and direct; to express how things are done, to open the black box, and to reveal to us how the building is made, where it bears its load, where it is strengthened, what is happening with the finishes. This understanding of the whole as a technical and material resource by default offers simple maintenance. An effort should be made to prevent the built detail from becoming a system of concealment but instead a way of making things possible, of making architecture take responsibility. It should help us understand the finished construction and simultaneously offer architects freedom in achieving their professional goals.

Intermediate Spaces

In order to understand and define intermediate spaces, we need to describe the climate in the tropics. It is also worth highlighting that such spaces are possible due to the fact that tectonics and stereotomics are dislocated to exchange and invert their qualities, and to blur their boundaries.

In a single day, temperatures can vary by more than 10 degrees centigrade. Torrential downpours and fierce heat and other changes in the weather can occur almost simultaneously and without warning. This is the situation to be addressed and appropriated by architecture conceived with a tropical mindset. Although the tropical space is generally considered to enjoy permanent, year-round springlike weather, its architecture needs to be designed for uncertain climatic conditions. The appropriate architecture for this territory calls for different but small variations in managing and defining boundaries and in defining space.

Intermediate spaces acquire a dual status. They consist of architectural devices that help stretch the boundaries of space to turn it into a living space, and not only a border zone or place of transit. This condition creates the experience of perambulating between indoor and outdoor conditions.

Although these spaces are born of the need to regulate the climate and the temperature, their side-effects are socially the most interesting in order to define the space. The space acquires greater depth due to the necessary filters to ensure the materials' durability and resistance to temperature changes, to manage light, shade or dimness, to provide shelter from the rain, and to create transitions.

Its afferent effects are not simply inscribed in the building's material perimeter or in the precise definition of its rooms and spaces. This normally non-programmatic "leftover" space is spontaneously used by visitors to these buildings, which broadens the sense of limits and the public space.

A public space is the result of a usable surplus and an interior spatial organization that acquires social value in a specific way. It is presented as an opportunity to erase the border between city and architecture, to become open to a diverse range of activities; energy efficient (there are no machines); enabler of built facts, the intermediate space is the materialization of architecture understood as generosity. By responding to a need or private request, it is capable of delivering more, of expanding the useful space, of adapting to various conditions without losing its spatial identity without this being relevant. We are simply referring to an open architecture.

This architectural approach makes an obligatory contact with the city; consciously addressing the side-effects of its positioning dilutes what is happening on the street and must happen between the walls. This spatial articulation gives a different meaning to the territory and to architecture's role in its reciprocity with the urban context, also ensuring that architecture is active within geography. Architecture can therefore describe the territory on its multiple scales; it can generously prepare new fabrics of relations with its immediate context and more distant surroundings; it can extend its component parts, openings, and filtering systems to give its interior a broad range of elements, figures, forms, spatial conditions, and atmospheric experiences that are not necessarily formed there but which, once introduced into the architectural experience as a form of designing and building relations in space, makes it possible to establish a new scale of spatial and critical values, no longer necessarily solely dictated by the nearest place but by the simultaneous conversation between typology, form, climate, matter, geography, available technology, and customs.

In the architecture of tropical ideas, this multiplicity of situations is not resolved on the basis of the dichotomy as in the case of modern architecture. It is understood with the chaining together of built facts and transitional forms that help construct a specific ambiguity created and configured on the basis of gradients, avoiding an object-based, absolutist, and totalitarian approach.

Although we critically appraise architecture's role in tropical contexts, particularly the glib analysis of its social aims, as well as the naïve regionalism and how the region's architecture has become a cliché, there is no doubt that—independently of the critical perspective that tries to explain or understand architecture in these parts of the world—it is clearly adept at responding to, understanding, and intervening in complex social, environmental, and economic contexts. The architecture here is constructed with an optimistic pragmatism. All good architecture is like a Trojan horse: it contains hidden capabilities, even going beyond questions of form, in its way of unfolding, housing, and allowing encounters, exchanges, and relations that create fairness.

Specific Ambiguity

Specific ambiguity is the action—the experience—of perceiving, organizing, and occupying space in the tropics. It is mediated by, and comes from, the architecture itself and in its own instruments. The project is the point where these coincide, in addition to being the tool that manages the confluence between ways of making and building techniques. Both need to coexist and belong to different material times in order to construct a boundary that expands, contracts, and breathes, creating an elastic and ambiguous space that is difficult to apprehend and describe.

Specific ambiguity is something kinetic, shifting, and liquid, and therefore difficult to record in photographs or graphically. This condition coincides with, and reacts to, ways of occupying space, the climate (in its many daily variations), which creates contrasts between atmospheres, scales of reference, and relations.

It works for itself and with surroundings based on redescriptions of the outdoors, mediated by architectural elements such as pergolas, awnings, courtyards, thresholds, zaguans (passageways leading from the entrance door to a central courtyard), and balconies that inform the experience as a narrative, multicolored thread that constructs transitions from the shifting realm of the living to the blur of the boundary.

Specific ambiguity is not an ideologically absolute or one-way process. It is supported by architectural issues that can become linked to a tradition of the practice that goes far beyond the building and can connect to the tradition of history, culture, and geography in a particular reality.

It is a critical approach to thinking and acting, a location-action-idea that is contradictory, uncertain, enigmatic, and defined. In any case, although in some contexts and moments it may seem opaque or impossible to bring about, it is heir and a participant in a universal history, including those references to which the contradictions of its representation have led to creating particular appropriations of improbable documents that are disassociated from their place of origin.

A good example of this condition is the appropriation of the patterns published in Owen Jones's *The Grammar of Ornament*,[16] a book [7]
brought over to Colombia by British mining engineers in the second half of the nineteenth century and that, in the middle of the Colombian mountains, and specifically in the regions of Antioquia, Risaralda, Caldas, and Quindío, were translated an adapted as carved openwork in in wooden doors and windows to help regulate the tem- [8]
perature of homes and public buildings. This appropriation was converted into a national heritage style.

Accepting this condition, these representations are as true and instrumental as if they were the living vestige of original and unique remains to inhabit and occupy the space. As the only document that has travelled in time, we approach it as if it were true, opening the narrative of Western and universal architecture to new references and notes, allowing and supporting a historical tradition of the expanded tropics.

As mentioned above, specific ambiguity is marked, defined, powered, and restricted by the tropical climate and geography, based on the form's ability to assume and respond to those confluences and contradictions. It adapts and changes simultaneously with it. In other words, the form assembles, constructs, translates, gathers, and distributes confluences of places and ideas, opportunities and restrictions, changes and traditions, utopia and history, instinct and discourse, matter and space, geography and territory, time and eventualities, which are mediated by architecture and its elements, with the deviations, surprises, and contradictions that this implies.

16 Owen Jones, *The Grammar of Ornament* (New York: Dorling Kindersley Pub., 2001).

The form operates as an instrument of negotiation and confluence, as a strategy and response supported by models of primitive material organization; in other words, the stereotomy and tectonics, albeit distorted in its actual operation. **Undefined spaces are possible if stereotomy is an architecture that inserts material continuity into space through the definition of the surface, and tectonics is both a regulatory and administrative architecture, when coexisting in a territory where architecture can be freed from the need for thermal insulation: being indoors as if being outdoors, denying the absolute possibility of the interior as a clearly defined place, losing its edges—Gestalt—to acquire continuity based on interior and exterior transitions.**

The specific elements of architecture contribute to the composition of the whole, mainly based on its individual act of regulating/administering the space, accessibility, the climate. These elements become vulnerable by being distributed and reorganized in the built fact through temperature-regulating criteria. This also takes into account the availability of artisanal rather than industrial processes, exchanging information that shape and are located technically and materially between environmental and spatial conditions. In specific ambiguity, architectural elements play with appearances, with walls made of pilotis, roofs without façades, porous edges, technical linkages in the structure, circulation spaces as living areas, dynamic partitions, lightweight enclosures.

This is tropical space: it expands and contracts as necessary. The architectural elements define limits in their direct expression and integrality: the structure takes priority over partitions. Beams, columns, and roofs are organized primitively and sequentially. This is similar to Laugier's hut, which basically imposes that primordial idea of defining, with borders, where architecture begins and, at the same time, where these edges are blurred. With this rationale, specific ambiguity does not refer to the sun in its strictly thermal sense. In the tropics, the sun is also relevant as a light source and not only to provide heat. In the warmth of the tropics, light enters the space from below rather than from above. If we were to take that approach, we would be building heat pockets much more suitable for more southern or northern locations.

Regardless of location, modernity always imposed the repetition of forms and geometries, and postmodernity always imposed different forms. Therefore, we need to explore the appropriate response of tropical space to geography.

Tropical space consists of layers that need to be discovered. An ample threshold defines the boundary between interior and exterior. The initial experience of being in the presence of tropical architecture occurs at this ambiguous boundary. It is a space that needs to be unveiled, patiently observed, explored. The architecture of tropical ideas is located halfway between states and conditions. It also documents and describes the territory through codes, instruments, and ambivalent spatial alphabets; based on its effects, perforations, frames, and indications.

Reaffirming or trying to validate ideas, projects, and interventions of architecture in a world that demands coherence and exactness from a position that encourages redundancy or contradictions may appear risky. In particular, it is unusual at this time when the fast pace of life demands quick, easy, and sometimes simplistic understandings reducible to diagrams that cannot be called architecture. Or, worse still, projects essentially become commercial slogans that spread like wildfire through a network of likes and followers. However, in the same way that specific ambiguity establishes a framework to be understood and operated, the architecture of tropical ideas needs to find instruments for it to articulate its raison d'être from the world of ideas to the possibility of experimenting and interiorizing the exterior without the latter losing its features, either through contradictory conditions or associations based on non-binary situations. This creates the opportunity for giving transitional forms to this system of ideas and action.

BYZANTINISCH
BYZANTINE Nº 3.
BYZANTINS
TAFEL XXX
PL. XXX

[8]

Transitional Forms

Architectural elements used in projects created with a tropical mindset are important not only to give shape as a unit but also to define borders by making them imprecise and elastic. These elements operate around the perimeter that defines the surface of the relationship between the exterior and the interior, and also as dynamic systems that define and characterize the use of space for it to be unstable: to establish links between the parts and the whole, as well as to give meaning to something broader, more complex. This role is based on multi-referential spaces, which avoid referring to themselves but instead constantly construct relations, not only between the works themselves but also with the conditions and restrictions imposed from outside.

Transitional forms are the typologies, elements, and instruments of architecture that question boundaries and are used individually or through combinations to define the tropical space, giving meaning to the whole.

These forms can dilate and articulate the interior with the exterior, preventing absolute dominance of the exterior understood as the world, and the interior as the totalizing point of self-reference. In other words, transitional forms are the specific instruments used to create specific ambiguity based on the built fact to mediate between living areas and flows, as well as to define the spatial condition between the inside and the outside, a limit that is intermediary and a point of confluence.

Transitional forms are not unlike other architectural forms, nor are they excluding or exclusive compared to other ways of defining space outside the tropics. As mentioned throughout this text, the architecture of specific ambiguity does not rule out the possibility that its principles and ways of understanding space are usable in non-tropical parts of the world and societies. Indeed, their greatest ambition is to participate in a wide range of references and narrative linkages over and above nationalisms, regionalisms, and identity-based appropriations. They are generous in the type of space that they build. Transitional forms constitute a spatial system that operates simultaneously, and dynamically articulates long transitions between interior and exterior with ideas, local realities, and universally applicable disciplinary autonomies.

Transitional forms can be established based on general questions about architecture, such as limits, perforations, voids, and platforms, giving them new value. Although this system of defining and characterizing elements is not exclusively tropical and can equally apply to any other geographical area—since they form part of the architecture's basic grammar—the way in which they have been combined or developed in the architecture of tropical ideas imbues them with a different connotation not only as a response to universal conditions but also as particular inventions that acquire universal interest.

Boundaries

As in any architecture, the boundaries of specific ambiguity, based on transitional forms, allow architecture to emerge. Without boundaries architecture cannot exist. Marking a boundary may be the first step in architecture, as it distinguishes between being inside and outside, according to a series of spatial ideas, beyond resolving the need for a dwelling.

Architecture is necessarily about imposing limits; a boundary that determines what belongs to the world, and what belongs to the space built around ideas. In this case, and in line with what has been discussed above, the limit in the architecture of tropical ideas consists of blurred boundaries and ambivalences.[17] Establishing the elements that define architecture's limits according to these characteristics forces us to initially define whether the limit constantly plays with the idea of inhabitation or not. Setting limits is not creating an absolute boundary; its main function is to mediate between an interior and an exterior, making it a livable space to create an inhabitable limit as well as another transition.

We have defined three types of boundaries. First, the structure as a technical system of thought and action. To think about structure and putting ideas into practice is to determine the field of action for architecture and to understand that both gravity and weight are elements that enter into negotiation with the instinct and the ideal of creating architecture. The structure makes it possible for the space defined by architectural ideas to exist. The second type of boundary is the roof, providing shade and differentiating the climate, the primitive act of distinguishing between interior and exterior. Finally, we can refer to the wall as marking the boundary to organize, regulate, and define the space in relation to the exterior as a filter and based on our ideas of an enclosure or space.

STRUCTURES

The structure, and specifically columns, probably constitute the component that enables us to define the most direct and objective multi-referential meaning when the space establishes extensive relations with the exterior—when simply a canopy—as well as when it establishes them in a limited way through windows and perforations. The structure, by creating a grid in the space, not only indicates the X, Y, and Z axes as a multidimensional spatial reference. Above all, without any tricks or deceptions, these give us the

17 We are aware of Toyo Itō's ideas in *Blurring Architecture*. However, here we refer to this concept in a way that is more analogous with, and dependent on, the most basic elements of architecture without considering digital technologies. In any case, we feel a resonance with Itō's perspective on the program and its possibility to allow temporary changes, and consequently changes in the space.

most basic pointers for how to understand the space. They indicate to us the scale, height, width, and length of the spatial modulation, the references established by the architect in addition to the measurements. Among other things, they are the most legible document in the space.

The distance between columns operates in various directions. When spaced at a sufficient distance apart they can define afferent areas and virtual spaces, defining a tacit boundary, an enclosure that hopes to be occupied that is free of programming. When relatively close and placed around the perimeter, they create a kind of filter, a wall of columns, a transitional space, a pause. This malleability of space in plan and its effect on the section based on points and lines of reference created by the columns reveal the logic of the order and different gradients of spaces, not only inside where they are visible but also outside, where they are expressed as colonnades that articulate the diffuse space between interior and exterior. In this way, they contribute generously to spaces to be used freely as public areas. In many cases, they can generate a public fabric despite being subject to the rules and conditions of the private space, producing porches, arcades, and colonnades.

The structure defines the shape. This is how to protect the project strategically and formally in order to guarantee the relations that can build areas for public use by establishing a porous system between the limit, space, and structure, as well as establishing how this system defines and characterizes the space. The structural system is also the form and indicates the type of space.

The structural system is understood culturally in the tropics as a technical rather than a formally architectural definition. Connecting the architectural form to the structure as a strategy automatically excluded arbitrary and subjective discussions about the architect's formal choices or conditions in the project. We live in societies that prioritize an engineering mindset over anything else, thus prioritizing efficiency over aesthetic or conceptual considerations. This indissoluble union of structural technique and form also makes it possible to discuss engineering, construction, and space, in a way that creates more solid entities to negotiate arbitrary with the predefined aspects. From a different perspective, this condition makes architecture possible over and above subjective and whimsical criteria. It is definitely the intelligent association between means and possibilities.

WALLS

In specific ambiguity, walls are not simple partitions, boundaries, or barriers. They play various roles, especially when closing from the outdoors, when they are responsible for defining a vague limit.

Walls in the architecture of tropical ideas are more akin to a membrane than a barrier. They let the space breathe. Their ambiguity and porosity lead them to being confused with windows. In these cases, the wall is constantly modulated by millimeters rather than centimeters. The distance between its elements is the crucial factor; in the calibration of the proximity between its parts, the wall becomes a veil, a curtain, a filter.

This distance is what gives them the ability to regulate airflow and temperature, define views, privacy, and sound insulation. If air can enter, then so can sound. Hence the wall is a succession of planes of varying thicknesses and characteristics. A static or dynamic skin that reacts to time, use, and climate.

In these geographical zones, the wall is usually a latent element that appears in accordance with the development of spatial conditions or needs, and the inhabitant's financial means. The wall is a textile, unstable, and mobile membrane. It is used to be displaced as a partition or solar protection from the air or the sun. It can also connect spaces and expand or contract them; it takes the shape of a blinds, panels, secondary flexible devices, flap windows, sliding or static partitions. The multiplicity of partition systems indicates and proposes that the space should be changing, dynamic, and elastic.

In the tropical architecture of the informal economy, the wall belongs to the household budget. It is simultaneously about savings and investment. Generally speaking, its concrete or clay construction means it can be bought in units, stacked up and accumulated. It is a resource pending use.

The wall is often constructed geology. When made of clay or stone, even concrete and sand, its color blends it into the geological background of the place of its extraction, preventing a differentiation between the geological layers of mineral architecture, expanding its phenomenological effect and revealing its geography, chromatic aspects, and visual relations. The wall is not only the second architectural act after the structure, but it also establishes ownership or relations.

ROOFS

Many types of roofs exist in the tropics: some simply provide shelter from the sun and heat, but they are not watertight. Others not only provide shade but also provide protection from the rain. An eave, pergola, or roof are some of the formal variations and choices for roofs to give shade, shelter from the rain, or control the intensity of natural light. Gradients exist between these extremes, in any number of combinations with an almost-infinite range of materials that enrich the experience of the expanded threshold and inhabitable space.

Here we should highlight the role of the section. Though it may appear obvious, once we see each component individually in the wide range of these elements' climate- and space-related performance in the tropics, we become aware that porosity, so often referred to and presented as perforations in the walls, is not only found in them. The idea of a shelter, a simple frame or clearly demarcated roof gives us, due to its conditioning and the skill in its manipulation and height, the sensation and experience of space that constructs, among other spatial references, the sense of scale. An interesting aspect of these places is that this horizontal plane, in combination with the structure, creates an ambiguous and dilated sensation to establish relations of continuity between the exterior and interior, while remaining entirely regulated by the conditions of exteriority or without fully accepting the interior domains. Their intrinsic value lies in the dim lighting rather than shade that they provide, thus establishing and creating an indefinite space halfway between the spatial experience of being in the woods or in the house, between being sheltered or in the open, between the inside and the outside: an eternal spring.

The roof's type of regulation defines the spatial experience. If we are talking about the warmth of the tropics, whether dry or rainy, the most likely scenario is that the architecture's organization will be based on spaces that expand or contract in its section. Protection from the sun or water will lower or raise the level of the roof's lintel on the building's most exterior section in order to provide shelter from the sun or wind-blown rain. Similarly, the roof, is built toward the exterior, the section will change again—becoming higher—in order to expel the warm air. Then it may become articulated again lower down to define an eave near the central courtyard. This constant variation of spatial references and heights is not exclusive to tropical architecture. What probably does solely pertain to tropical architecture is its unique way of producing linkages and successive experiences of perceptual simultaneousness of its multiple scales. In this way, it connects interior and exterior as an undefined space within its boundaries, questioning our spatial perception and reaffirming the sense and experience of liminality.

Perforations

DOORS AND WINDOWS

In the history of architecture, the development of perforations on surfaces that distinguish the world or relate it to the realm of architecture could be explained not only as the success story of technical freedom—separating the load-bearing wall from the exterior's contact surface—but also as the constant ambition to create a connection with our surroundings and to make connections between inhabitants and societies, between "nature" (the exterior) and the "building" (the interior). Perforations in the tropics establish relations on multiple levels and scales. On the one hand, they complement the wall's role as a thermal administrator by establishing themselves as dynamic filters but at the same they build living areas. Perforations are installed as spaces in which to live; they are not merely devices. Doorjambs, barred windows, and wide thresholds are hybridized with the intrinsic properties of these elements to produce fenestration, as well as to control air flow and privacy, relations, or intimacy.

Doors and windows are often organized as a system of articulated layers to regulate relations with the exterior and, in turn, they project the interior outward (but without exposing the exterior) since they operate as a system of veils and filters. The window, for example, is made of three or more layers, and performs a regulatory function. An initial part of the system is the direct contact with the outdoors, generally consisting of wooden or thin metal bars, providing security. Immediately behind this is a woven system, similarly to openwork, usually located in the lower third, as an architectural curtain that provides visual protection from the outside and generally brings in fresh air or protects from the sun. The remaining two thirds of this system are open but protected by the aforesaid bars. In some cases, this portion is sealed by thin glazing. Then, a third system of double-wing windows divided equally in the bottom third and two thirds in the upper part can seal the space completely, to provide absolute darkness, or only one of the systems to regulate dim lighting. Finally, and in an act of absolute ambiguity, the wall, which is generally thick, becomes deep and stepped, making it possible to sit behind the window and put your feet up comfortably and, due to its symmetry from one side of the window to the other in the interior, it stimulates conversation between two people sitting opposite one another as they watch the world go by outside.

Similarly, doors play a dynamic role in administering space and how it relates to the outdoors. Double-wing doors are common, and often with its upper quarter operating independently. The upper quarter can be opened or closed independently of the door. In another act of ambiguity, the door can also be a window. Its surfaces can be made of layers, light textile fibers that protect from mosquitos and insects or perforated to bring in light and air.

The perforations are understood as dynamic devices that articulate, connect, or disconnect the realm of the private in relation to the intimate, the public in relation to the domestic, or the social in relation to the context: they are intermediating elements. And as in almost every system of specific ambiguity, doors and windows are unstable elements in their use and operation, radically becoming devices that regulate atmospheres, accessibility, intimacy, and privacy that, at the same time, are inhabitable and places to use. They never perform the role of objects.

VOIDS

The void is not only the distance that exists between things or the absence of material or infill. It could also be considered as the place that occupies the perception of what we read as space, or the subject of work and the space's structure itself; something filled with air and temperature, feelings and memories in the ways of living and that acquire aesthetic and social conditions. The void in the tropics is also the formal action that opens the space and strips it of its cover, its roof, its absolute interiority; to rule out the threatening possibility that it is a self-referential structure. This makes it possible to enter and construct an exterior for the interior, without it being completely outside. It is even possible to construct the interior quality of the exterior.

ZAGUANS

The zaguan is one of those enigmatic figures/forms of Mediterranean and tropical architecture. The idea of bringing the forms of architecture close to the concept of skin as described by Michele Serres in *The Five Senses*[18] is undoubtedly the most specific and precise way of interiorizing an exterior. It is the continuity of skin that gradually marks a change of state by folding onto itself to construct an interior from the exterior, conserving its material quality. This way of allowing the deepest and most external aspects come into physical contact is important to articulate and construct the transitions of the public to the private, like a sophisticated way of placing different media in contact through the visual veil and the flow of air. The zaguan combines almost every type of transition: structure, void, filter, perforation, regulation, and administration of scale. **The zaguan is the epitome of tropical space.**

COURTYARD

A courtyard is not simply an empty space, but the possibility of bringing in nature, permitting it to transmute the landscape into

18 Michel Serres, *The Five Senses: A Philosophy of Mingled Bodies* (London/New York: Continuum, 2008).

nature and vice versa. In other words, it is the spatial system with which we construct a mediated and close relationship with the outdoors. The courtyard establishes various levels of privacy and intimacy. With the simplicity to open up to the sky and natural lighting without absolute mediation; to bring in heat, air, and living elements. A courtyard establishes a territory of its own and appropriates an existential meaning, of creating an affective relationship with a plot of land, air, sun, light, and nature that we can register and quantify not only with our eyes or movement, but also as the dominion that is only possible due to architecture's role in establishing limits through inserting the void into the mass. It is therefore no mystery then that, since antiquity, regardless of the climate and the culture, the central void has been a place of shelter and reflection, of constructing the "I," of everything that we can call internal or external to ourselves.

Platforms

Based on the most conventional meaning of the platform that defines it as a flat, uncovered, and elevated horizontal surface, built on a frame on the soil or other large surface that provides a base or foundation, we can deduce that this is no more and no less than the spatial device that allows us to observe, experience, and live in the space on a different level. Over the course of history, platforms have been a result of technical ingenuity similarly to the cultural and environmental need to occupy the air and the heights, not only in order to construct density but also to observe from above. In the tropics, platforms acquire multiple capacities: terraces, balconies, and staircases.

As terraces, they are inserted as transformations of the landscape and the earth, helping rescue a slope's changing level by making geography inhabitable. As balconies, they are observation decks overlooking the city from above, in contact with the tree canopies, and provide intermediate spaces in the generic residential spaces of today. And finally, the succession of small platforms creates staircases that connect the public with the private as livable spaces, similarly to hills replicated and mediated by architecture. When they are exterior, these make it possible to observe and experience the theater of public life. On the inside, in the design, with the handling and quality of the staircase, we can ascertain the architect's talent at building a coherent structure.

In the architecture of tropical ideas, platforms are transitional forms for us to experience and occupy geography not only making flat surfaces but constructing oblique relations that we most enjoy socially and culturally: to see and be seen.

TERRACES

In the Andean tropical region, terracing is the primordial act of preparing the ground. This technical step is taken even before marking out and defining the boundaries of the architecture. The terrace is necessarily an act of geographical adaptation to let architecture emerge, first while retaining is natural state, and then turning it into pure artificiality.

Terraces, as Carles Muro defines in "Mundos paralelos. Dos notas sobre Jørn Utzon,"[19] connect the rational and the intuitive act, so that the need meets the aesthetic purpose:

> [Utzon says] that the essential quality of the Mayan temples was the intense emotion of moving from the dark and limited jungle to the experience of endless space and light offered by the elevation.

19 Carles Muro, "Mundos paralelos. Dos notas sobre Jørn Utzon," in *Circo*, No. 33 (1996).

> [...] On the platform we can still discover a new, fleeting and changing roof that are the clouds [...] In Utzon there are always also two other parallel worlds. [...] one, the solving of technical and functional problems, which operates within the discipline and which is approached through reasoning; and the other, more intuitive world of evoking and recovering memories and dreams [...]

Thanks to this interpretation and Utzon's 1962 work *Platforms and Plateaus* we can redescribe the role of the terrace, either as a necessary technical act or sublime action, either to raise the building up into the sky or to anchor it in the ground.

In the tropics, the terrace regulates the climate, allows observation, and manages the surface so that life develops as a spatial experience.

BALCONIES

Balconies can be small protuberances or clefts in a façade. In any case, these spaces of spatial intermediation exteriorize the interior to bring us closer to fresh air; they invite us to perceive them as devices to capture the landscape. Balconies work like a camera: they frame, indicate, represent, and differentiate what we see from what we experience. Balconies create extensions and outlets for the interior. They contain gardens, regulate temperature, and provide links to a world observed from a height. The balcony in the tropics is simultaneously an extension of street life, a private box with views onto the public realm. They are the eyes on the street, the ideal space to exist between different ambiences.

STEPS

In the city of invisible frontiers, steps are the extension of the street, where neighbors and pedestrians can meet and have a chat. In this sense, steps are theaters and spaces of observation and exchange. In low-income neighborhoods, steps are often part of the façade, a filter containing and sheltering the circulation routes and apartments from the sun. There, in the vernacular, steps are not just functional connectors but the formal expression of a technical need to connect and link various levels. Steps work in unexpected ways. Sometimes their existence enables shared housing on narrow, deep lots. In other cases, they dominate the geography, so that porosity can be articulated as multiple accesses to small towers that use different levels for different purposes, thus creating Piranesi-esque spatial conundrums. Steps are one of architecture's expressive resources that give shape to movement and therefore let us enjoy the surrounding space. These tropical steps generally flee from the center of the plan and occupy the periphery, achieving connections and bringing the exterior into the domestic space.

3.

A Tropical Laboratory

AGENdA agencia de arquitectura

AGENdA agencia de arquitectura is a confluence of ideals, attitudes, and actions. From this perspective we see architecture both from the inside and the outside. To have an agenda is to have an aim and to plan ahead: from thinking about projects and building them—with all the associated architectural implications and cultural impacts—to reviewing on a constant basis what has been done.

It is always beneficial to take a step back from ourselves and look with detachment at the architecture that interests us and that we make, while formulating a position that is not only theoretical and critical but also material and inhabitable. AGENdA is also the acronym of **AGEN**cia **d**e **A**rquitectura.

The decision to call an architecture firm an "Agency" is not fortuitous. We want to move away from the idea of a closed and self-referential space reflected in the terms "laboratory," studio," "team," "workshop," or "atelier." We must also be coherent with the idea presented in this text in various ways: the aim of being necessary both in the built realm and in the world of writing, in communicating and strengthening critical architectural ideas. Therefore, we believe in the idea of *agency*, of the capacity of an agent (whether an individual or other entity) to act in a given space.

Hence our ongoing commitment to develop our theory and teaching work in addition to putting our ideas into practice and managing spaces of architectural culture. We wish to establish that our interest is directly and clearly based on disciplines committed to the management, administration, and design of space with an aesthetic value and purpose, whether this be called architecture, urban design, landscape design, or theory. Therefore, our logo is a slash: /. In contemporary culture, the slash connects multiple activities and spaces.

The projects described in this book are experiments, trials, and achievements that consciously participate as built architecture in different territories of the discipline in the tropics, as well as in its potential transformations. While acknowledging their differences and opportunities, we are convinced that projects raise critical questions for contemporary architecture and review historical narratives from a contemporary perspective offering a possible interpretation of an unpredictable future. Backed by the projects described in this book, we can claim that tropically inspired architecture gives more than it takes; it also draws a boundary that shelters, integrates, and creates confluences. It is an architecture that also establishes a dynamic relationship with history, capable of an interpretative or documentary perspective on the past. This creates parallel narratives which, despite not seeking to dominate circulating arguments, establish themselves to stimulate discussions and add new elements and criteria only achievable through distance and a penetrating gaze.

Our approach confronts and sets up a dialogue between local values and globality for a critical perspective on what has been made. In turn, this enables us to devise possible outputs that are less deterministic but perhaps more instrumental.

This perspective on architecture does not draw distinctions between vernacular and "pedigree" architecture. It respects and builds on spatial ideas, never on budgets or materiality, making them play an active role in constructing the universal narrative of architecture. This gaze is rooted in the belief in the built fact: we design what we can build for history (typology) to function as an open document simultaneously establishing order and opportunities, particularly in order to avoid dogmatism or whimsical experimentation of the kind that believes that the more dissimilar ways there are of understanding a project, the greater its originality or display of knowledge.

The ability to appropriate specific aspects of architecture in order to build ambiguous spaces is only the starting point for us to face up to the challenge of our time: to provide an interior quality to the exterior, without this implying distance, hollowness, or isolation between conditions. Understanding that ambiguous architecture designs relations in space and time is therefore essential to define the limits of our practice and profession. Moreover, this awareness shows us that these relations can only be measured on the basis of the strategic relevance of form, accompanied by the observation and translation of actions and conditions into specific architecture; in other words, into the creation of built facts. Imbuing exteriors with an interior quality, while still preserving their openness, requires spaces that consist of layers and thresholds, and a use of transitional spaces as structural elements rather than by-products of the interior-exterior relationship.

To believe in the opportunities for change implied by this way of thinking and doing requires a constant monitoring of spatial organizations where archaic and primitive aspects prevail, since they imply an action rather than a gesture, an aesthetic rather than a decoration, an idea rather than a whim, a tradition rather than a technical illusion. Above all, these spatial organizations start a conversation in time that brings up the elusive concept of space, an issue so difficult to define plausibly and instrumentally in our daily lives and that, only occasionally and from a distance—after spelling it out, making a clean copy, and disseminating that idea—allows us to look in the mirror and sit on the divan, staring ahead without looking at the wall or ceiling. Since our generation is not fully literate in creating images compared to younger generations, and also lacks the broad experience of building and producing many projects in contrast to some members of the older generations, again we need to place ourselves in the center, between conditions, to patiently await our turn to act. This turn already appears complex and variable because, although we know how to critically appraise images, we are also interested in the built fact and in presenting our thoughts and ideas. The world around us asks us for other abilities, and our era poses new challenges. The best way of taking our turn may be precisely by clarifying a long threshold of ideas, reflections and critical gazes, both in terms of what our predecessors have left us and in regard to our ideas about the present. This may at least help those coming after us and extend a conversation about problems and ideas that perhaps have always been with us over time and history, in the profession of architecture and in culture.

Projects: a) Structural or Pivotal, b) Articulating or Intermediate, c) Speculative

Most of the projects included here were produced between 2010 and 2021. As the result of the aforementioned ideas on tropical spaces, they display the specific ambiguity inherent in this approach to architecture for such places and in line with the strategies, intentions, and inquiries mentioned throughout the text.

Some architects draw from a limited catalogue in relating to forms. They pick more or less the same elements and spend their careers combining them in an attempt to give meaning to their ambitions and interpretations of space and architecture through small variations; they also redefine themselves using their own rules throughout their career, constructing small certainties and barely deviating from their course. In this way they set out to produce a body of work presented as the conscious and consistent search for a set of precisely defined set of ideas.

Others take a diverse and divergent route to explore any form, element, or spatial idea. By making many different things in separate projects, they accumulate knowledge, sticking close to the trial-and-error approach. They hope their work will be seen as a permanent, dynamic laboratory; they distance themselves from their prior work and even from themselves, disavowing their own past and unashamedly claiming to be disinterested in their earlier projects as they strive to exist in a state of infinite novelty.

In our case, we try to understand how ideas develop over time. We distill ideas that initially appear to be discoveries or findings before leaving them gradually to permeate our work to find the right forms and connections for each project and, in that way, escape from the prison of language as something absolute or as a label of identity and authorship. Of course, we always believe that consistency is achievable over the long term and is not necessarily based on the formal repetition of a certain element that we find useful for our general purposes. Instead, we choose to delve deeper into sets of ideas by carrying out small-scale tests and experiments that produce the desired spatial conditions that are not tied to the absolute search for a unique and characteristic language in our work.

In other words, we consciously avoid a hermetic language or style and the inconsistent variations inspired by the pleasure of creating new forms; we are also uninterested in following the zeitgeist.

We are not presenting these projects as canonical or exemplary in any way; they simply contain these ideas. In many cases the projects themselves were vehicles to stimulate thought processes that led us to alight on some of the ideas.

Obstinacy and obsession were essential ingredients for these built and unbuilt projects. We took every opportunity to simultaneously check and query our beliefs and desires. Today, forced by the need to put ideas down clearly on paper and in a retrospective and post-rational gaze, we are now close to achieving a logical accompaniment and understanding of the ideas expressed as a self-critical and retrospective manifesto.

However, our aim is not to justify the projects and their criteria in light of these ideas. Instead, these works are more the result of a critical gaze of the surroundings and a universe, in an attempt to look backward and forward on what our studio has done, always in an attempt to link this outlook to architectural questions.

Some of these ideas run parallel to the projects; others cross and interlink with them, complicating the task of explaining their origins and lessons learned. An undeniably arbitrary relationship often exists between some of the ideas in the text-manifesto and within the projects themselves, but helps construct more speculative realms that may acquire meaning along the way and open doors to new concepts.

Some of these proposals will certainly become applicable outside the scope of the project itself, opening a window onto other aspects of the world, although they will be ineffectual to shape and implement the processes of designing and approaching other conditions of architecture. Migrations or small discoveries will also assume a more central, even structural role in our work, which will be the sum of new interests and issues already existing within the projects but that we are not yet aware of.

In other words, the need to review our projects and the conscious drive to reflect on them necessarily creates a critical field that in no way seeks to justify what has been made or to presuppose a building's configurations. On the contrary, this text and these projects are an ambiguous canvas for us to think about what has been done, and to do what has been thought about.

The projects are categorized into three groups, determined through a retrospective analysis to find meaning in them, in addition to their methodological and critical importance during our history as a practice. In other words, they represent the self-critical gaze designed to initiate a public and open conversation about what has been made. From this perspective, we have realized that, in our own work as in the work of many other architects, projects can be: a) structural and pivotal, b) articulating or intermediate, and c) speculative.

Structural and pivotal projects are the conscious and unconscious result of an accumulation of ideas and prior experiences; they lie at the crossroads between arrivals and departures, offering conclusions of addressed previously themes or ideas, as well as new opportunities and areas of work. These projects mark an important shift in how we make things, because they indicate a new source of information and resolution, encouraging new routes that generally prove to be enduring and become long-term themes or interests; routes that begin to repeat themselves not necessarily as a formal solution but in the sense of how we structure and conceive our idea of space. Through *structural and pivotal* projects, we can structure a comprehensive system of thought, guiding us in terms of what is non-negotiable; such projects raise questions and develop themes of general interest and areas of research. They are milestones in our portfolio of work.

A *structural and pivotal* project arises from the accumulation and subsequent evolution of *articulating* and *speculative* projects. It is the result of many previous trials, experiments, and small tests. Such projects are also described as pivotal because they make it possible, simultaneously, to open and close previous ideas to link them to new ideas which arise precisely during the project. These projects are both speculative and articulating at the same time, hence they are sporadic and limited in the work of architects, because they supply intellectual nourishment and ideas for most of their careers and acquire a certain encyclopedic quality. They are not just the compilation of many sources of information and references. In most cases, they explain architects' way of doing and thinking. To date, *structural and pivotal* projects are essentially the Orchid House (2006) and the Farallones Community Coffee Wet Mill (2014).

Articulating or intermediate projects combine a series of experiments or tests, expanding and putting into practice lessons learned. These projects make some bold moves, accompanied by some certainties gained over time, because they benefit from proven instruments while also incorporating new areas of interest. However, despite sometimes leading to discoveries or opening doors to interesting new ideas, they do not always achieve transcendence or the ability to change our way of seeing and doing. *Structural or pivotal* projects imply a certain conclusiveness since they are the exceptional result of trials, tests, and new gazes from which we can continue extracting content and positions, whereas through articulating or intermediate projects we can offer continuity to themes and ideas over a shorter and more modest timespan, thus verifying temporary interests and questions. These are *intermediate projects* because they are halfway between *speculative* and *structural* projects: they are bridge-projects, routes traveled, the space in-between milestones.

The word and the idea of speculating is very attractive: not only does it refer to the act of reflecting on an exclusively theoretical level and to make conjectures on something without enough knowledge, but it also inspires us to look at primary meanings, something belonging or relating to a mirror. *Speculative* projects oblige us to look at ourselves when we occupy unknown spaces of knowledge. From a complementary perspective, we can state that speculative projects help us accumulate theoretical and practical knowledge or to make conjectures so that later, as we look at ourselves, we can search for other methods of taking action.

The idea behind *speculative* projects is to reveal our way of thinking and acting. Generally, they have been immersive experiences that, without intending to be art, make it possible to abandon temporarily the need to respond solely to functional or extremely technical aspects of architecture. Speculative projects are bridges that connect time and ideas. They are investigations and inquiries, encounters and ruminations.

10B Housing (2002–2003)

In association with JPR Arquitectos

5G Housing (2004–2006)

In association with JPR Arquitectos

ARTICULATING OR INTERMEDIATE

We should begin the self-critical and analytical journey of our work by examining two projects which, despite pre-dating 2010, are still worth describing and analyzing. These are articulating projects, although as they belong to the multi-family housing typology they remain structural due to their intrinsic connection to all aspects of architecture and the city.

As housing projects, they require a focus on architectural and urban space, on individual and collective issues, in relation to time and society through their economic and urbanizing models.

To think about housing is to think about the city and how to organize society. Although housing has inspired all manner of ideas, none more bold, true, and incisive than Mies van der Rohe's claim that "the housing of our time does not yet exist." Although this may appear like a simple witticism, such a statement simply reflects an eternal impossibility: architects struggle to understand and reach solutions for living spaces in our own time and in connection to daily life. This requires an opportunistic (in the positive sense of the word) reading of housing and one that is therefore capable

[1]

of establishing a clear and visionary system of living, responsive to our shifting social dynamics. Such adaptations continue to be a challenge for architecture, particularly nowadays since housing forms part of urban real-estate speculation that prioritizes profitability and returns on investment over meeting essential needs.

Although Mies's statement emphasizes conceptual and formal issues, today's housing is undoubtedly a product or almost a surplus/leftover of the city and its economic transactions. In truth, housing today is more about economics than property; it is entangled in the complex web of transactions, relations, and real-estate, technical, and financial mechanisms instead of playing a complementary role to monuments and primary urban elements as a means of organizing and understanding the city, as in Aldo Rossi's thought-provoking definition.

To understand the failure of housing policies, we also need to consider that over the past several decades government bodies have largely overlooked factors of quality, location, density, and even ownership. After ceding housing construction to the private sector, the state has prioritized quantity over quality. As a result, housing became a poorly regulated instrument for political maneuvering which, in certain areas, strengthens links between corruption, regulatory modifications, and illicit enrichment. In other words, the state's role in housing is more as a useless guest that only profits a select few while having a negative impact on urban development. This leads directly to profound social inequalities and unsustainable states.

Given this situation, how can architecture help produce housing that can establish itself despite such forces? We must circumscribe and define the area where architectural and design thinking can somehow affect technical and economic decisions. We would even venture to say that it is essential to understand where housing is located, in which territory, and how it performs. In this way, we could select and configure a series of typologies potentially catering to different ways of living within perimeters that are limited to a certain degree, subject to severe technical restrictions and to the commercial pressures of the real-estate industry, which supposes that typologies are indiscriminately replicable, at any time and for any user.

Typology is a means of spatial organization that has survived over the years and that describes and explains the territory and how cultures have settled spatially. Like architecture and the built space, typology has changed and adapted our way of living by offering many ways of leading our daily lives as well as the opportunities to absorb and introject new ways or changes in this sense. Typology helps generate a spatial order so that housing can offer opportunities for social mobility, thermal comfort, cultural identity, and appropriation. Hence typology is how we can understand and expand on ways of living and the possibility for it to negotiate with time and establish relations between the home's performance and its inhabitants' needs.

Time plays a fundamental role when we consider how housing will be developed once occupied, how it will grow, and how it will be transformed. In other words, and to use the words of Ana Elvira Vélez—an architect from Medellín and our former university professor, perhaps the only one in Colombia focused on the architectural aspect of social housing—we see that typology must be adjusted and calibrated to foresee how it will be used and how it must react and how typology in that specific territory must react and allow daily activities, adjusted to the various pressures and needs of the times and variations in each family grouping or social organization.

Time and typology within real-estate dynamics or financial considerations define a certain standardization based on a market, meaning that the housing's size may be more or less in line with different budgets. We must be clear about this: size does matter in housing. How big is big enough, and what form is needed for people to go about their everyday lives? It is important to connect the issue of size to time because no housing should be born complete or as a closed system. Based on our chosen typology and outlook in time,

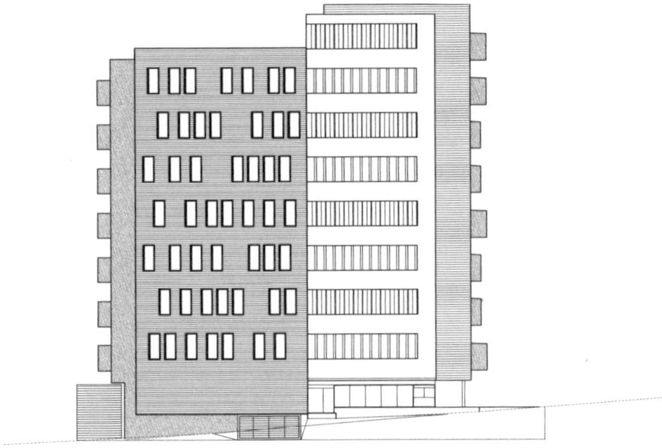

a.

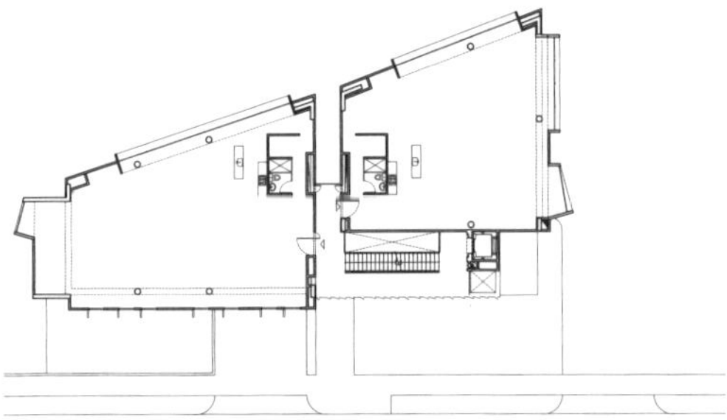

b.

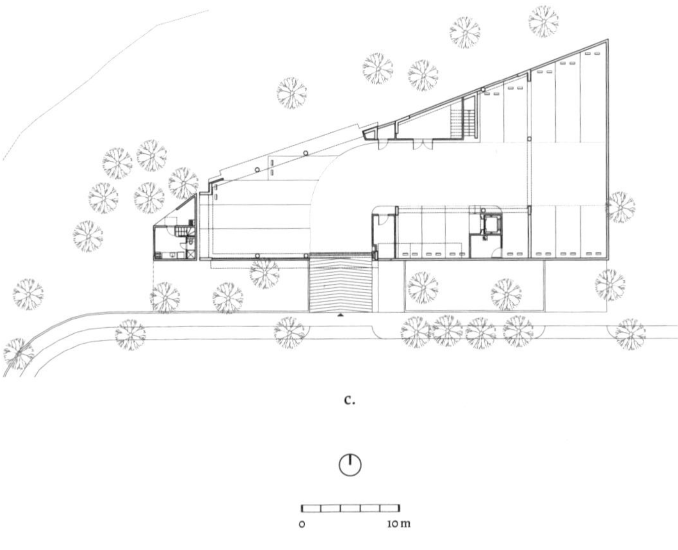

c.

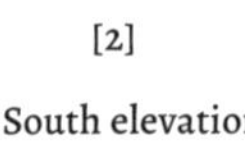

[2]

a. South elevation
b. Typical plan
c. Ground floor plan

[3]

we can understand and glimpse possible measures that will fit and empower users' various activities.

Housing areas and sizes have been the subject of many speculations. We would even venture to say that ultimately it is the only indicator that interests real-estate developers and governments, but areas and sizes are more than numbers based on statistics and budgets. Size can be understood not as the surface area but as the volume of necessary and optimum space to create options and opportunities for users to adapt their life to the space and not vice-versa.

If we are to connect the challenges outlined in this text in a rational and beautiful way, we require the support and realism of technical systems: how projects derive their inputs and discharge their waste. These systems are what provide social mobility and enable the adaptation to new or different characteristics within each unit. We propose that technical considerations should coherently consider materials and how they are assembled according to the spatial opportunities provided by the typology, demanded by the territory, required by time, and permitted by size. Technique is how we intelligently understand the performance of available materials and installations for us to achieve our goal.

The 10B and 5G housing developments were built in association with J. Paul Restrepo between 2002 and 2006, five years after Colombia's possibly greatest social and economic crisis prior to the COVID-19 pandemic.

From our perspective, these projects are important not only for the importance of considering today's housing in social, urban, and environmental terms, but also because they allowed us to establish ideas and to prove them in a limited period and within the restrictions of the real-estate market. This experience provides us a series of structural ideas for our practice that we consider remain relevant.

10B Housing

First came the commission for Calle 10B: the brief was to deliver a project offering relatively large apartments ranging from 150 to 200 square meters. The triangular plot was a leftover from previous de- [2]
velopments. The location beside a ravine reduced the proportion of usable land, and the building molds to the shape of this area: a triangle demarcated to the north by the ravine and to the south by 10B street, and to the east and west by pre-existing constructions.

Due to the plot's characteristics, we concluded that the building's internal organization needed to provide domestic and office spaces. At the time in 2003, mainly thanks to mass online communication, we saw that this housing development had strong potential to become a mixed-use project for office spaces and housing.

Without losing sight of this premise, we considered that a dwelling should, above all, offer possibilities to organize itself internally—through its typology—as well as to express its ventilation, view, and lighting conditions on the outside.

Therefore, we began by dividing the triangle into two parts, ensuring that the lower section, the slightly larger one on the western side, measured 205 square meters, while the upper section was set back from the street, with the vertical circulation system (staircase and elevators) attached on the southern side. This gave independence to three elements: Type A apartment (205 square meters), Type B apartment (175 square meters), and the vertical circulation. This formal strategy prevented the staircase from becoming the typical left-over space but instead a pleasant, well-ventilated zone where people [4–5]
could gather. This also gave independent entrances to every apartment, so the corridor gave access along two sides of each unit and two doors could be inserted: one for the house and one for a potential office space accessible from the outside. The building has seven floors, including the ground floor which, apart from having an

[4]

[5]

entrance lobby, has car parking spaces. The building has fourteen apartments.

The corners of each apartment were used for a series of shafts. The interior ones bring utilities into the building and house the graywater drainage pipes, reserving the exterior ducts solely for blackwater and rainwater. Concentrating these pipes within a central shaft to bring in water, electricity, telecommunications, and gas means each typology can function almost independently, as if the system were plots of land stacked up as autonomous and independent units.

To determine the operation of each floor, we created an open system in two ways. First, the client was offered a bespoke typology, simply with a bathroom, kitchen, and independent access for the working space. Second, buyers could hire an external architect to work within the perimeter space gained, using the designated chimney-type ducts. Both models necessarily affected the façade since it would be completely illogical to expect the different interior organizations not to impact the exterior. Therefore, we decided on the need for seven windows on the southern side, each one measuring 2 me-
[3] ters high by 1.20 meters wide; each owner could position them according to each owner's needs in the Type A apartments. On the east façade, for the Type B apartments, we chose a glass-door and half-balcony system, divided into two units, one longer than the other, which could also be located on any part of the façade while respecting the same heights for the windowsill and heads, which
[1] could also be arranged in any order. The north façade, the largest, had long glass doors affording a direct and clear view onto the trees. Finally, the west façade was simply a small preponderant cube on the façade that adjusted to different typologies of bathroom, bedroom, or studio for the Type A apartments.

The typological system, which rarely proposes open systems, could be adapted, transformed, or remodeled according to users' wishes and habits, allowing them to move or change it thanks to the drainage and supply systems. These aspects were reinforced by a simple and resistant material system with artisanal and semi-industrial finishings. Concrete floors were used for the apartments, and metal mesh flooring for the communal areas. Both create very pleasing spaces, as their surface and transparency filter the light entering from an upper light well. Brown-stained concrete block was used for the walls, combining with the metal mesh flooring to create a calm and straightforward ambience.

5G Housing

In the case of 5G housing, the lessons learned and intentions were [6]
already on the table. The same client for 10B asked to make some smaller apartments for a market sector with a smaller budget. For this purpose, we defined four types of areas that, in turn, would define the same number of typologies: Type A (80 square meters), Type B (90 square meters), Type C (100 square meters), and Type D (110
square meters). They were laid out in a rectangular bar with façades [7]
on their four sides. Despite having adjacent properties on the western and eastern sides, the block is set back from the edges of the plot due to building regulations. On the southern side, the block looks out over a ravine and a woodland with mature trees while, to the north, 5G street already had various pre-existing constructions.

For this new project, we decided to put into practice the lessons we had learned with 10B. Once again, we saw the vertical circulation as a defining characteristic of local contemporary housing. In this approach to fixed points and staircases we applied the observations made by Carlos Pardo, design director of Obra Negra, who had achieved the same result with an interesting and powerful series of residential projects in Medellín. Following in their footsteps, we decided to use a two-section staircase system on the north façade, which provides acoustic insulation from 5G street at the same time as revealing the volume to the public. The stairs are open at the
roof and covered in a gray-painted sheet metal. [8]

At each corner of the units, we installed a system of drainage pipes to be distributed and operated internally, while the entire utility supply (gas, electricity, water, etc.) is installed in the space between the stairway and the building's main block.

For this project we left the decision-making system even more open. Each buyer could acquire apartments with basic services already installed, such as the bathroom and kitchen, or they could also buy pre-designed kits with different types of bathroom and kitchen, cabinets, etc. As a third option we proposed Type A, B, C, and D apartments with different typologies. Similarly to 10B, we opened up the system for other architects to be able to design apartments for other buyers, even allowing them to buy two units and to connect them to create more spacious apartments. The building has forty units in total, on twelve floors. During the construction process, at one point there were sixteen other architects working simultaneously alongside us, enriching the design process and introducing many variables and typologies within the system.

In terms of the buildings' material and exterior, the language was informed by decisions taken within the typologies and whose importance became clear especially on the south façade, where they consisted of two elements: the windows and a possible balcony. In relation to the former, we decided on four windows, each measuring 2.6 meters high and 1.2, 2.4, 3.6 or 4.8 meters long, while for the balconies we established measurements of 1.5 by 3 meters, 1.5 by 4.5 meters, and 1.5 by 6 meters. The idea was for the balconies to be attachable even after the building was finished, and these additions have often been made since 2006 until today. For this to work, we decided that the metal balcony should be attached to a 60-centimeter concrete beam on the block's perimeters.

The formal result is a random interplay of windows and balconies that is not only defined by the decisions for the interiors but also by time. The building's structure is made of concrete poured on-site and clad in yellow concrete blocks.

[6]

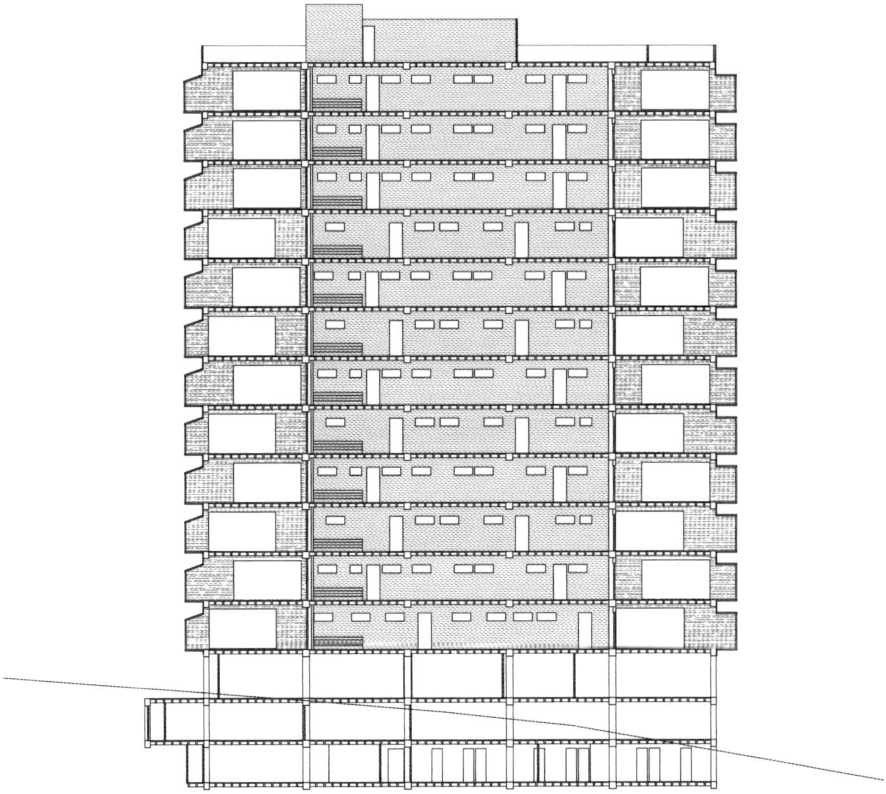

a.

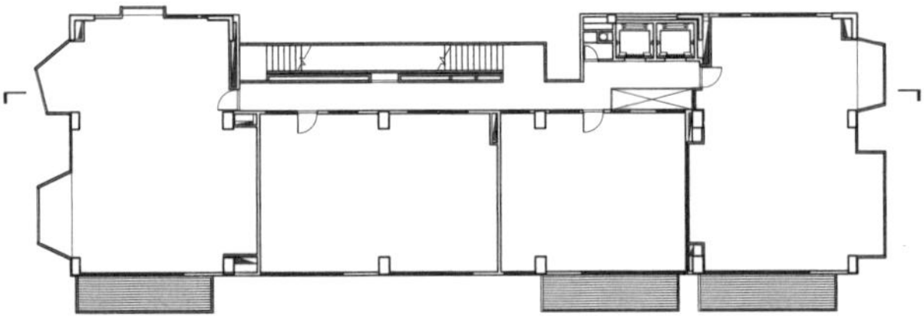

b.

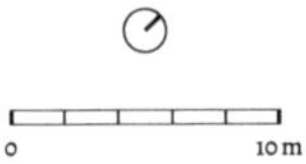

a. Section
b. Typical plan

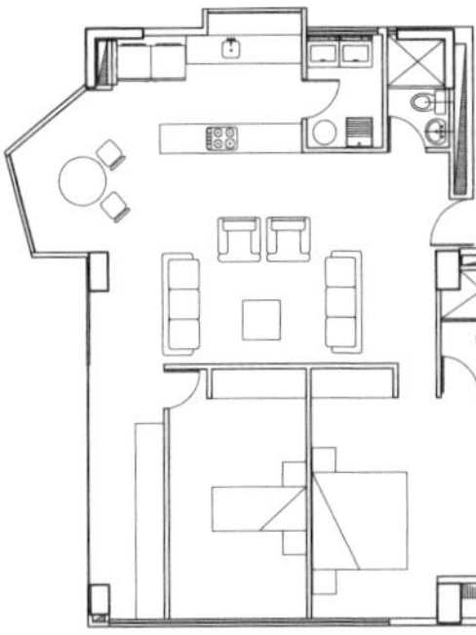

c.

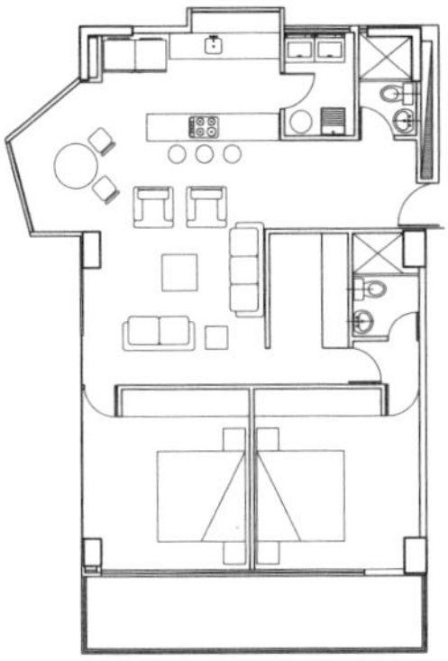

d.

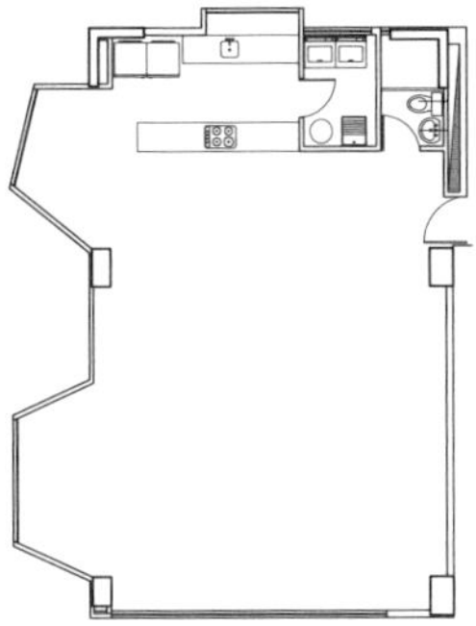

e.

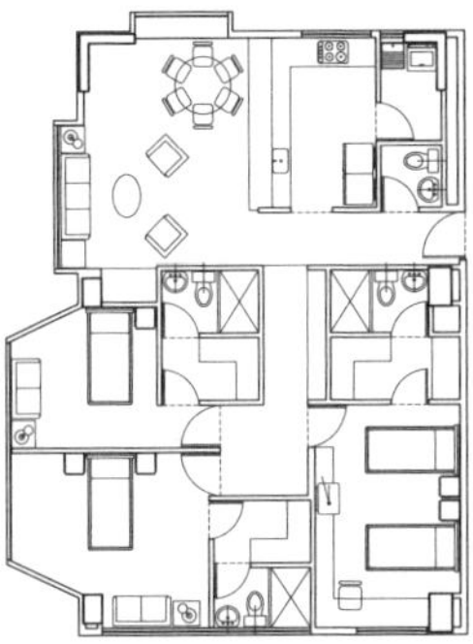

f.

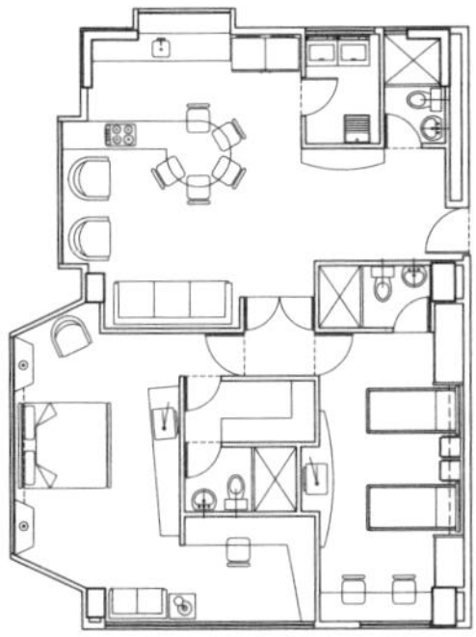

g.

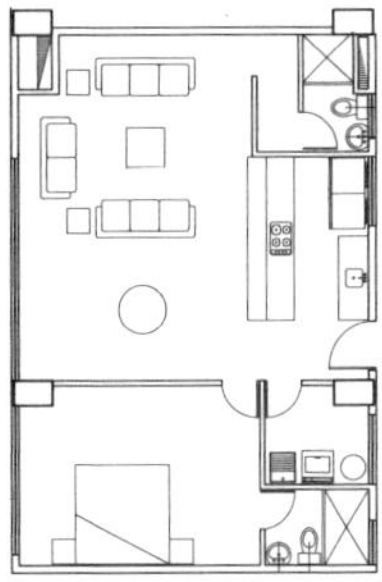

h.

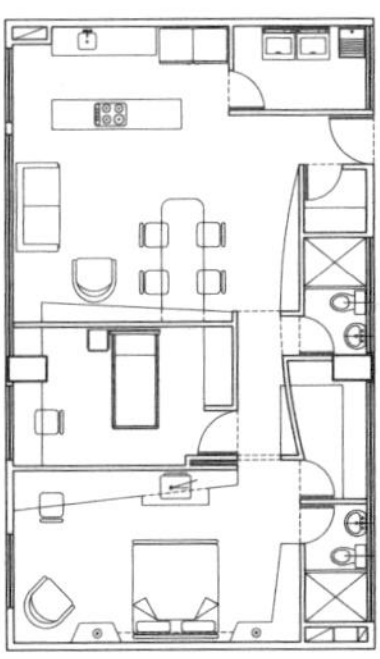

i.

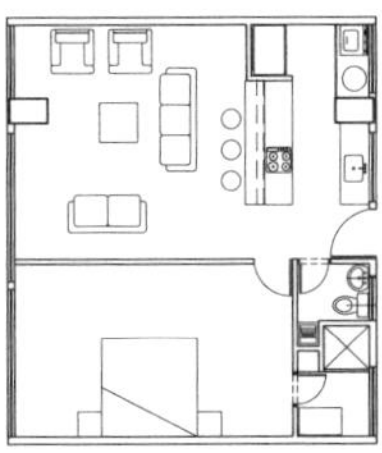

j.

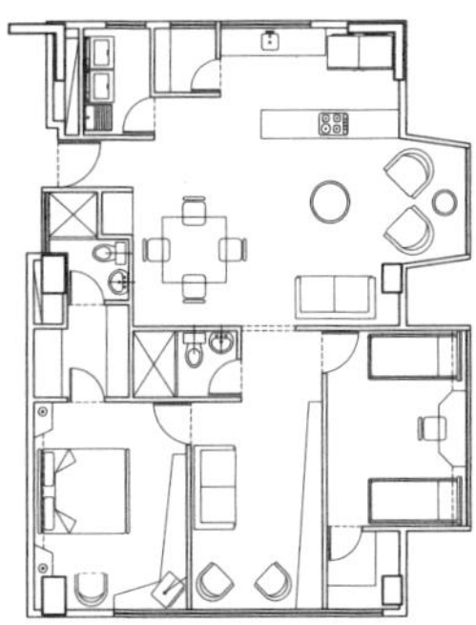

k.

0 10 m

[7]

c–k. Typological variations

[8]

For us, these two projects were an important learning process in terms of how the buildings take shape and develop over time. In retrospect, we realize that projects imply (fixed) decisions relating to infrastructure and (negotiable) decisions relating to time. The former are those decisions that we deem necessary on the grounds of form or function to guarantee a certain permanence and are more respected during the construction process. The latter decisions, relating to time, enable the processes and different actors to be in fluid negotiations and, generally speaking, they also help protect those parts that cannot be altered; those which, if they are changed halfway, can jeopardize the system as a whole, and the project's integrity.

Orchid House (2005–2006)

In association with JPR Arquitectos and Plan:B Arquitectos

STRUCTURAL OR PIVOTAL

Orchid House, a project with J. Paul Restrepo and Plan:B Arquitectos was a competition we won in 2005 and built in 2006. It displays a series of changes in our working methodology before and after the competition, a new perspective that continues to this day as a series of theoretical, strategic, and material continuities. An interesting aspect of structural projects is that they can be re-interpreted to extract new ideas from them or to understand them differently. We can learn lessons from them over time.

In that period, it seemed clearer and more interesting to explain this project's concept as the result of the overlap of architecture understood as a system and based on more phenomenological ideas. The explanation for the competition was based on an idea closely related to naturalism and that expressed the aim of connecting architecture to life itself. A reactive architecture that could respond to the characteristics of the places where it would be inserted and transformed thanks to its geometric properties, mainly in plan. A formal interweaving in which the components were able to tessellate—with hexagons in this case—and appear and disappear according to the social and financial conditions. As we said in the project description, "architecture developed and laid out as if planting a garden."

By taking this approach, the plan was organized around ten
[2] “tree-flower” modules. In plan, each tree-flower always keeps the central hexagon as an open-air garden-patio. The seven hexagons shaping the tree-flower have the formal appearance of a geometrical flower whose height, branch structure, and extension means we can
[1] also call it a tree.

Each of these modules is spatially and structurally autonomous, and has its own water supply, drainage, and electricity systems. It is precisely this modularity that makes it possible to create architecture as if planting a garden—adaptively or repetitively. Each tree-flower functions as a replicable and standardized module; each one is a steel structure soldered on site, clad in patula pine from a certified sustainable reforestation plantation, with concrete floor pavers and a polycarbonate and metal sheet roof.

The jury awarded us first prize primarily on account of this modularity because it enabled a rapid construction based on a single system of structural details. This condition also helped adapt the project to the budget, because in the competition entry we proposed thirteen tree-flower modules, but in the end we only built ten.

In retrospect, the idea for the system may have been too focused on the power of the shape in plan and unwittingly we overlooked the importance of the section and our spatial approach, an essential aspect of our work and one that interests us today: the idea of an umbrella-type shade structure or canopy. As an intermediate space, without a façade, its spatial characteristics expand to the surround-
[3] ing woodland and the section can develop its entire spatial capacity to introduce architecture as a dynamic threshold that allows air to pass through, thus dispensing with the need for air conditioning systems.

This method of defining the tropical space through the idea of a canopy is one which, over the years, has helped us to position ourselves more precisely when accepting commissions that entail a commitment and requirement to use architecture in interaction

[1]

with the city and the landscape. In the case of the Orchid House, it was essential to articulate Carabobo street as a public space and as a boundary at the same time as the heart of the complex.

As such, the Orchid House acquires dual meaning: as a roofed public plaza activated when connected to the border of the botanical garden, or as an additional element within the garden and to function independently in its center. Therefore, the canopy becomes a way to play with this dual-use aspect, making an impact on and organizing the property's interior while displaying a generosity toward the exterior. The canopy exists in-between different conditions, between the public and private space, and forges connections between ambiences, something that would be impossible to regulate by using walls and façades. Hence the relevance of prioritizing openness in the section and the roof.

The project is structural and pivotal because, even today, almost fifteen years later, it represents a different approach to what has been done. The project contains ideas that perhaps have always existed. However, at the time we were not conscious of their deeper architectural meaning. From our perspective, the ideas that fed into the Orchid House were influenced by Stan Allen's *Field Conditions*[1] and Jorge Wagensberg's *La rebelión de las formas*.[2] Furthermore, in my recollections I will always have in mind Moneo's *La vida de los edificios*,[3] particularly since my final years at university. Seeing that Orchid House was almost a program-free building and instead one marked with a strong spatial condition, we could not pass up on the

1 Stan Allen, *Points + Lines, Diagrams and projects for the city* (New York: Princeton Architectural Press, 1999).

2 Jorge Wagensberg, *La rebelión de las formas o cómo perseverar cuando la incertidumbre aprieta* (Barcelona: Metatemas Tusquets, 2004).

3 Rafael Moneo, *La vida de los edificios*, (Barcelona: Editorial Acantilado, 2017).

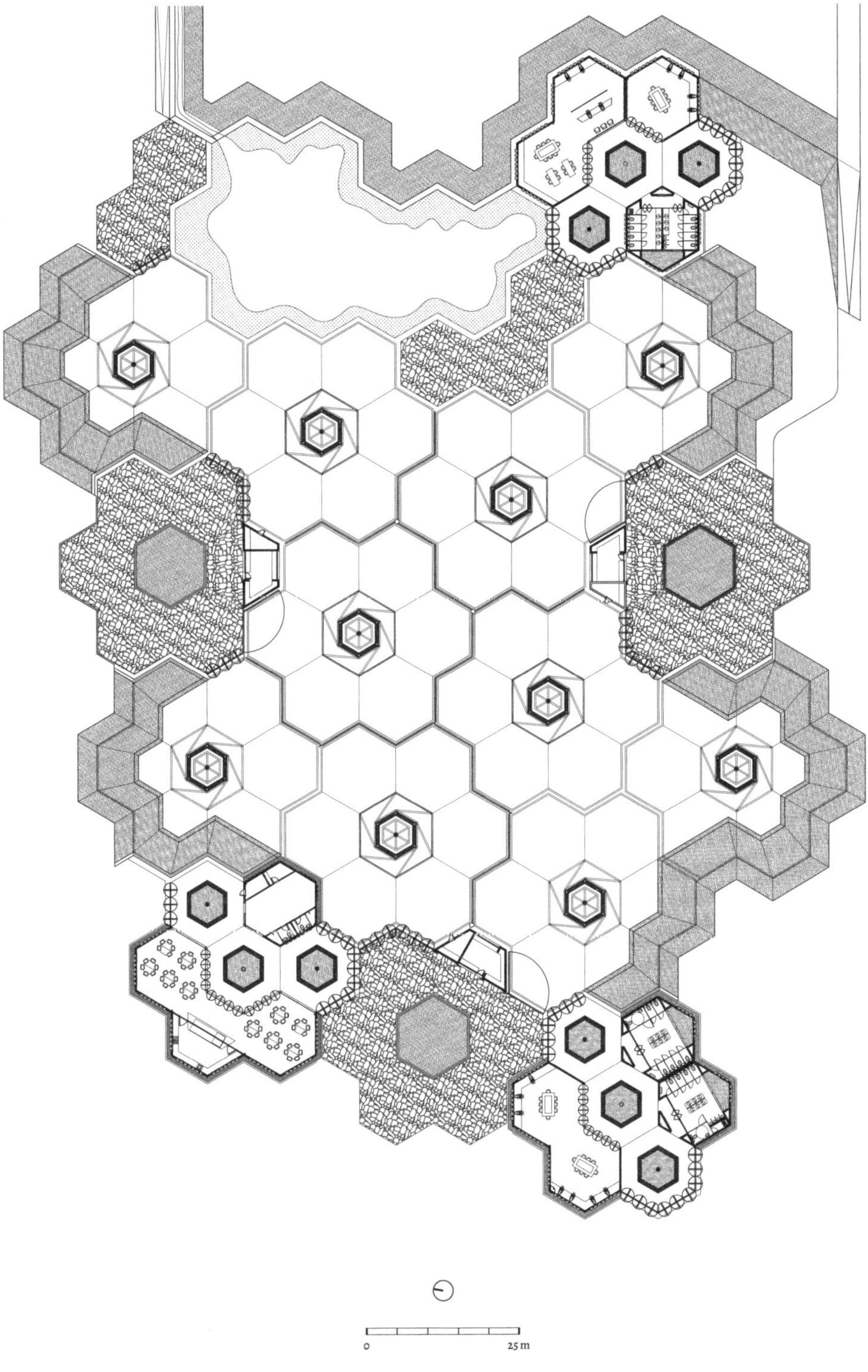

[2]

a. General plan

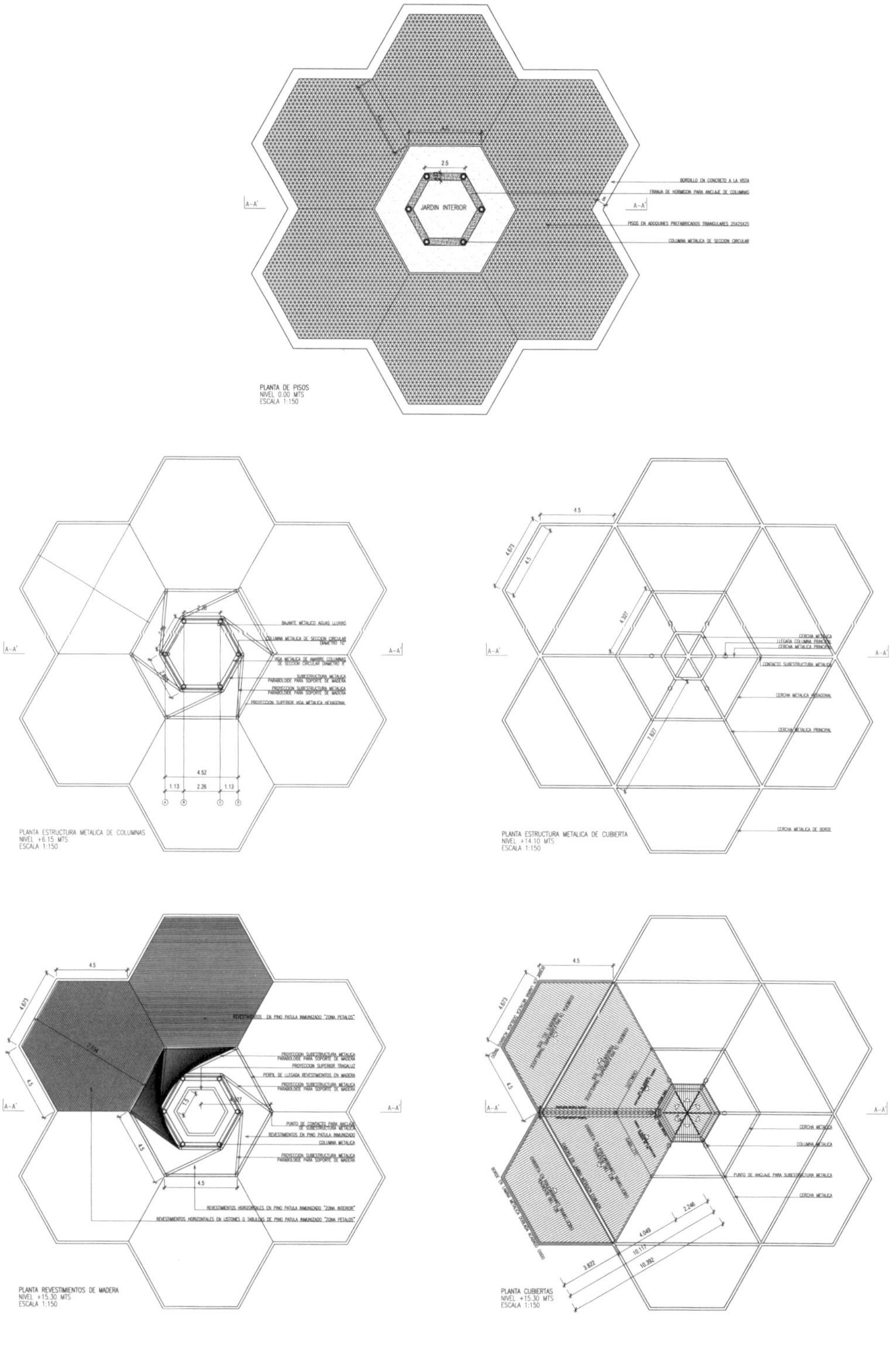

JARDIN INTERIOR
BORDILLO EN CONCRETO A LA VISTA
PISOS EN ADOQUINES PREFABRICADOS TRIANGULARES 25X25X25
COLUMNA METALICA DE SECCION CIRCULAR
A–A'
PLANTA DE PISOS
NIVEL 0.00 MTS
ESCALA 1:150
BAJANTE METALICO AGUAS LLUVIAS
PROYECCION SUPERIOR VIGA METALICA HEXAGONAL
4.52
1.13
2.26
1.13
PLANTA ESTRUCTURA METALICA DE COLUMNAS
NIVEL +6.15 MTS
ESCALA 1:150
4.5
CERCHA METALICA HEXAGONAL
CERCHA METALICA PRINCIPAL
CERCHA METALICA DE BORDE
PLANTA ESTRUCTURA METALICA DE CUBIERTA
NIVEL +14.10 MTS
ESCALA 1:150
PROYECCION SUPERIOR TRAGALUZ
COLUMNA METALICA
PLANTA REVESTIMIENTOS DE MADERA
NIVEL +15.30 MTS
ESCALA 1:150
CERCHA METALICA
COLUMNA METALICA
CERCHA METALICA
2.246
4.049
10.117
3.822
10.392
PLANTA CUBIERTAS
NIVEL +15.30 MTS
ESCALA 1:150

a.

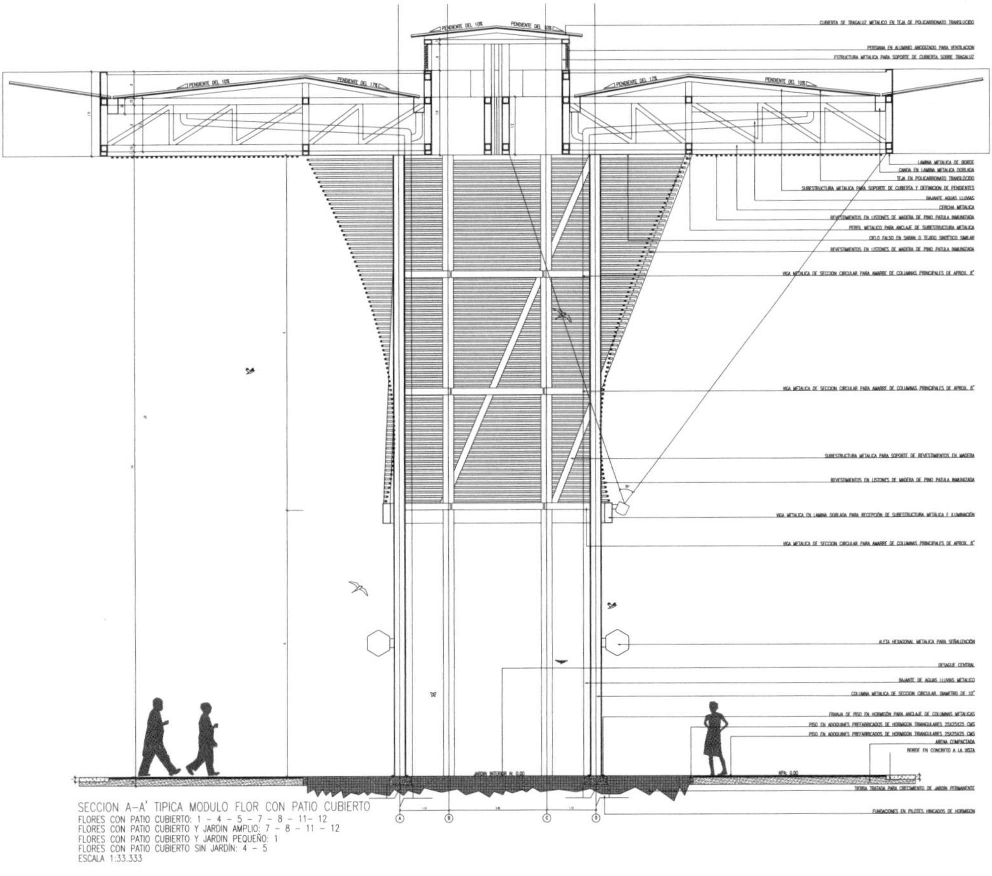

b.

[3]

a. Construction floor plans
b. Construction sections

opportunity of attempting something from that perspective. Therefore, the building—inspired as much by Moneo's text as the Mezquita in Córdoba—concentrated on the role of structural elements and of the roof. We could therefore develop ideas about allowing architecture to adapt to our time so that it can be updated without losing its spatial identity.

The sum of these texts and the program, its location, and building's characteristic, which is halfway between the pergola and a greenhouse, introduced the possibility of giving defined geometrical forms to nature, as well as responding to the indefinite program in order to establish a work of architecture that could be in harmony with a botanical garden in a location with a permanently spring-like climate. To organize the project geometrically and in its form, as Wagensberg mentions in his text, we assumed that the *hexagon paves*. Given this formal aspect, defined through precise and measurable geometries, we found Allen's text to be wonderfully inspiring. Why not think that architecture has that capacity to extend, adapt, mutate, and receive the unexpected?

The construction of the Orchid House and its validation as an architectural experience marked a change of direction. A few years later we realized that we needed to abandon the idea of organizing the space based on the same repeated form because, by trying to make various programs and ideas fit into a single system, we learned rapidly about the limitations of the spectrum of forms, and therefore this cast doubt on the relation between systems and exceptions. The system normally swallowed everything, turning its units into generic and undifferentiable responses to a context or program. But the distancing from the formal system as a repetition gave us another idea: the perimeter of the plant contributed interesting conditions because it was contained yet at the same time diffuse and meandering. By setting out in different directions, with clefts and protuberances, the perimeter of the plan was a line that could be the by-product of the shapes that order the system, or a whimsical line. It was created by the result of the collection of orthogonal figures, articulated to generate a kind of perimeter membrane, enabling the construction of convex surfaces or concavities that, in different ways, contained a relationship with the exterior that questioned the very edge of the membrane.

During a period, this formal decision permitted co-dependency between primary geometries (defining the space toward the inside) with the exterior of secondary geometries (suggested by the void between them and usually occupied by gardens). Thanks to the idea of the diffuse perimeter, we realized that the perimeter could relate to the surroundings in various ways, opening up to the landscape to bring it near and into focus, to receive and embrace it. [4–5]

As a result of this formal strategy, after Orchid House we abandoned the idea of the whole as a system, because we sought to create these long and flexible perimeters. This mainly displaced the construction of the perimeter as a surface, where architectural features rarely worked as a system. On the contrary, they became more like individual elements that, by adding or subtracting matter, made it possible to construct the windows and make connections to the exterior.

As a second lesson learned, after we completed construction it gradually dawned on us that the underlying ideas for the Orchid House meant that the structure could protect the form and methodologically initiate the project's spatiality. Undoubtedly, the structure is the most precise pragmatic resource to create a spatial principle. In this case the lesson learned not only brought into view the structure's potential use, but also the instrumentalization of the section. **The power of the section in tropically inspired architecture is clearly explicit in Orchid House** and, as we mentioned above, the façade and the walls were not the essential aspect of the project. Architecture is often related to the intelligent and strategic location

[4]

[5]

of walls, and most of our work as architects depends is based on establishing appropriate boundaries, based on social or climatic factors, and to give shape to the void as an aesthetic intention that belongs to the condition of architecture, a standard practice since the late nineteenth century.

Type, plan, and layout are just some of the key themes, interests, and bases that form a part of our profession. They have been discussed and implemented in designs, drawings, and displays of the vertical limits that constantly separate the interior from the exterior, creating a dichotomy that, for centuries, has fed the debate among civilizations for social order and its architectural manifestation; in other words, the idea of the interior, private space in contrast to the exterior, public realm. The traditional order is diluted when the purpose of another kind of architecture is not to create interiors or to define them using vertical partitions but instead to blur the boundaries or define the space in other ways, mainly through the section.

The practical logic of defining space through walls and layers of insulation, a constant narrative in societies with seasonal climates, runs through the history of our profession. It is even a key to understanding, learning about, and foreseeing the evolution of architecture's disciplinary core. But the exception also makes the rule. In tropical regions, where temperatures and climates are relatively mild, walls are useless and are not usually registered or incorporated within the definitions of the architecture practiced in those areas. This non-usefulness of walls and their resulting disappearance was the lesson learned from the Orchid House, where spatial boundaries are not defined by walls; limits are created by a canopy that allows cross-ventilation. Discovering the power of the undefined boundary, marked by the section and moving away from the distancing between perimeter and structure, becomes a fundamental condition when considering public projects. This also amplifies the definition of the tropical space, helping to create an imprecise and ambiguous condition, a liminal space of intermediate conditions consisting of specific elements.

As Orchid House shows, this structure is an expansion of the tropical narrative as built space, which belongs to the discourse and tradition of an architectural discipline constantly under construction.

MAE House (2010–2011)

Abanico House (2009–2011)

ARTICULATING OR INTERMEDIATE

These domestic projects display a mixed relationship with the outdoors. MAE House is the result of managing architectural elements and the articulation/transition between interior and exterior. For Abanico House, meanwhile, the clearest architectural intention comes from a contact surface that folds and is molded to keep the exterior closer through a diffuse perimeter, although not to contain it or to activate an ambiguous condition in the space.

Although most projects made between 2006 (when Orchid House was completed) and 2014 (the start of the design process for the Farallones Community Coffee Wet Mill) form part of the aforesaid tendency, these were small-scale laboratories, mainly single-family dwellings, where we could begin a series of experiments that would overlap most radically and interestingly in Farallones as a structural or pivotal project.

These experiments in articulating or intermediate projects, exemplified by MAE House and Abanico House, focus on their structure and role in terms of organizing the space; they also explored the idea of the diffuse perimeter.

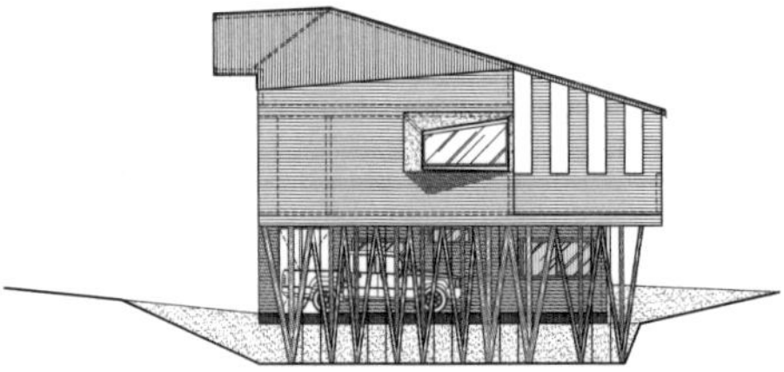

a.

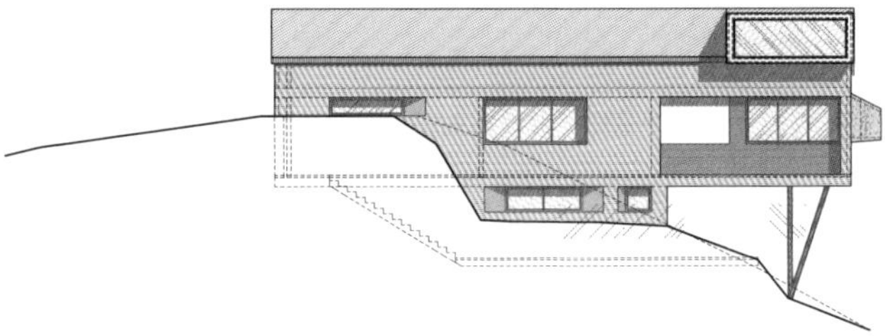

b.

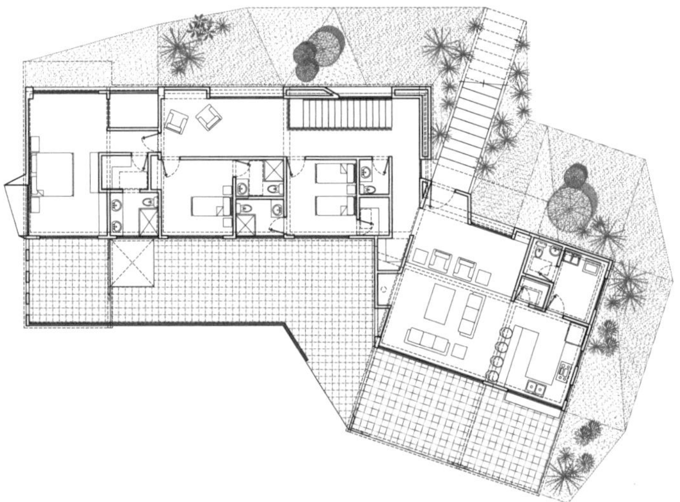

c.

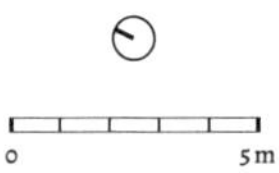

[1]

a. North elevation
b. West elevation
c. Plan

[2]

MAE House

In MAE House, the terrain's slope and drop in level called for an articulation of the programs on the ground floor and basement to create space for a garage and a second entrance. The project is constantly investigating the interior space in relation to the roof, as well as the vanishing points of the flat roofs and the attempt to make a connec-
[2] tion with the surrounding landscape. It is interesting that the idea of the greenhouse begins to penetrate our work, not yet as an underlying spatial concept but rather as the chromatic and formal solution found throughout this eastern part of the Antioquia province where flowers and food are often grown in greenhouses.

During this period, most of our projects, mainly houses, sought the material quality of a monolith. The houses are generally clad in dark stone and wood, and with thick textured plaster, in dark color schemes. This unifies how it is read materially, and it is unusual to see changes in its definition and in its relationship to the volume. In most cases, the formal and volumetric manifestation tries to express uniqueness. On the whole, the floors have a long and winding perimeter, or they work as a succession of fanned-out volumes. They also articulate volumes to bring the exterior into the house, although this attempt may not have succeeded in transcending the walls' solid limit to incorporate the vegetation.

Abanico House

Abanico House is distributed and organized through orthogonal vol-
[4, 5] umes. Articulated boxes create clefts at their contact points, which also adds a new volume to contain gardens. These apertures were clad in untreated Choibá wood. This will make noticeable the passage of time as the wood acquires a patina and changes color. Calle 10B —a multi-family dwelling made in association with J. Paul Restrepo—had already put this idea into practice. There, the façade clads

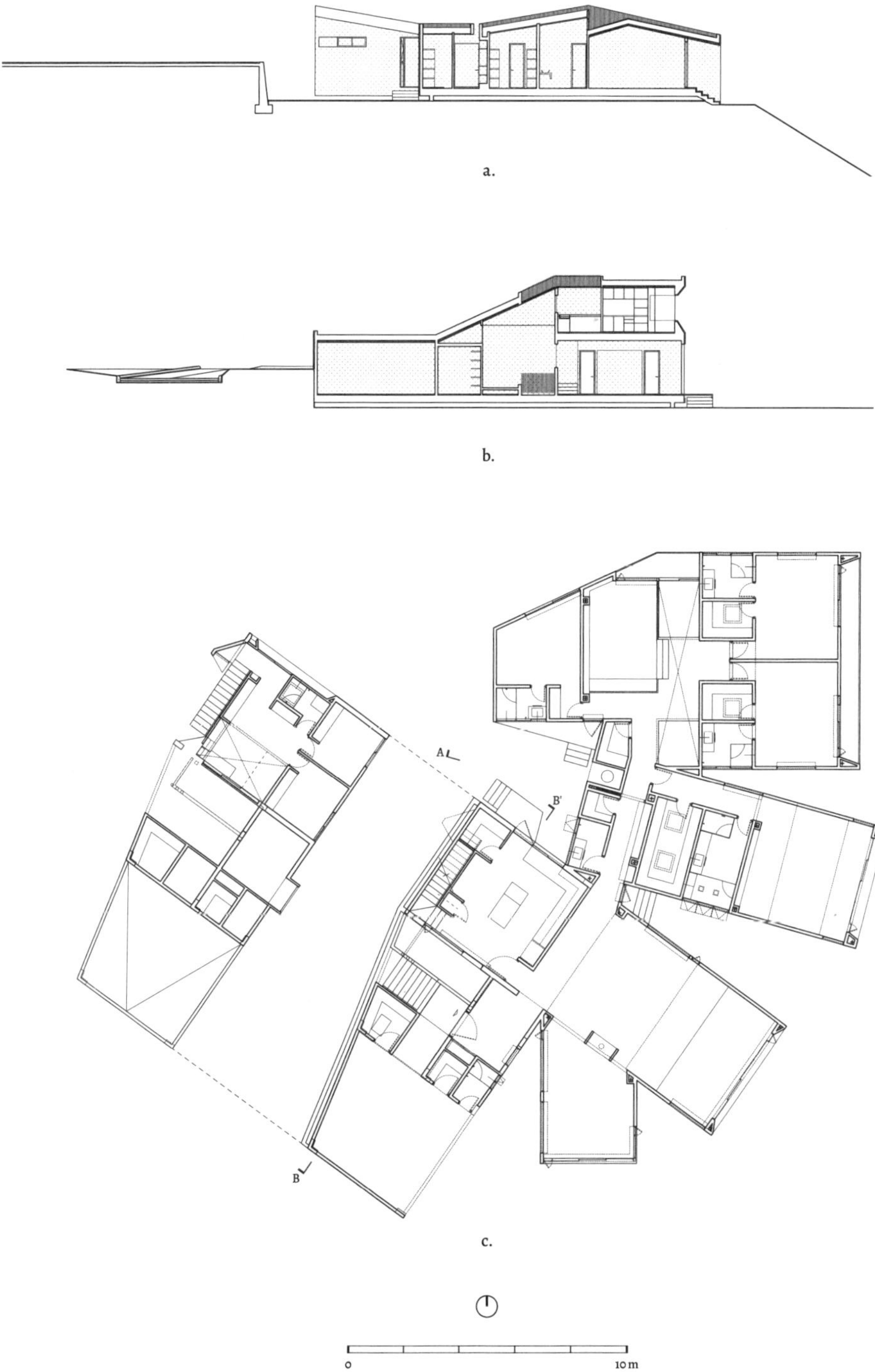

[3]

a. Section A–A'
b. Section B–B'
c. Ground floor plan and upper floor plan

[4]

the vertical circulation system; rusted iron sheets envelop both the lift and the stairs placed in such a way as to stain the skirting board and the base of the door, as well as the building's entrance. This bursts with the bright colors of the site's pre-existing paper bark tea tree (*Melaleuca quinquenervia*).

In the case of Abanico House, the programs have four volumes:
one for the parking area, another for the family area and kitchen [3]
—the join where the house's entrance is located—and another for the master bedroom, and finally one for the children's bedrooms and a studio. This organization gave a certain autonomy to each volume and section, the roofs with their different pitches were formally referenced to the mountain silhouettes. The contours of each of these parts became expressive, becoming a complete surface.

This phase of projects up until 2014 was a period when the plan encompassed everything, from the layout of systems in relation to the exterior in terms of their surface, to the possibility of understanding how to create opportunities and opportunities within tightly defined limits. Although most of the plans respond more to a diffuse perimeter, the silhouette/mountain—the section—and the built space always seeks variation within the surface of the enclosure and of the volume's definition. The section, with its mountainous silhouette, acquires meaning if we bring into the picture a naturalist
approach to architecture that connects processes both to its uses and [1, 3]
occupations and to the dynamics of what is alive.

Although today we might perceive this to be a slightly naïve initial foray, the produced spaces and the opportunity of having experimented and reflected on the built environment has undoubtedly produced interesting and very welcoming spaces, particularly because they are experienced as a succession of volumes of varying heights. This effect is heightened by the variable roof pitches and a series of conditions that, once articulated in the circulations, create a whole.

[5]

Argos Innovation Center, EAFIT University (2012)

ARTICULATING OR INTERMEDIATE

EAFIT University's Argos Innovation Center in Medellín was an invitational competition, with a brief to develop a building that communicated its product and could resolve various problems on the campus. In particular, the idea was to improve the relation with the existing buildings and to strengthen the park's identity.

As this was a project for a university, our design set out to make building an open document. The project is near the gothic cathedral, whose façade and surface tell a story. Therefore, we designed
[1] the façade to tell a narrative about the industrial process of concrete, and also to describe construction systems over the years. On the ground and first floors, monolithic limestone upright slabs support concrete plates, evoking primitive dolmens. On the second floor, a stack of hewn, mid-sized rocks houses the laboratories, which need very little natural lighting. This layer created the impression of a Roman building. The third floor employs a mixed system of glass and smaller rocks, bringing in more light; the rock surface evokes pre-Hispanic constructions. Prefabricated, terracotta-stained concrete was used on the fourth floor that provides a home for various animals, plants, and birds, reflecting the fact that Medellín and the university are located on the flight path of migratory birds. Finally, the fifth-floor façade is clad in translucent concrete. The idea was not

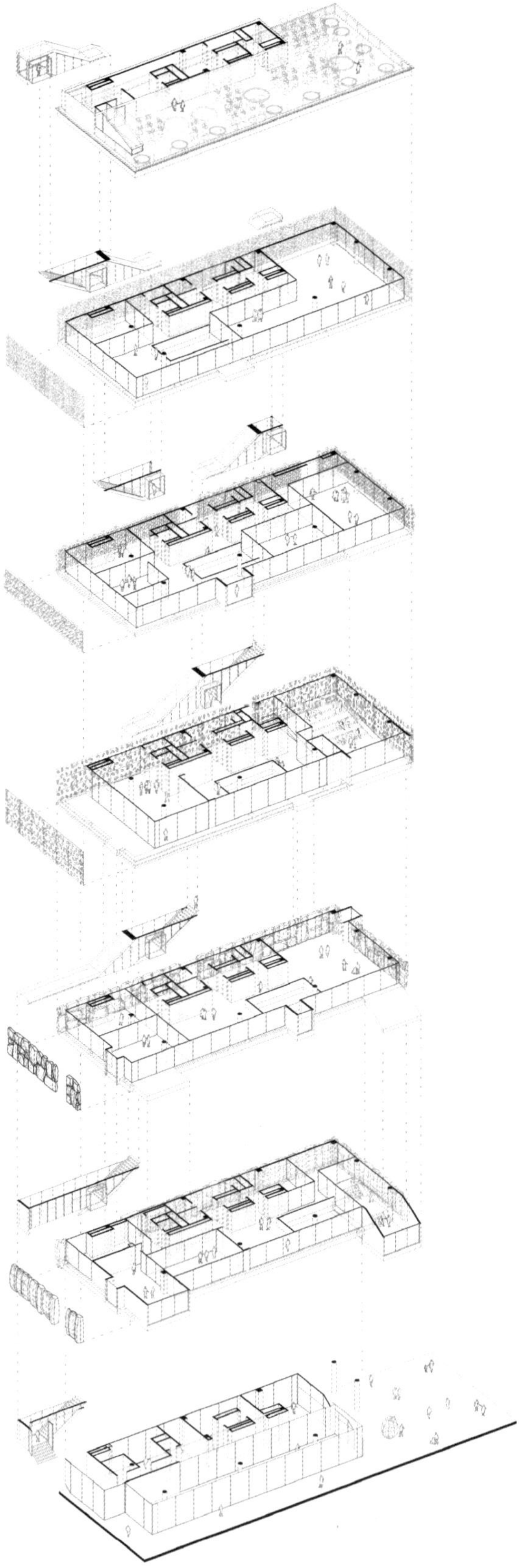

Axonometric

[1]

only to show this stratification in the construction, either with rock or powder treated with the latest technology, but also to construct a gaze on architectural processes over time.

[2] Outside, we created a park on a slight slope so that each tree well could collect rainwater to supply the building.

The park is organized around a network of tropical trees that blossom differently throughout the year. This grid consists of jacaranda (*Jacaranda mimosifolia*), bucayo (*Erythrina Fusca*), Malay apple (*Syzygium malaccense*), pink poui (*Tabebuia rosea*), and the yellow guayacan (*Handroanthus chrysanthus*).

In terms of plan and section, the spatial system was designed to function as a building for education, with a staggered void that, from the upper level, gives views onto the teaching taking place on the lower floors.

[2]

Gabriel García Márquez Public Primary School (2013–2016)

In association with JPR Arquitectos

ARTICULATING OR INTERMEDIATE

Designed in collaboration with JPR Arquitectos, the Gabriel García Márquez public primary school contains ideas that developed out of our first journey to São Paulo, Brazil, in 2013. On that trip we could [1, 4, 5] grasp and directly witness Brazilian architecture's ability to create extended thresholds as intermediate spaces between interiors and exteriors, thus managing the scale of the public space, taking it inside through subtle transitions in the structural organization and its presence in plan as an articulating filter. The program's interpretation and opportunities were also crucial in its highly complex social and geographic setting.

Initially, the project needed to use the land occupied by the pre-existing school. The topography created a complex plot, with a slope of more than 45 degrees. The materials of the shoddy pre-existing construction were unsuitable for local temperatures, that range between 25 and 34 degrees centigrade. Given these geographical conditions, and in the knowledge that the college was a donation, the client wanted to minimize maintenance costs. Through a LEED certification we minimized energy expenditure and kept down the cost of future maintenance, creating the first state-run school to be awarded this certification.

[1]

The school is located in a marginalized area with high unemployment and school drop-out rates and widespread family violence. Furthermore, as in so many other peripheral neighborhoods in Colombia, the local population are often caught in the middle of turf wars between rival criminal groups. The neighborhood also lacks government presence, public space, or meeting places.

We began by proposing a different construction site than the one chosen by the local authorities; at the rear of the plot we could make a corner entrance instead of making the access through the middle. This would also avoid us having to start by demolishing the existing school, which would have entailed a high social cost for the children by forcing them to attend schools far away from their neighborhood [during the construction process].

Working on this basis, we not only wanted a more public, democratic, and institutional presence, but also easier access for local inhabitants so that the community could appropriate the space. However, the land on the initially assigned lot was of terrible quality and the structure alone would swallow 60 percent of the budget.

After changing the site, we considered it focused on a courtyard
[2, 3] typology for the center of the building and the ground floor to func-
[6, 7] tion as a community center outside teaching hours and at weekends. Following that rationale, we placed the classrooms on the first floor, and on the ground floor all the other spaces that could be easily accessed and used by the public as a center for children's early stimulation, a library, cafeteria, multipurpose hall, and bathrooms. The classrooms themselves were surrounded by a 3-meter-wide corridor/ring as somewhere children could gather. This corridor shelters the classrooms from the strong sunlight and gives children somewhere to play. This ring appears suspended. It has a yellowish concrete sill—a color created by the local silicate—lending it a powerful presence within the local neighborhood.

Since the building's completion and initial use, the project has become a neutral territory and easily accessible for families. It has even encouraged many children to return to school; drop-out rates now remain low. The school has become a center for the neighborhood, with spaces that do not require any mechanical ventilation or air conditioning systems to keep them cool. The interior is naturally ventilated and affords spectacular views over the Cauca valley.

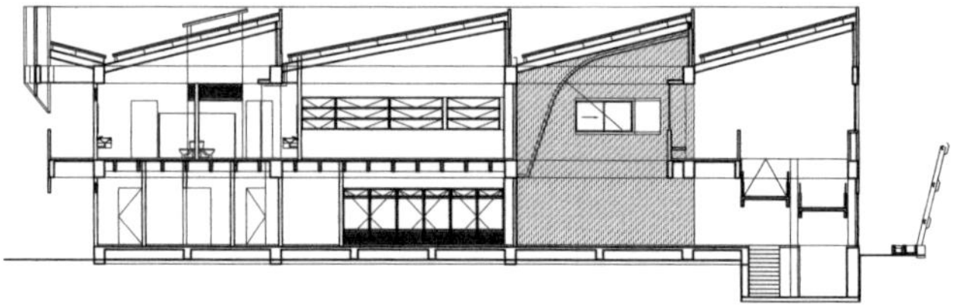

a.

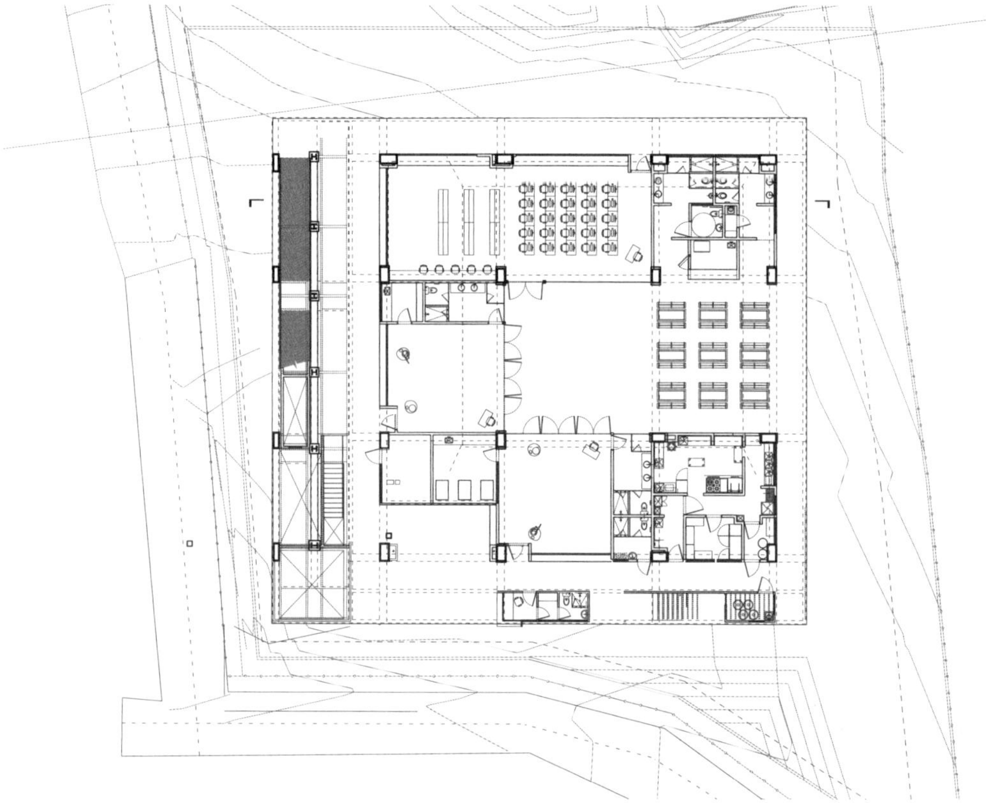

b.

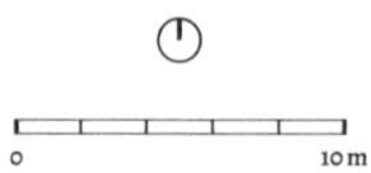

[2]

a. Section
b. Ground floor plan

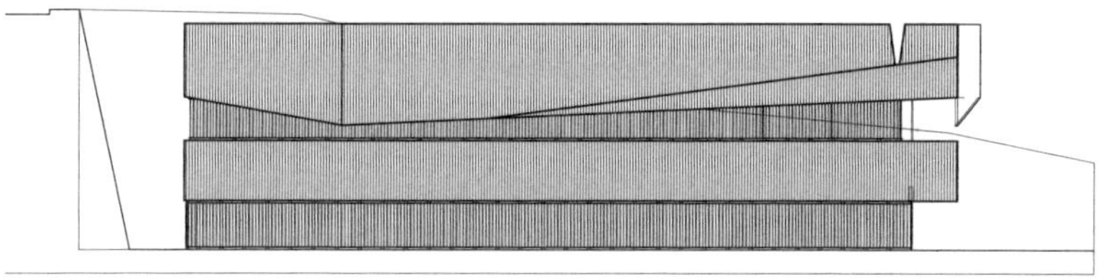

c.

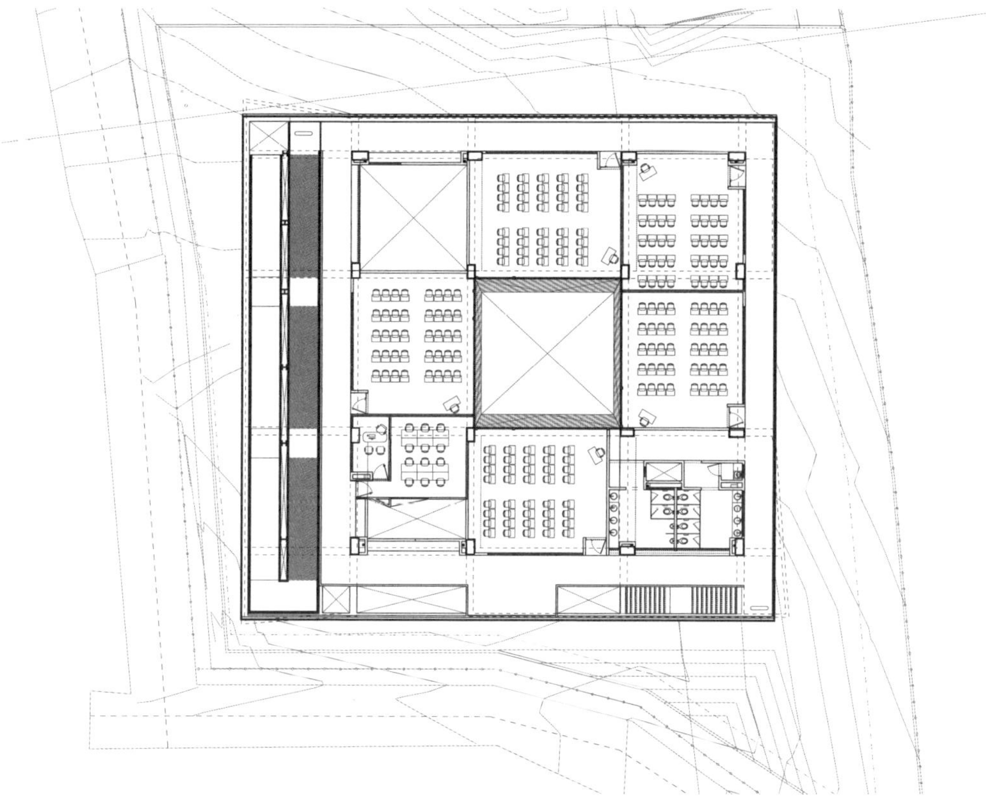

d.

[3]

c. South elevation
b. Upper floor plan

[4]

[5]

[6]

[7]

Gramalote Community Center (2014)

ARTICULATING OR INTERMEDIATE

The competition for the Gramalote Community Center formed part of the reconstruction of the town that had that to be abandoned because of a geological fault posing an extremely high risk of its potentially tragic disappearance. The government assigned a new tract of land for the construction of new social and cultural buildings along with hundreds of homes to rebuild what the earth had buried.

We approached the competition based on the premise that it was necessary to remember what had happened, and to give visibility to what geology had altered. Therefore, we understood architecture as a system of materialization and convergence that, to shape the built and unbuilt space and make it livable, enables the increase and association of relations among different agents co-existing in a particular geographical area. Our project is a system of convergence that articulates human geography and landscape through specific architecture. Such architecture is organized around a geographical location with layers of activity materialized and expressed through vertical, spatially interconnected sequences internally and in relation the immediate context and distant surroundings. Blocks of local clay and earth show the living memory of the houses of the time and the geology that transformed its daily life and inhabitability.

Specific architecture also establishes material, climate-related values based on the combination of regulatory and relational factors

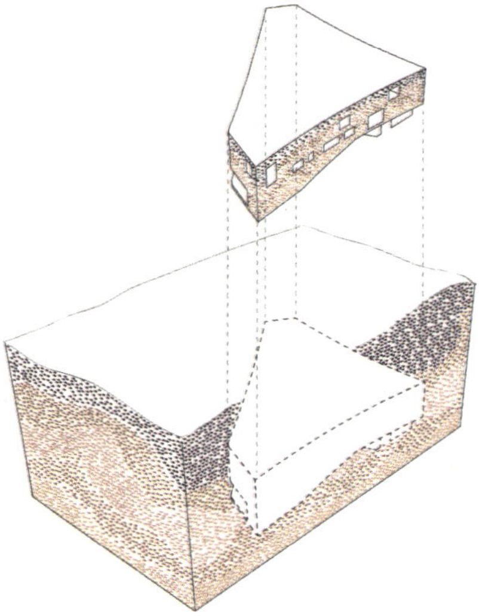

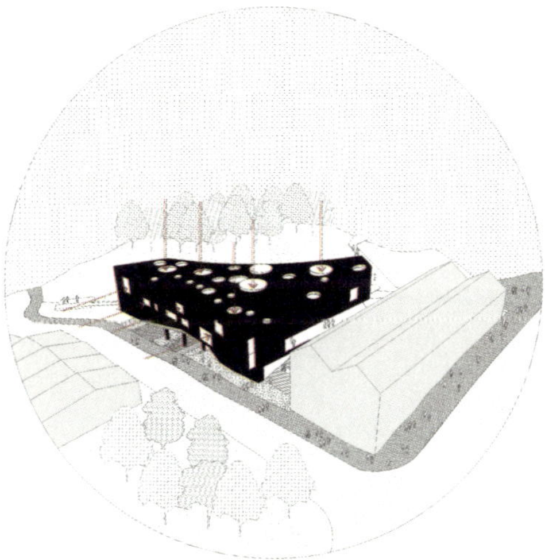

Axonometric

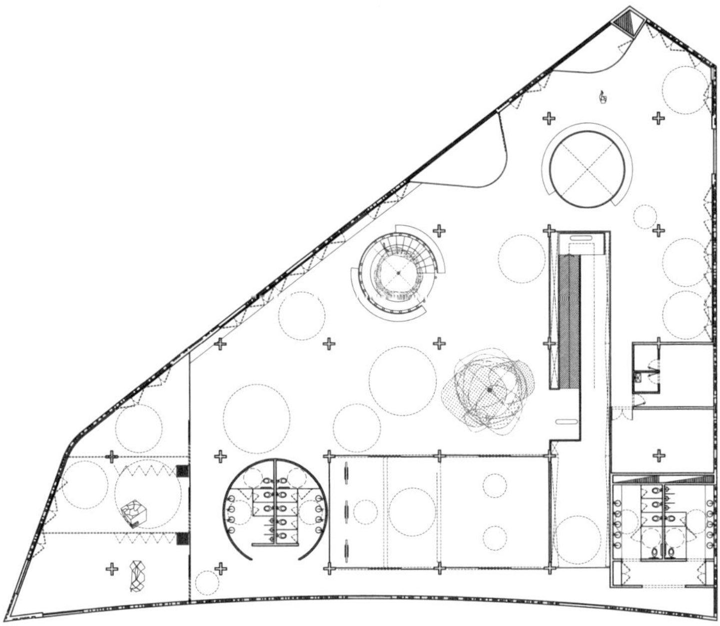

a.

0 10 m

a. Ground floor plan

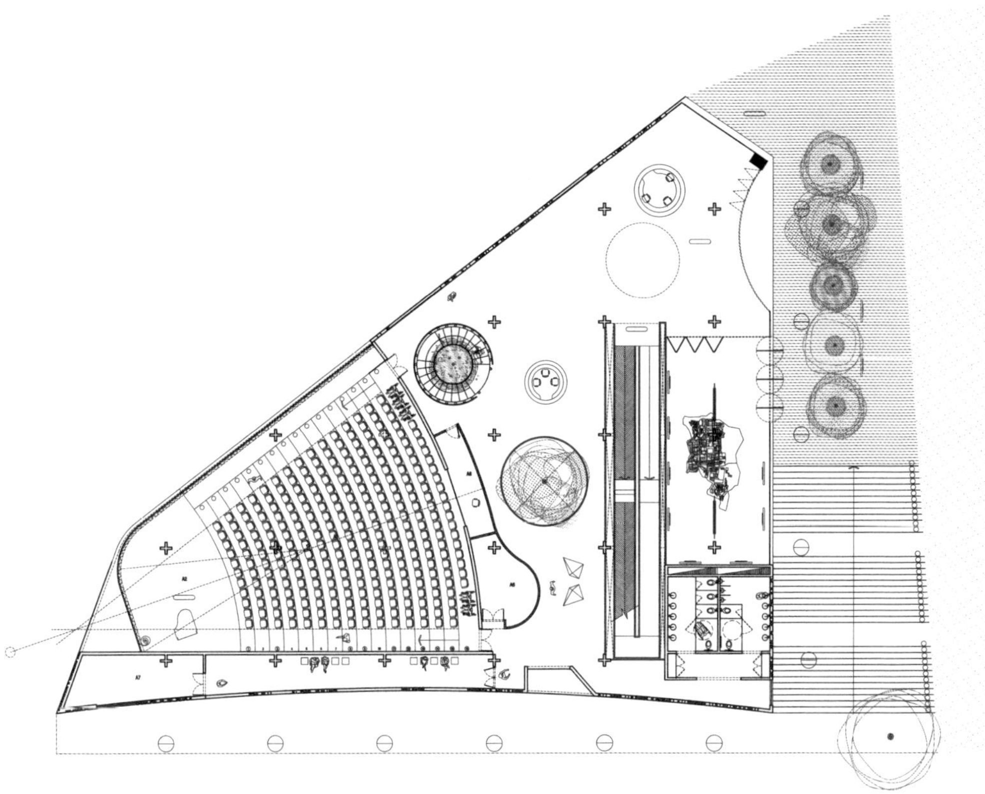

b.

b. Level 1 plan

[1]

[2]

to make it work in its tropical mountain location: thick walls, vertical ventilation systems (courtyards that intersect every level) and cross-ventilation systems (openwork).

These aspects create a porous structure for an intermediate/intermediary space as a work of relational architecture.

1. Porosity

Porosity is the spatial condition understood as the place for the exchange of information and experiences. The porous space exists to create social infrastructure for communities. Porosity has a twofold value: first, it refers to the perforated material condition, lightened and veiled, for the exchange and regulation of temperature by letting
[1, 2] light and air to filter through openwork in the façade or perforations in the volume. Second, porosity is that space of negotiation and blurriness that allows appropriation; it is the space where social groups can go about their daily lives, similarly to the appearance of new, unexpected behaviors. In this project, the ground floor is for public use, a quality that encourages spontaneous activities.

2. Intermediate space

Porosity creates the intermediate or intermediary space. Due to its lighting and ventilation, as well as the undefined and flexible program, intermediate spaces create an elastic architecture closely related to the passive administration of energy exchange. This architecture has the ability to be changing, reactive, and adaptive to new social needs such as budgetary changes, new functions, and unexpected behaviors. The intermediate space is a space created by, and for, the tropical climate.

3. Relational architecture

Architecture becomes relational by incorporating—and functioning as—active geography, and also by connecting and creating bonds between topography, human population, climate, and surroundings in an inhabited system with codependent pieces and parts. These parts provide comfort, identity, and formal links; they articulate and accommodate spaces for encounters, to indicate the landscape, to recognize a community space on the street.

SITUM Business Center (2014)

ARTICULATING OR INTERMEDIATE

The invitational competition brief for the SITUM Business Center essentially called for a conventional office building. However, this gave us an opportunity to reflect not only on the contemporary office space but also on megastructures that remain empty half the time —at nights and on weekends—and that, in their megalomaniacal desire to attract and provide services, become filled with parking spaces.

Before explaining the project, readers should note that this description was written in 2014, six years before the outbreak of the COVID-19 pandemic. Therefore, some aspects may now appear obsolete or, in some cases, visionary.

We began to prepare our submission by analyzing the workplace, where four generations of different ages and working cultures came together at that time, supported by dissimilar technologies and platforms, giving the office a different meaning for each one.

a. Baby Boom Generation

The generation born between 1946 and 1964. Many baby-boomers are now retired, and most of the group born between 1955 and 1960 should begin to retire in the next five years. This group is characterized by their inflexible idea about the workplace: its members felt that their work should be in a fixed space and as private as possible, with firm office hours and sacred weekends. Late adopters of computers and systems.

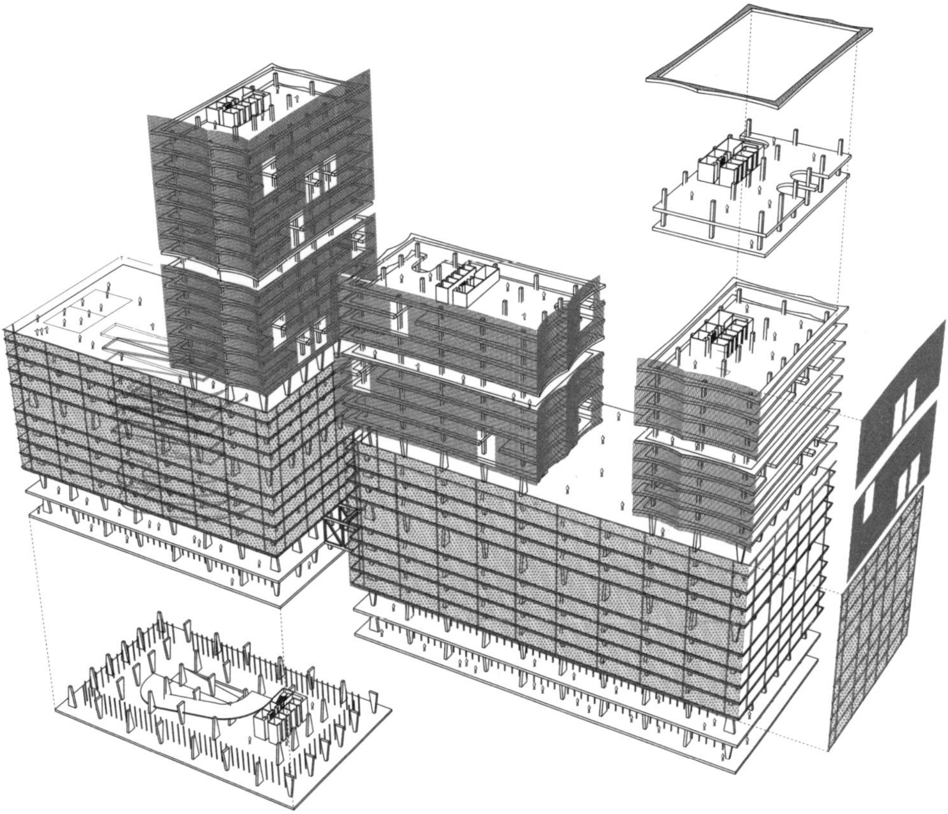

[1]

Axonometric

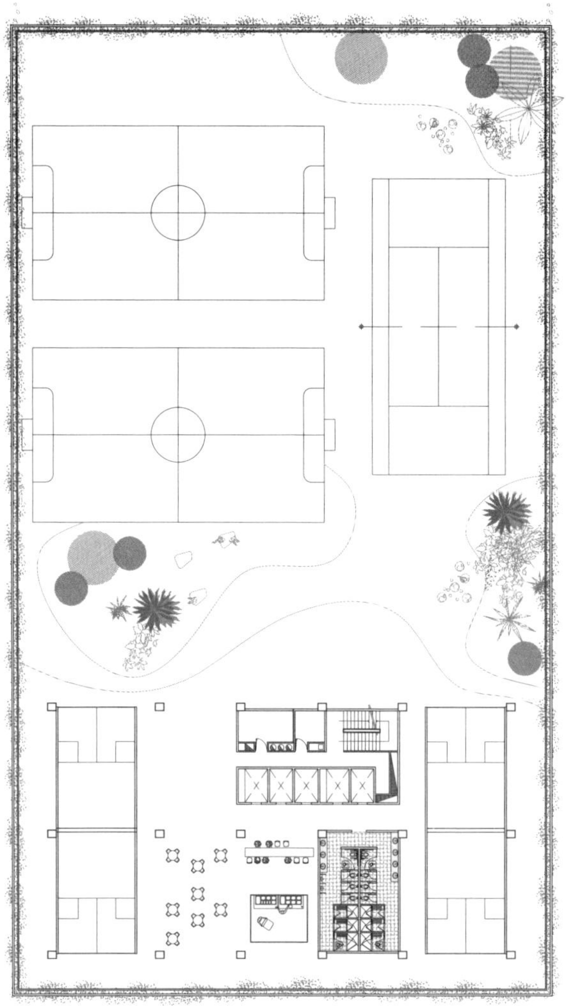

a.

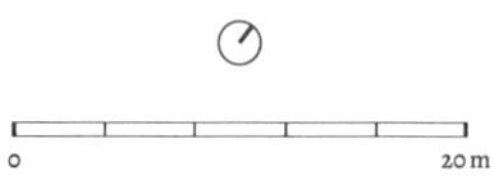

a. Level 11 plan. Sports pitch

Communal and meeting areas are kept to the minimum necessary: meeting rooms, bathroom. The transition to the cubicle was traumatic and complex. For this last generation of large industrial companies, the factory is the epitome of the workplace.

b. Generation X

The cohort born between 1965 and 1981. Ambitious, competitive, individualist, its members directly experienced the development of communication systems, from television to the latest-generation portable devices, including the appearance of video games. The first to receive education in computer systems from a young age. They will reach senior management and board-level positions in the next ten years.

Open attitude to working culture: they consider it unnecessary to have a fixed workplace or an office cubicle. Office hours do not cause problems. Priority given to work over family, therefore, the office is an extension of the home and members of Generation X are prepared to spend as long as necessary there to achieve their objectives.

c. Generation Y or Millenials

Those born between 1981 and 1997 belong to an ecologically and socially conscious generation, whose members grew up in a world revolutionized by digital and mass culture. Office hours of little relevance to them. Sharing is part of their culture: they are the creators of new companies such as Uber, Airbnb, etc. Naturally entrepreneurial. Little job security within companies. Proficient consultants and with an open, free, and flexible attitude in their perspective on the workplace. The office is anywhere with an internet connection. The factory as a space does not exist for them; production is not tied to any particular place.

d. Generation Z

Born between 1997 and 2015, the generation of the digital revolution. Being disconnected is not an option. Social networks and communication media are their meeting place. Skillful communicators; their idea of work is related to entrepreneurial projects, mainly in the services sector and on digital platforms. Everywhere is the same for this generation, for whom work and geographical location are unconnected. Jobs come and go. They do not stay long in companies and are uninterested in careers in the traditional sense of being tied down to a company.

Confluence in the workplace has meant that offices have had to cater to four generations simultaneously. Everyone needed to feel comfortable in their work surroundings, despite their different working methods and tools.

THE FUTURE OF THE WORKPLACE

The office cubicle—inefficient, unconducive to teamwork, and irre-
[2] sponsive to individuals' needs—is undeniably dead. Therefore, and at that time, the theory of distributed work—where people work in interstitial locations instead of assigned, stable centers—began to evolve.

During the competition, we concluded that given that the contemporary work context of that time did not yet meet the needs of privacy and teamwork, and due to the intermittency between these models, people are taking the following steps to cut themselves off and find a moment to concentrate:

1. Workplaces encourage users to stay put, promising a comfortable and pleasant experience.

2. Various types of space are designed, with varying levels of formality.
3. Individual and shared spaces are in equal proportion.
4. Spaces can be adapted to different needs. [3]
5. Creating dynamic, mutant spaces.

Ubiquity and technology

Technology and the internet have profoundly altered the working environment. We expected to be able to work anywhere but, contrary to what many people thought, the internet does not appear to have displaced the office as a place of confluence. What was clear at that moment was how the office needed to offer variables to handle different rhythms of work and different lengths of stay. Despite remote working, between 80 and 85 percent of activities took place in the workplace.

Speed

Communication and connectivity are vital in the workplace, not only in terms of connections and the internet, but also in links to the physical world. How do people meet in the corridors? Where do people take a break? How can we create dynamic environments where people can meet and exchange ideas? By answering these questions through the design of spaces, we can meet a wide range of needs and demands for the workplace, both now and in the future.

Doing more with less

In companies, the goal and tendency in the administration of the workplace has been to reduce costs by 25 percent in the space used. This represents substantial savings in terms of annual fixed and operating expenses. This reduction is essentially planned to increase the efficiency of available spaces without the need to increase the number of square meters built or used, as the usual aim of efficient

furniture design and a versatile and flexible distribution and assignation of jobs.

The Ciudad del Río Retail and Office Complex was designed to be built in the order considered necessary by the promoter. It had an underground parking level in each block and potentially having three towers in total. [1]

a. 3-phase construction

Phase 1: Build car parks and Tower 1 on Block A5. Once the construction of block A6 was complete, it was necessary to connect the walkway of level +7.00 to block A6, linking to the Entre Orillas project, a private development to connect both sides of Medellín River by using a walkway/bridge over the river.

Phase 2: In Block A6, car parks could be built up to Axis 14 and Tower 2. The car park would be closed and protected by a wall on Axis 14

Phase 3: From Eje 14 we could build the remaining car parks and knock down the wall that enclosed the car park. Build Tower 3. Both towers shared a car park.

b. 3-phase construction, second version

Phase 1: Build both car parks and Tower 1 in Block A5 and, once the construction of block A5 was complete, the walkway of level +7.00 could connect to Block A6, linking to the Entre Orillas project.

Phase 2: All the car parks could be built in Block A6, and Tower 2.

Phase 3: Tower 3 was built. Both towers shared a car park.

c. 2-phase construction

Phase 1: The car parks as well as Tower 1 in Block A5 could be built. Once the construction of block A6 was complete, it needed to connect the walkway of level +7.00 to Block A6, linking to the Entre Orillas project.

Phase 2: The building of all the car parks and the two towers of block A6.

Reviving the Dead Zone

a. Wide availability of mass transport infrastructure and potential construction of a new Metro station between Poblado and Industriales, was combined with a stimulus package for alternative, green means of transport by the city's land-use planning department, and an extended public bicycle network. *Cicla* turned the project's area into a large car-parking space: more than 54 percent of the construction would be occupied by cars. We saw great potential for creating a new space for other programs by repurposing the car park area.

b. Therefore, thinking about its short-term use, we designed parking levels as flexible and versatile spaces, readily modifiable to host temporary activities such as the MAMM gallery and urban events. This could generate permanent revenue at a very low cost, only requiring an efficient administration of the car park's use and occupation.

[2]

c. For the medium term, we believed that the car park areas on the upper floors could be rented as office space. The 4-meter height between floors was almost the same as in typical office buildings. With this aim in mind, the vehicular access ramps to the various parking levels needed to be made out of a metal structure that is removable in case of the need to increase the rental area, provided that this process was proportionate with a steadily increasing reduction in the use of car parking spaces. This operation was accompanied by natural ventilation and bioclimatic policies. Removing the ramps will turn these spaces into courtyards with natural ventilation and lighting.

The materials for the façade and enclosures would work exactly the same as for the upper levels. Around each parking level there was chain-link fencing, along with sun-protection systems—using various kinds of climbers and plants—to regulate the temperature. Upon

[3]

conversion, the fencing would simply be removed and the walls replaced with prefabricated perforated GRC concrete panels, as used on the offices' façade.

The rental area to be increased per floor would be 7,786 square meters. Passive air conditioning is a reality and a promise that can be kept. Compared to the expense of mechanical air conditioning, this very low-cost solution would guarantee spaces that did not need air conditioning or other temperature control systems. Simply managing the temperature and humidity levels properly could create comfortable year-round temperatures using systems with lower installation and maintenance costs.

Each office floor had: (a) an outer skin that provided shelter from sunlight and other meteorological elements, (b) a thermal buffer zone or "maintenance corridor" for passive temperature control and maintenance using plants and humidity, and (c) a second layer of glazing to control the air flow toward the interior, made of projecting windows and lattices. They are located both in the lower area and in the upper part of the second envelope. Finally, (d) a vertical ventilation duct, located in each floor's elevator lobby, to funnel air up from the ground floor to the top floor. The duct is created by using a mesh floor that lets air flow up from below:

a. The first envelope (a) was located on the outer perimeter, and it receives sunlight from the west and east. The skin was made of dark gray, micro-perforated GRC concrete panel with a 60 percent light filter. Each panel measures 3.5 meters high, 30 centimeters wide, and 3 centimeters thick. This panel receives the initial impact of the heat and defines the outer membrane and finish of the façade. The system reduced solar gain by 60 percent and also ensured that the rain does not all enter the buffer zone created precisely to regulate the interiors' exposure to sunlight.

b. The thermal buffer added humidity to the air passing over the plants located around the perimeter. These plants are irrigated with the rainwater harvested from the building's roof and from the surface of the sports pitch. On extremely hot days, a spray system could increase humidity for the plants by distributing microparticles of the same irrigation water. The thermal buffer also created somewhere for workers to take a break and a corridor for maintenance and cleaning.

c. The second skin was glazed and had two projecting windows: one on the lower part, 15 centimeters from the finished floor surface and 50 centimeters high; on the upper part, 50 centimeters from the level of the slab, is a 70-centimeter-high, top-hung window. This window system defined the entire perimeter. It provided acoustic insulation and cooled the building through cross-ventilation. If necessary to close off the offices to make exclusive compartments, it was simply a question of moving the upper mesh to above each office door to ensure continued ventilation.

After potentially transforming the parking levels into office space, the system would continue working because the entrance ramps are removable so that each resulting space can become a courtyard.

Farallones Community Coffee Wet Mill (2014–2016)

STRUCTURAL OR PIVOTAL

Our second structural or pivotal project is the Farallones Community Coffee Wet Mill. This project came at a moment of increasing interest in historical structures and in the absolute determination to approach our tropical work as an opportunity to revise current and previous narratives to discover new seams in our practice. This tropical approach does not represent so much a naturalist intention as a shift toward an uncompromisingly disciplinary gaze. As such, we have been able to gain a fuller understanding of historical architectural processes and their implications for our work. Tropical architecture implies a fragmented idea of heritage and the city. Therefore, we are forced to find small-scale foundations to carry out our work.

My work at the Harvard Graduate School of Design as a Design Critic undoubtedly inspired and accelerated this interest, thanks to the support of Rahul Mehrotra and Giancarlo Mazzanti's invitation to take part in his course and, subsequently, to the infinite generosity of Iñaki Ábalos to receive us for three years at the Department of Architecture. This experience continues to this day thanks also to the trust, support, and generosity of Mark Lee as the chair of the department. This has certainly marked a watershed in our way of reflecting on and carrying out architecture, and in the ways of guiding and structuring our studio.

Social and environmental factors defined the Farallones project from our earliest discussions with the client. The objective was to ensure that the small coffee producer did not lose its crop due to a lack of resources to maintain its coffee processing facility; Farallones also needed to secure a better price for its product, preventing the contamination of more than 25,000 cubic meters of water per year and thus providing a social service to the local campesino population. The project benefits 750 families in the area of Ciudad Bolívar, Antioquia. This coffee-rich part of the country is eminently rural and currently being transformed into accessible countryside.

Before we began the design process, we deep-dived into the coffee production process; we traveled to the region several times, visiting various kinds of processing plants. During these journeys, apart [1]
from understanding industrial processes or entering into contact with rural Colombia, we gained first-hand knowledge of vernacular architecture that shows spatial, climatic, and material intelligence in their layout. At the same time, it was essential to discover

[1]

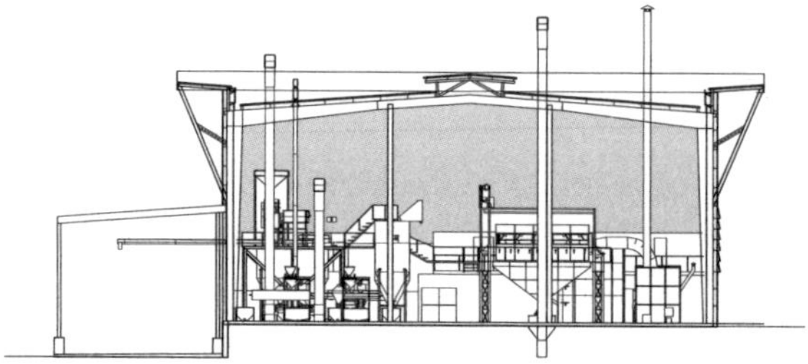

a.

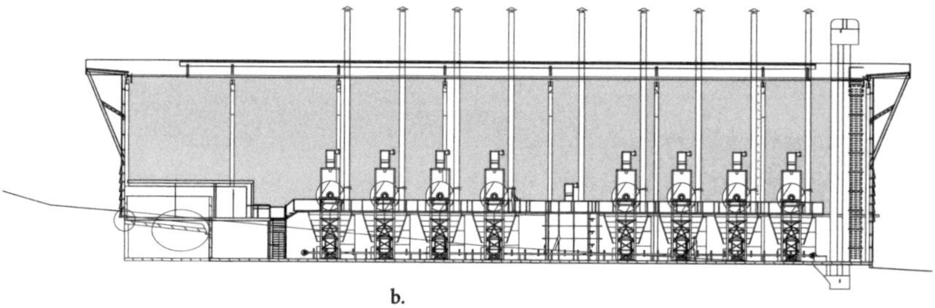

b.

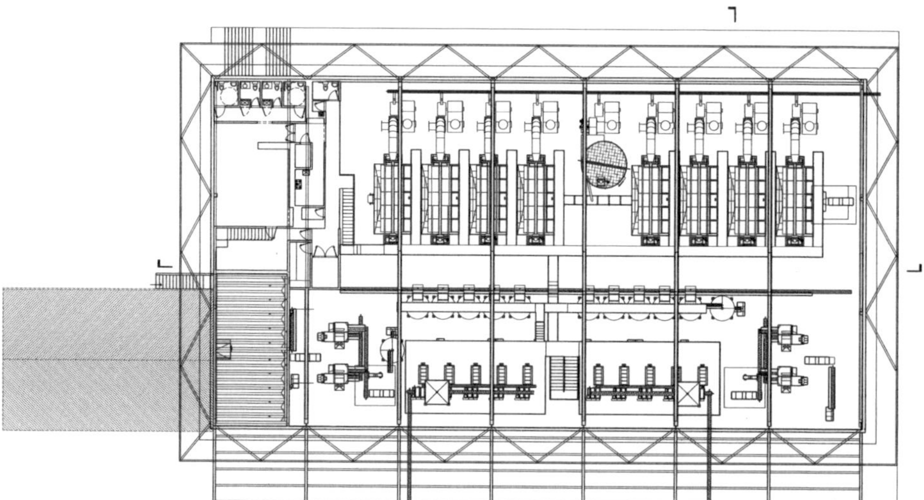

c.

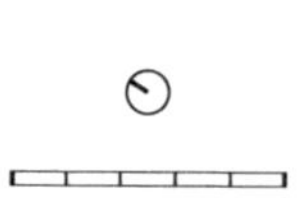

[2]

a. Transversal section
b. Longitudinal section
c. Plan

the reproductions and interpretations of *The Grammar of Ornament* by Owen Jones, whose book was brought over by the British mining engineers in the latter half of the nineteenth century, amid the mountainous and traditional coffee-producing regions of Antioquia, Risaralda, Quindio, and Caldas, and adapted its decorative patterns, such as the wood-carved latticework, to ventilate and cool housing. Today this is considered one of Colombia's heritage styles. Although these findings were not new, they have remained on the radar of various generations of architects, including our own.

Located around 75 kilometers southwest of Medellín, the processing plant is where the coffee beans are washed, depulped, fermented, and dried. The project is the result of an initiative to join forces between a cooperative of coffee producers and Colombia's largest trading company. This community and business association is rethinking the use, role, and operation of coffee processing plants, in order to give coffee producers more free time and to generate greater economic and environmental benefits.

Inside, the project encompasses two seemingly contradictory functions as a community center that provides services to families working in the coffee industry (education, training, entertainment) at the same time as being an industrial processing plant, from the bean to the dry parchment coffee.

The rectangular floor plan measures 28 by 58 meters, with an [2]
eaved roof cantilevered 3 meters to provide shade to the coffee
pickers while they queue up to deliver their harvest. Given the lo- [3]
cal weather conditions, the curtain-wall façade is not designed to be transparent or to artificially regulate the interior temperature. On the contrary, it allows cross-ventilation and provides visual protection by using terracotta-colored GRC concrete panels attached to a structural iron frame.

These panels are arranged into three layers. The lower layer has [4–6]
bas-relief patterns extracted from the typical iconographies of the region, derived from Owen Jones's patterns. This approach creates a

[3]

[4]

[5]

[6]

link between pre-existing elements not far removed from local references. In the intermediate layer, a series of panels with pyramidal sections were poured on burlap-fiber textiles, the same material used in the sacks used for transporting coffee. This allows cool air to enter, essential for the escape of the vapor produced when the water leaves the beans as they dry. Finally, on the upper layer, a series of panels with rhomboid-shaped perforations helps the vapors to escape and natural light to enter.

The processing plant evokes the typical constructions of the region where the structure defines the volume and, based on the articulation of the eave and the structure, it establishes the relationship with the mass of the roof. This canopy-based design gives importance to the air and sun for how the space is organized, conditions that truly inform the formal principal and primary functional ideas. Given these requirements, the project needed to be a practical construction system to speed up the construction process, using materials capable of withstanding the exterior and interior conditions.

As in the Gabriel García Márquez Primary School, the specific, well-defined, and regular floor plan displaces the force of the interior to the spatiality of the absolute void. As an industrial processing plant, an immediate and obvious response is to create a box to house many production activities, except that here the box is made porous through the curtain-wall system. The GRC panels' perforations help create an exterior system of environmental and thermal exchange, and by doing so create a beautiful and phenomenological atmosphere thanks to the natural light penetrating through the perforations. This quality is powerfully expressed when the vapor can be seen escaping through the orifices.

Boulder House (2016)

ARTICULATING OR INTERMEDIATES

Boulder House is a concrete canopy made of concrete poured on site and stained with local silicates. A 9-meter-high volcanic rock marks the middle of the plot, which is located in the traditional coffee and citrus growing area in the Cauca river valley, 70 kilometers to the southwest of Medellín. The house uses previous strategies and aims considered innovative at the time. Through confluence, the project combines and articulates several intentions: a prior interest in a diffuse perimeter plan and a growing but subtly expressed proclivity toward defining the space using specific yet ambiguous ele-
[1] ments. This house's X-shaped layout is designed to envelop the rock without touching it; to connect it to a diffuse interior that is also defined by an almost obsessive repetition of thin concrete pillars, simultaneously integrating them as part of the structure and as the façade. The house incorporates a series of tropical gardens and transfers them to the perimeter, cooling the temperature that rises to 30 degrees centigrade during the daytime and drops to 15 degrees centigrade in the early morning.

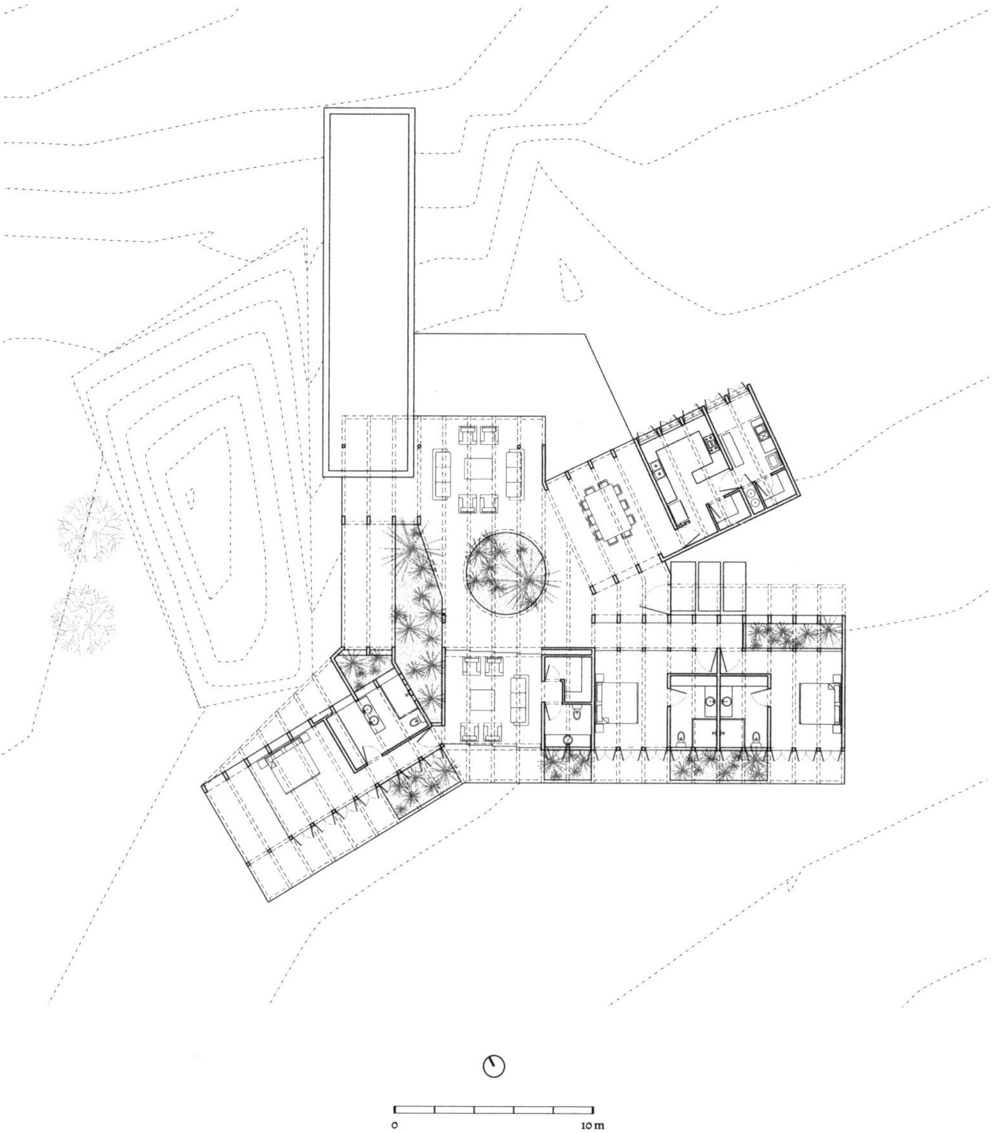

[1]

Plan

MiesUnderstandings (2017)

SPECULATIVE

MiesUnderstandings is the result of an invitation by Johnston Marklee, chief curators of the 2017 edition of the Chicago Architecture Biennial called *Make New History*. We were assigned a corridor measuring approximately 40 meters long by 4.5 meters wide.

MiesUnderstandings was our first speculative project. Although LIGA D.F. Canonical Tropics was the first one to be built, this was our initial approach to the idea of an architecture of textiles and to the ideas about tropical space condensed in this experiment. The idea of putting together a display called MiesUnderstandings directly referred to that ambiguous yet specific understanding of Mies's work, of his way of creating spaces and of (our) arbitrariness in sensing and believing that Mies always dreamed of a tropical spatial idea: a fluid space with blurred boundaries that increases the perception of nature through a lightweight roof and several plant-related and geological reference points, built as an abstract graphism by manipulating stone slabs and with the idealism of glass.

Our project also wanted to be inserted in the dual meaning implied by the biennial's title. On the one hand, it can be read as "Making history new" as an invitation to look at what has happened, and on the other, it could mean "Making new history," which we interpreted as reviewing the existing narrative to construct a new present. Our project locates itself at once in both these interpretations: reviewing the history of the narrative of the tropical space not only

in its references but also in its component images, from the vernacular to the most genealogical—Mies. We believed that by juxtaposing local images of the tropics and their context next to canonical images for architecture such as "Laugier and Eisen's Primitive Hut," we could expand the conversation beyond the often-naïve policies and narratives. In this sense, we considered it necessary to appropriate for ourselves the history of architecture, considering that we needed
[1] to participate in it with our Farallones Community Coffee Wet Mill project. Its particular location, use, and context made it possible to play with ambiguity and be open to interpretation.

Our initial approach obviously led us to reflect on the work of
[2–3] Mies van der Rohe, given both the historical context (the biennial's title) and the geographical location (Chicago).

We started out working on the idea of the curtain wall. First of all because Chicago was a veritable laboratory for modern architecture and an early adopter of the curtain wall. This structural system maximized transparency, light, and a controlled connection to the outdoors, and regulating the indoor temperature. Afterward, in reference to the first MiesUnderstanding, we considered Mies's curtains for Café Samt und Seide (1927), co-designed with Lilly Reich. In the café and then in Barcelona Pavilion (1929), textile is an ambiguous, dynamic yet specific, abstract and phenomenological partition. Mies used textiles to construct an unstable space activated by the vibration of time and flow; a space that also distances itself from the transparency for which he would later become known. Textiles helped Mies and Reich conceive space both ambiguously and specifically. Their strategically located velvet and silk panels suggested a fluid, multi-relational space consisting of flat, concave, and convex surfaces that indicate, welcome, and distribute. Café Samt und Seide, along with the Barcelona Pavilion, are structural and pivotal projects of the first phase developed in Berlin. Thanks to these small experimental laboratories, Mies found a source of ideas to accompany him for the rest of his life.

[1]

[2]

[3]

Our second MiesUnderstanding derives from Villa Tugendhat (1928) and Barcelona Pavilion, also made with Lilly Reich. The project moves in two directions. The first points toward constructing the fluid space and transparency of Barcelona Pavilion that is already foreshadowed by Tugendhat Villa; the second, toward the material and formal surfaces that defined space in Mies's two works, specifically the stone and wood cladding that not only creates a boundary or partition but also a pictorial and graphic construction.

In the case of transparency, we found an anonymous photograph of Tugendhat Villa's terrace showing it as a small interior garden which, thanks to the light and glass door system, reproduced and multiplied the effect of the greenery on the surface. This action was later repeated in the Barcelona Pavilion's series of glass doors, although no longer with the presence of plants. Instead, these were abstracted in the stone and marble. This interpretation led us to imagine reproducing these surfaces, though no longer with rock or marble but with tropical vegetation. This approach introduced a multifarious codification of the space and the construction of a relation on several scales based on the graphic pattern, using it progressively, among polychromatic mushrooms and tree canopies, lichens and orchids (*Cattleya*), ceiba tree bark and calatheas.

After selecting the graphic patterns, we set about experimenting with different surfaces. This took us back to Café Samt und Seide, since we defined that the patterns needed to be stamped in velvet and had to function as curtain walls to be distributed all along the assigned corridor. Once again, we arranged the curtains as concave, convex, and flat shapes, creating a series of niches. In that position, we located a series of Camilo Echavarría's photographs of the coffee-growing region of Antioquia, the location of our Farallones project. These niches also included some photos of our project, taken by Echavarría, as well as a series of images referring to the idea of Laugier and Eisen's Primitive Hut like Mies's Farnsworth House, registering the transparent limit as the threshold, at an oblique angle to the kitchen; Lake Shore Drive under construction, just as a structure; Farnsworth House under construction, just as a structure, floor, and roof, without enclosures. We also displayed a vernacular coffee processing plant, photographed at the edge, between the inside and the outside. Similarly, we added Humboldt's plant geography, a small roof to receive harvested beans in the coffee producing areas, a vernacular hut-like coffee processing plant, photographs of the coffee-growing region and engravings from the eighteenth and nineteenth centuries depicting Caribbean sugar-production facilities, combined with images of our project under construction and completed.

This project was undeniably influential on our work. On the one hand, and although it may sound naïve, it gave us the chance to connect differently to the history of architecture. We could now relate to this history in a more essential way, appropriating it as a personal, local, and universal narrative. This was far removed from the canon we learned as students, when we were taught that the architect was a creative artist and his inspired genius would generate completely new forms, solutions, and compositions without any trace of history or prior learning: without any precedents, only the present.

It was also clearly feasible to implement a series of references and positions, all described in this text—mainly in the first part—ranging from the interpretation of the primitive hut, passing through the material and spatial understanding of stereotomies and tectonics, to the repositioning and definition of tropical space.

Canonical Tropics - LIGA (2017)

SPECULATIVE

Canonical Tropics is another speculative project where we could objectively and instrumentally reveal and propose a series of ideas already latent from the first decisions taken. This project forms part of the magnificent series of exhibitions at the LIGA architecture gallery, directed and founded by PRODUCTORA and Ruth Estévez.

Along with the Chicago Biennial, this invitation gave us an im-
[1] mense responsibility since it was the first time that we reflected on our work through an installation-like exhibition as opposed to the regular formats of models and drawings.

We took this opportunity to develop a series of parallel ideas for our proposal for the Chicago Biennial. Whereas for the second exhibition of MiesUnderstandings we focused on the tropical narrative and its possible links to Mies (the curtain wall) and the primitive hut, for LIGA we wanted to establish an inventory of relationships with images, historical or material precedents, as well as exploring our understanding of an architectural work to show it as a spatial experience outside the regular context of our projects, now condensed
[2] into a temporary, 10-square-meter exhibition space.

Our real starting point is a superimposition of conceptual ideas, theoretical interests, and the possibility of building a spatial experience closely related to exploring or inhabiting the tropical mindset. Canonical Tropics is a good example to explain the idea of architecture as a confluence. To create this exhibit, we began by returning to silk,

[1]

since we were working around Café Samt un Seide. If MiesUnderstandings was velvet, Canonical Tropics needed to be silk, in order to [3]
close the circle of references.

We decided that it was interesting to consider a system of curtains as a space consisting of layers, as if we were passing through the forest to which we referred in this text, when we mentioned the description of the territory created by art. By structuring this spatial experience we saw an opportunity to refer to the diorama, a system already being used in the nineteenth century, where travelers recounted their experiences by candlelight—a method that prefigured cinema—with drawings on silk cloths, that passed by, one by one, as the tale of the journey unfolded. This idea inspired us to look for an architectural reference that might allow us to establish the spatial experience of layers as an organizational system. With this objective, it struck us as an interesting idea to invert the experience and material quality of the Pavilion in Sonsbeek Park by Aldo van Eyck, a strong critic of tropical space, although someone undoubtedly admired for his work. By making this choice, we wanted to redescribe his pavilion's linearity from a tropical perspective: not to read it or experience it along the Y-axis, but to make it vulnerable along the X-axis. We could therefore build an unstable, dynamic space activated by breezes and in the wake of the semi-transparent and multi-referential route, inverting the qualities of van Eyck's work while remaining connected to it. We maintained the firm intention to enrich the visitor's spatial experience, purposefully distancing ourselves from minimalist preciousness. We thought that the curtain system should be more than a simple ornament or decoration: it should come close to the spatial system proposed by Jesús Rafael Soto with his penetrable works.

Canonical Tropics needed to possess and build an atmosphere of veils, layers, and superimpositions that would guide or refer, either tangentially or directly, to the context in which we go about our

LIGA 25 | CAM
PO / AGENdA (COL)

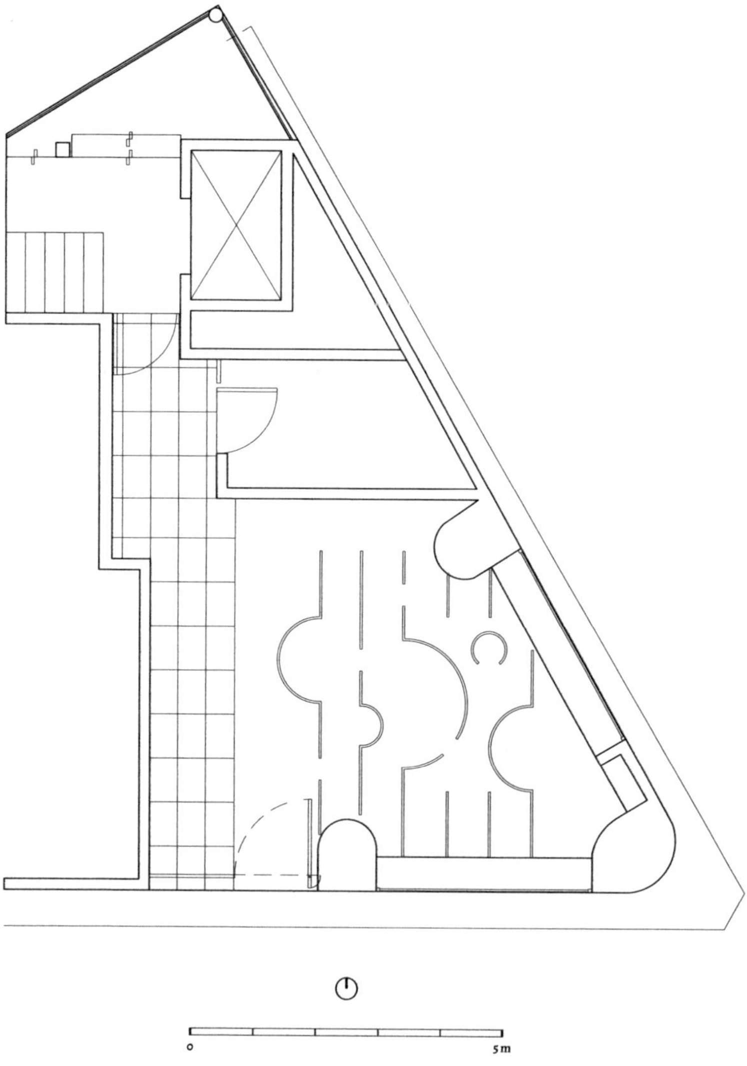

[2]

Plan

daily lives. To this end, we took photographs of a series of plants, bushes, shrubberies, flowers, and leaves in our house's garden and in our studio's garden. We followed in the idea of Church who represented multiples scales of nature on a single plane, together with the superimposition of improbable and threatening images as visible in Fischli and Weiss's photographs of nature, we created a system of expanding scales of living entities in each layer corresponding to van Eyck's plan.

In this way, our intervention underlined a series of values already explained in this text and worth exploring briefly: ideas that established, temporarily, the principles of a tropical canon.

Essentially, these values are about accepting and searching for a non-absolute, multi-referential, dynamic, and unstable space made up of layers. The construction of an elastic threshold.

[3]

Puebla (2017)

ARTICULATING OR INTEMEDIATE

The housing project for the historic center of Puebla (Mexico) combines three fundamental objectives: to appropriate, recover, and encourage habitation. It also offers affordable housing in one of the city's prime locations, generating social and urban value. Thus we conceived and designed three strategies, using history as a system of continuity; materials as a strategy of understanding and dialogue; and typology as an instrument.

1. History as a system of continuity

The challenge of intervening in a historic center requires understanding history as an open text available to be edited or interpreted in accordance with the spirit of the present. With this aim in mind, we have carefully and responsibly observed two particular issues. First, typology understood as a way of organizing space through time produces a particular spatial order that interconnects with social variations and their opportunities. The second element is the material quality. Matter is the organizational form for typological orders to endure and for time to be expressed in a joined-up fashion with the knowledge of the place itself and its cultures. Hence this

[1, 2]

articulation between typology and material makes it possible to adapt and to start a dialogue with the urban fabric and domestic intimacy.

2. Materials as a strategy of understanding and dialogue

While exploring the streets of Puebla, we noted that materials appeared in many forms. We were impressed by the value given to ornamentation and its technical and aesthetic implications. We thought that this decoration needed to remain and be readapted for today's conditions. Our recommendation was for a prefabricated, terracotta-stained concrete to occupy a part of the façades'
[1] surface. The color gave continuity to the city's chromatic identity. Concrete needed to be poured in formwork containing a pattern (see Image 1). Although the pattern already exists in the city, its beauty and ornamental density gave us the idea that it would make the façade more expressive.

The decision to use concrete stemmed from the opportunity to have a malleable material that is also capable of resonating with historical forms, as well as ensuring low maintenance.

[2] We considered that other parts of the façade required handcrafted Puebla-style talavera ceramics in blue and white. This made a connection to ancestral knowledge that echoes artisanal traditions (see Image 2).

3. Typology as an instrument

Typology plays a special role in the organization of the intermediary space, where it articulates the public with the private and creates
[3–4] community. For this purpose, we used typological space based on the Puebla-style house built around a courtyard. We think that this typology helped connect the local climate and the opportunity to create spaces for social interactions.

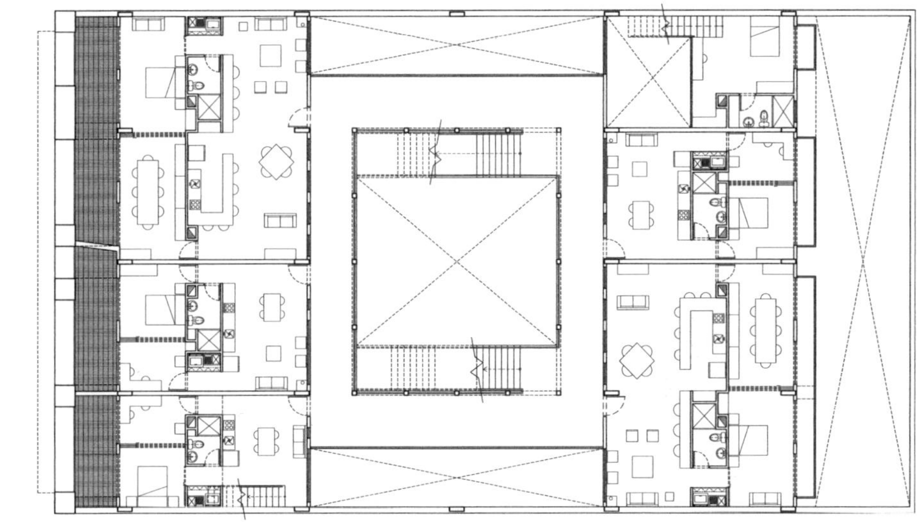

a.

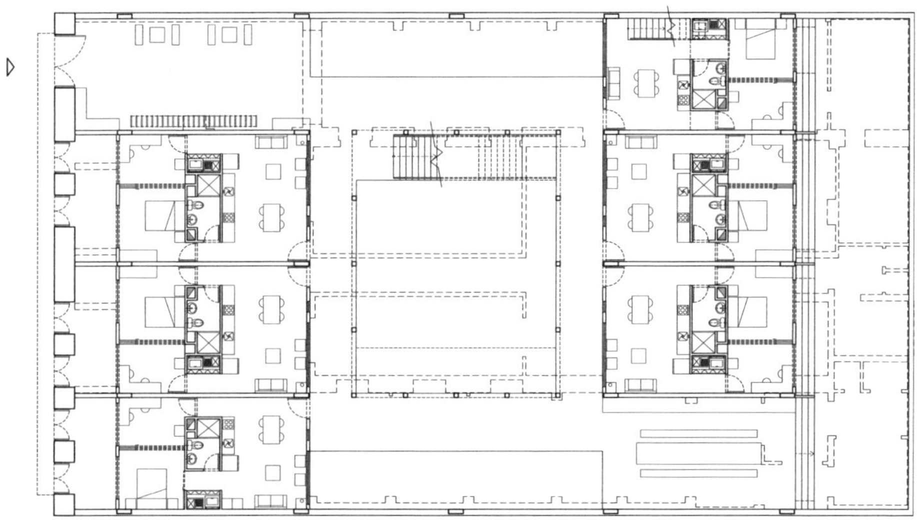

b.

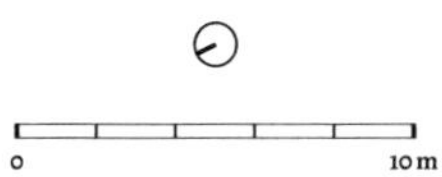

[3]

a. Level 1 plan
b. Ground floor plan

[4]

On another scale, we have opted for a housing typology distributed in thirds, where we inserted all the functions containing technical installations into the second third—the middle one—with a determination to leave the extremes available for a more flexible use and also to ensure cross ventilation. For this typological purpose, we proposed five typologies that guarantee social interactions and exchanges. These were designed to be adaptable for social changes and potential adjustments, as shown by the possibility of having commercial premises on the ground floor and the concept of accommodating members of non-direct family members independently while still under the same roof.

We believe that the best home is the one that not only offers opportunities but can also respond to the demands of time and new social configurations.

Groundscraper Hotel (2017)

ARTICULATING OR INTERMEDIATE

After the Colombian Peace Agreements were signed with the FARC guerrilla on 26 September 2016, large areas previously off-limits for tourism suddenly became accessible to all Colombians and foreign investors. The agreement opened the way for many people to finally visit, get to know, and enjoy the wonders of Colombia's vast biodiver-
[1] sity. The hotel—located in the Sierra de la Macarena National Park—was made possible thanks to this development.

The Andean, Amazonian, and Orinoco Basin ecosystems merge in this region to create a unique biodiversity and beauty. Our client acquired a property that was partially deforested in recent years after the only existing local authority (which was, until very recently, the FARC itself) withdrew from the zone. Based on the premise of this area's social and environmental fragility, we worked with the client to help limit deforestation through the responsible stewardship of the area, and to raise awareness and protection with scientific and adventure tourism.

The property is a one-hour boat ride upriver, and the river itself is ten hours from the nearest city (Villavicencio, Meta). Given the remoteness and difficult access, we decided no single structural element could measure longer than eight meters, to make sure it would fit in the trucks or barges commonly used to transport cattle in the area.

[1]

Furthermore, in this wilderness there was no aqueduct, drainage, electricity supply, or drinking water. The only access to the property was by river. The water can reach up to 30 degrees centigrade and humidity can reach 100 percent. In other seasons of the year, the temperature drops to 20 degrees centigrade and torrential downpours can last up to a week. This isolation, level of technical complexity, environmental fragility, extreme weather, and lack of a local workforce steered us toward assembling the building on site out of parts prefabricated in Medellín and Bogotá. At the same time, we also considered that the building could be disassembled at any time if necessary.

As a result, the construction was placed on a platform raised two meters above ground level for fauna to pass underneath. It also contained a landscaping system designed by Bas Smets, which displays plant and tree species as in a museum. Therefore, at the lodge visitors can become familiar with what they will see on their expeditions and explorations. The building manages water, purifying it in natural wetlands for treatment after its use and processing. The lodge's 3,500-square-meter roof has photovoltaic panels. The area around the hotel was reforested with native trees.

[2] The building is a large eave, a metal, almost vernacular structure where columns, beams, roofs, and handrails are expressed as a purely tectonic system of a large primitive hut: a building that allows direct contact with the surroundings while enjoying protection from the sun and the torrential rain.

The lodge has applied for a Living Building Challenge accreditation that certifies the proper management of materials and the work, and that the hotel and building operations are not only net zero but also regenerative.

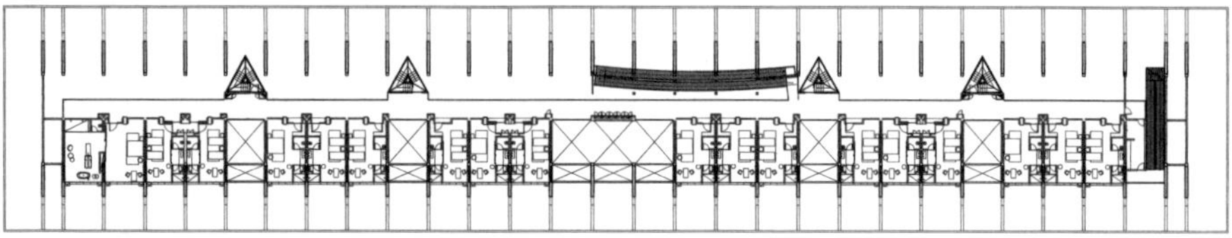

a.

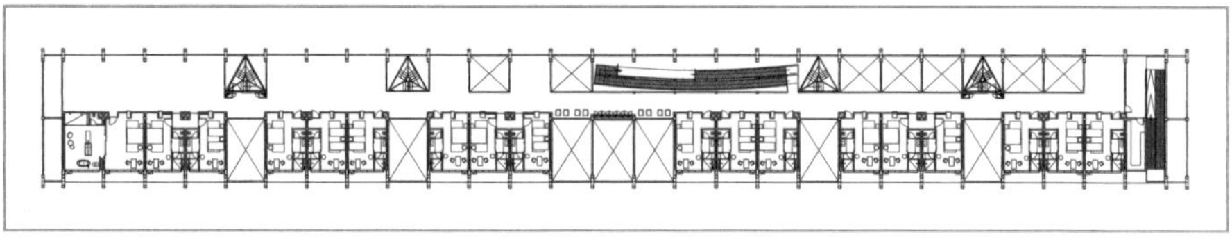

b.

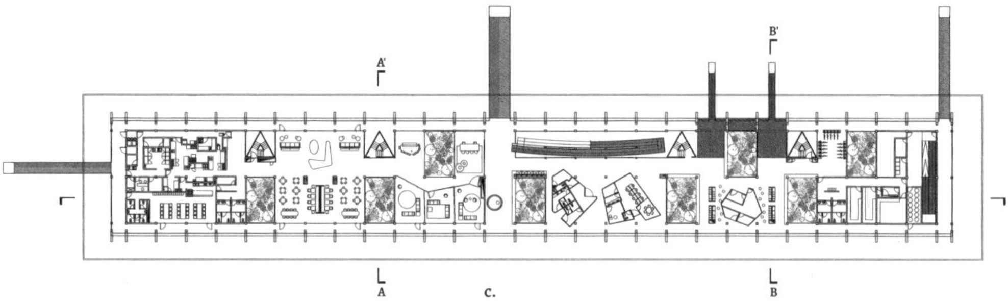

c.

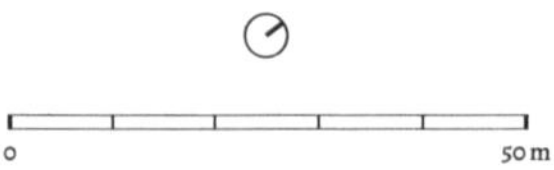

a. Level 2 plan
b. Level 1 plan
c. Ground floor plan

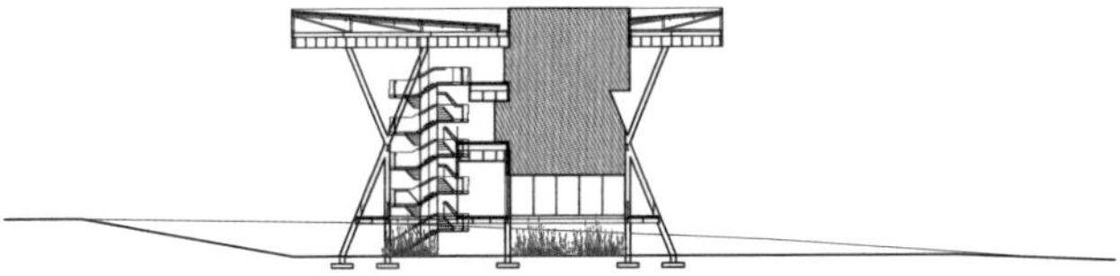

d.

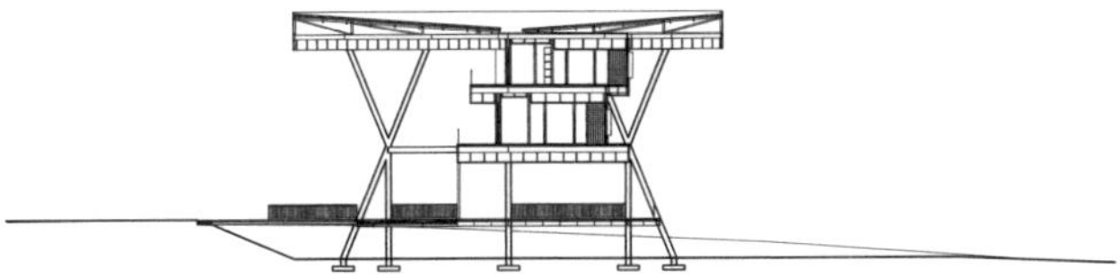

e.

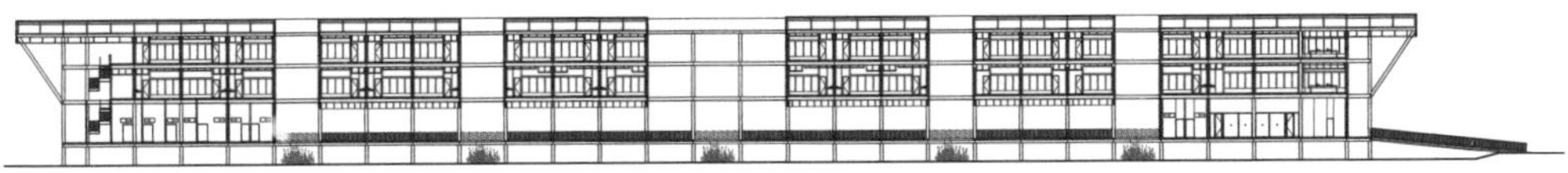

f.

d. Section A–A'
e. Section B–B'
f. Longitudinal section

El Higuerón Community Center (2017)
Shrine of Our Lord Of Tula (2017)

In association with Dellekamp Schleich

ARTICULATING OR INTERMEDIATE

The sudden and massive impact of Mexico's earthquake of 19 September 2017 was matched by the unexpected reaction of actors and agents of change, particularly in the municipal district of Jojutla in the state of Morelos. Despite vicissitudes, the collaboration between community leaders, supervising architects, visionary politicians, and the handling of the available techniques and conditions, all renewed hope in the midst of the chaos, supported by the transformative power of architecture. This offers an interesting case study of leadership and efficiency, teamwork, and the capability to respond through high-quality, enduring architecture well adapted to its social and climatic context that includes local cultural identities. In other words, a specific work of architecture for a specific location in keeping with broader discussions of what constitutes architectural culture today. The events not only made architecture a point of confluence for many forces and actors; its specificity and material condition also articulated long-term responses that go beyond what is urgent. In other words, it helps construct the social fabric based on what is community-based and shared.

The earthquake destroyed more than 2,600 homes in Jojutla, and left almost all public infrastructure—schools, plazas, the central church—in ruins. The design, management, and construction needed completion in record time: less than eighteen months. More than twenty different actors were involved in the decision-making process, including the National Institute of Anthropology and History (INAH), the National Workers' Housing Fund Institute (Infonavit), the municipal, state, and federal government, charitable organizations, NGOs, neighborhood groups, the local diocese and the Church. Given this scenario, many people considered it unnecessary to rebuild public works. Some demands to build privately even turned violent. Strategically, and thanks to the leadership of Carlos Zedillo Velasco, working at the time as director of Infonavit's Research Center for Sustainable Development (CIDS), resources and support were channeled through Hogares Foundation to rebuild public infrastructure.

This approach challenged the usual priorities for such interventions and disrupted the standard formula by examining the housing situation with support from technically qualified personnel before the implementation phase. This undoubtedly risky approach prioritized public projects over private developments. Moreover, experienced and knowledgeable architects were selected for specific projects that required and permitted the reconstruction of the social fabric ahead of residential projects.

Our team was commissioned to rebuild the Shrine of our Lord of Tula, a religious site with more than five centuries of history, and also El Higuerón Community Center, a park and library with a program for cultural workshops, administered and used by the community. Both projects, despite their differences in formal design, respond to similar ideas resulting from conversations between our studio and Dellekamp Schleich, our partner in both projects.

The urgency of the situation obliged us to use local and affordable materials and workforce, hence the decision to use concrete for both projects. Furthermore, the understanding of the social context and local climate encouraged us to consider typologies and models suited to the place and its opportunities. Therefore, the projects seek to build threshold spaces with blurred boundaries, making it difficult to tell apart the interior from the exterior. This ambiguity enabled occupation and a variety of uses.

El Higuerón Community Center

For the Higuerón project the spatial structure had to instigate a geometric and spatial order. The new construction needed to incorporate a pre-existing tortillería owned and used by the community; demolishing it was out of the question. The park, covering almost an
[1] entire block, called for a link between a fabric of public spaces, not just as the tree-filled area as it was before the earthquake.

To the rear—although this could also be understood as being to the front because it was on the route from the town center—there were already roofed sports facilities that we needed to connect to thc building.

[2] The center has an L-shaped layout, with the middle opened for people to be able to pass through and to connect with the sports facilities. On the shorter side of the L-shaped plan, we connected the tortillería by repeating the pattern of the structural portico. The need to make the structure porous in relation to the street, and the portico's solution to relate and link to the pre-existing construction, determined that the spatial system needed to be a precise grid around the perimeter. Once this grid was complete, the program was contained by setting it back from the structural perimeter and raising its level 1.20 meters above the park to create an expansive threshold, a useful intermediate space for retreats and concerts, somewhere to enjoy and share urban life.

The park, meanwhile, is structured in the same way by using a grid that introduces strips of endemic vegetation and living spaces, including a small children's playground.

[1]

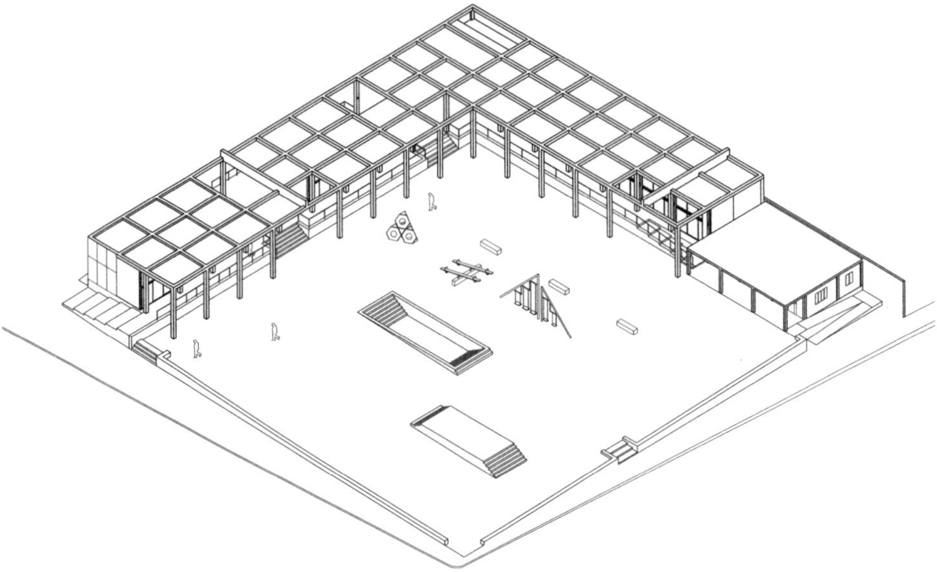

a.

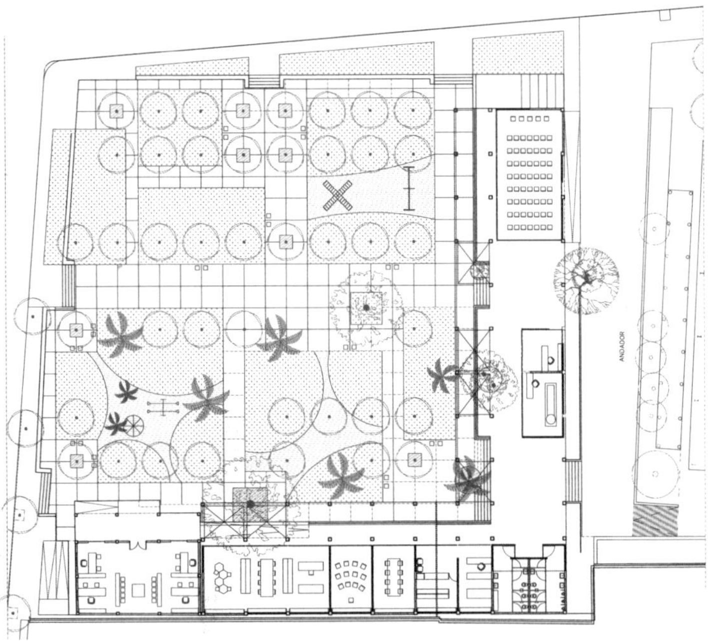

b.

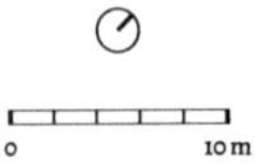

[2]

a. Axonometric
b. Plan

Shrine of Our Lord of Tula

After a natural disaster, it is normal to focus on housing reconstruction. In a surprising twist, Carlos Zedillo Velasco skillfully managed to steer the immediate reconstruction process of this municipality toward private developments. This was significant, because by prioritizing the collective we succeeded in restoring the social fabric for the community and in creating places where people could meet.

Based on this premise, we focused on the church's role as a public building before addressing its ceremonial function. Without ignoring this ritual aspect, our initial approach was to consider this role and the need to articulate and act in ways that would bring
[1–2] people together. As such, we cast our minds back to the Mexican typology of open chapels, particularly the one designed by Félix Candela in Cuernavaca in 1959 that itself was heir to a long tradition.

The chapel needed to be easily accessible, a simple canopy where air could pass through in a shaded and sheltered space. The chapel's
[3] plan is based on the classical cross-shaped basilica, while the elevation—both for the altar and the confessionals—is ordered and de-
[4] fined by curves. For the altar, a curved, 1.80-meter-high concrete wall contains the ceremonial area, while a sloping plane receives the reflection of the sun and the glow from the floor create pleasant lighting conditions. At the same time, when it rains the surface becomes immaterial thanks to the reflection of the water that creates an ephemeral mirror of the sky.

The section also plays an important role in defining the space,
[5–6] which is determined by a simple roof, supported at four points and unfurled as a structural concrete arch on the four sides. The floor plan slopes down gradually from the outside to the inside, ensuring a shelter by becoming detached from the exterior and also the space's possible use as an auditorium.

To emphasize this relationship built through the section, the choice of the flooring and roofing materials, especially with exposed brickwork, creates a sensation of continuity that not integrates the public space with the surroundings but also imbues an aura of warmth.

[1]

[2]

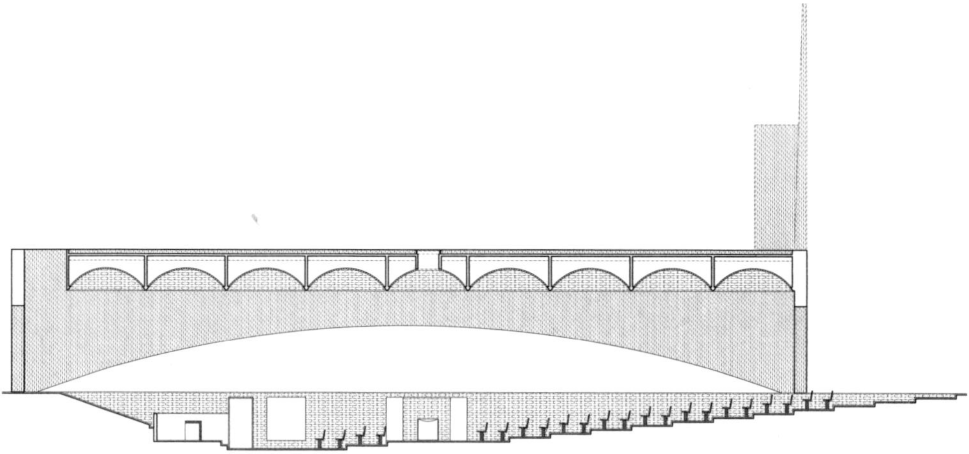

a.

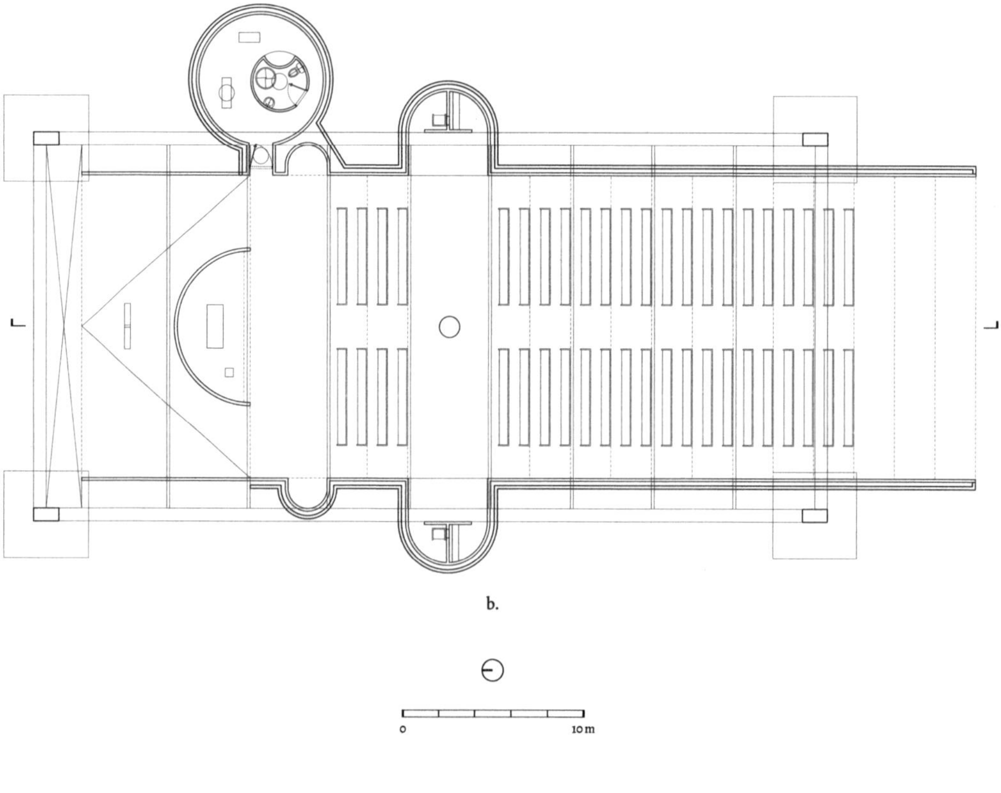

b.

[3]

a. Section
b. Plan

[4]

[5]

[6]

Santa Ana Mixed-Use Apartment Complex (2018)

ARTICULATING OR INTERMEDIATE

The Santa Ana apartment building articulates the city's urban dynamics and the comfort of tropical housing. The tower is located just a few blocks from Panama City's historic center, a neighborhood undergoing a regeneration process. By understanding the urban dynamics and making the most of the lot, which has entrances on both sides, we decided that the best way for incorporating the city within the project was to create a landscaped shopping passage that
[2] would benefit from the site's lush exoticism. The tower's first three floors are designed as public spaces and contain cafés, restaurants, bicycle parking areas, gardens, a gym and an area for coworking.
[3] The twelve upper apartment floors have three typologies measuring 45, 55, and 70 square meters. The residential floor plan has a typical vertical circulation in the middle and around the circulations, providing an entrance to the apartments. Each plan has ten apartments per floor, and the typologies offer residential solutions for single occupants as well as for couples and young families. The top floor has some complementary services, both for the apartment building's residents and for visitors; this area includes two restaurants offering spectacular views over the bay and the Panama Canal.

[1] The building uses terracotta-stained concrete, post-tensioned beams, and a series of GRC elements that can regulate the temperature and provide shade for the apartments' interiors. Every apartment has a balcony, giving local inhabitants direct contact with the surroundings.

[1]

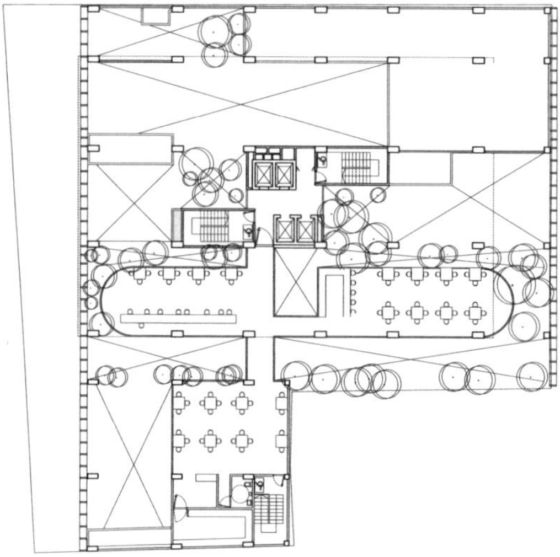

a.

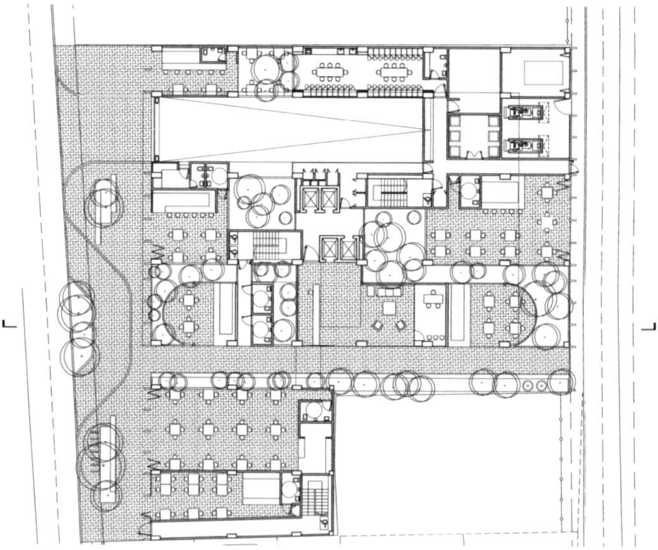

b.

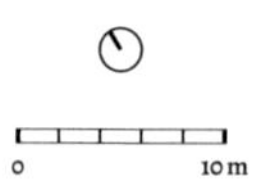

[2]

a. Mezzanine plan
b. Ground floor plan

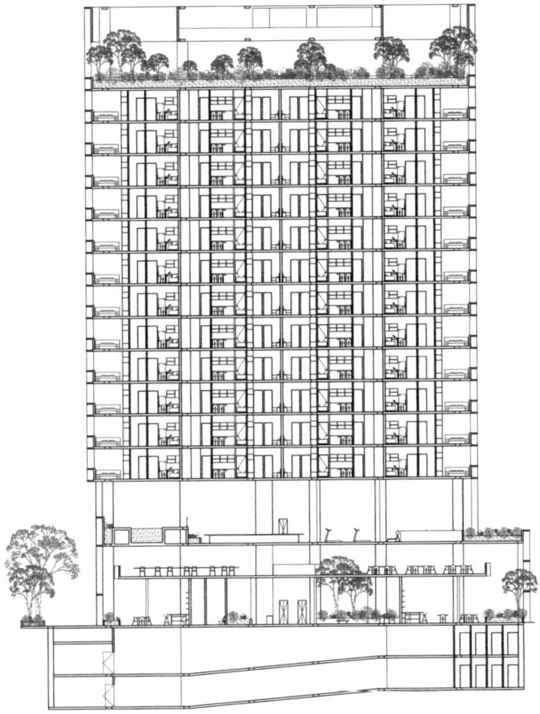

c.

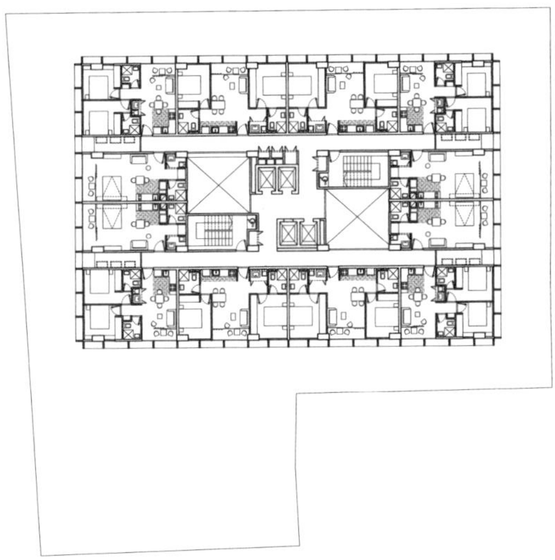

d.

[3]

c. Section
d. Typical plan

Garden of Earthly Delights (2019)

SPECULATIVE

The Garden of Earthly Delights is an architectural installation created in the Schindler House in the Mak Center, Los Angeles, United States, for the Soft Schindler exhibition curated by Mimi Zeiger.
[2] Our proposal is based on the social dynamic of the table of Mr. and Mrs. Schindler. Every Sunday, the couple opened their house for gatherings and parties. At these parties everyone would be drinking, eating, smoking, and dancing, since the substances, materials, and delicious drinks of the tropics were the perfect accompaniment for this invitation for socialization. Coffee, tobacco, linen, and cotton were omnipresent as silent witnesses to the various conversations, encounters and arguments, a simple backdrop to a non-neutral territory, beyond the domain of Mr. Schindler's masculine behavior or Mrs. Schindler's desire to mark the house with a feminine touch.

[3] We used linen and cotton as textile support to die various curtains with coffee beans, roasted coffee, tobacco, and dried tobacco. These substances are the materials used to provide a chromatic quality to the curtains, creating various hues of brown, red, terracotta, beige, etc. This atmosphere resonates with the colors and ambiences of the Schindler House.

[1] To inform the intervention's spatial logic we used gridlines taken from the Schindler House's floor which were later edited to create less of an absolute space and more a sensation of a tropical space of ambiguous experiences and layers derived from daily life; domesticities to create tension between the solid and the void, the hard and the soft, the wall and the curtain, which also departs from the neo-plasticist grid hidden in the plan.

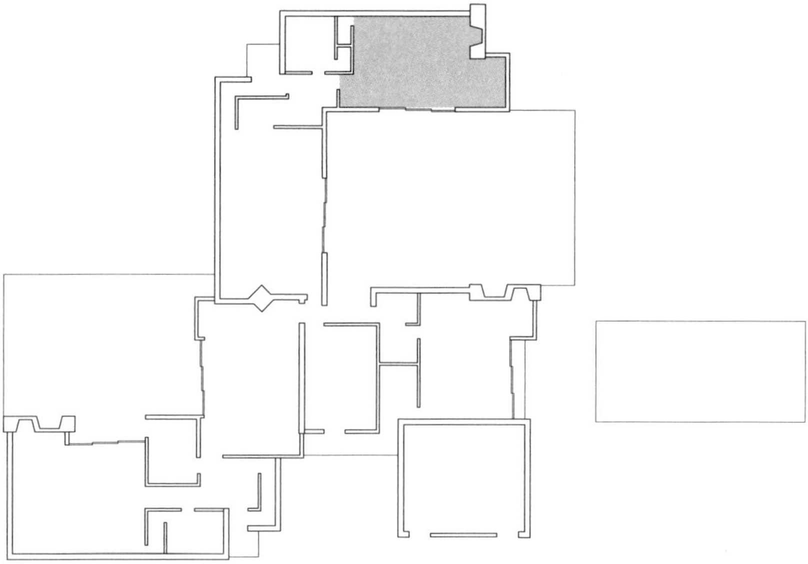

a.

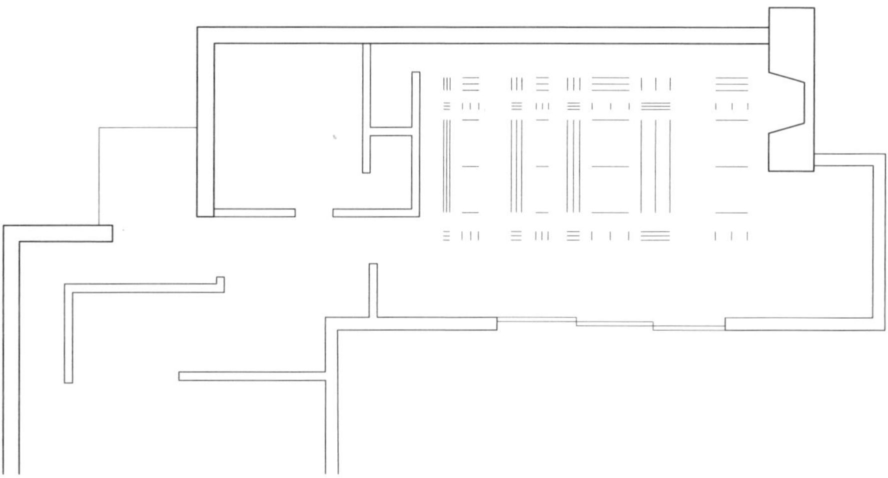

b.

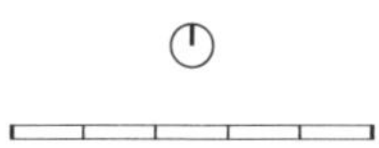

0 5 m

[1]

a. House plan
b. Project plan (gridlines selected for the curtains inside Mr. Schindler's studio)

[2]

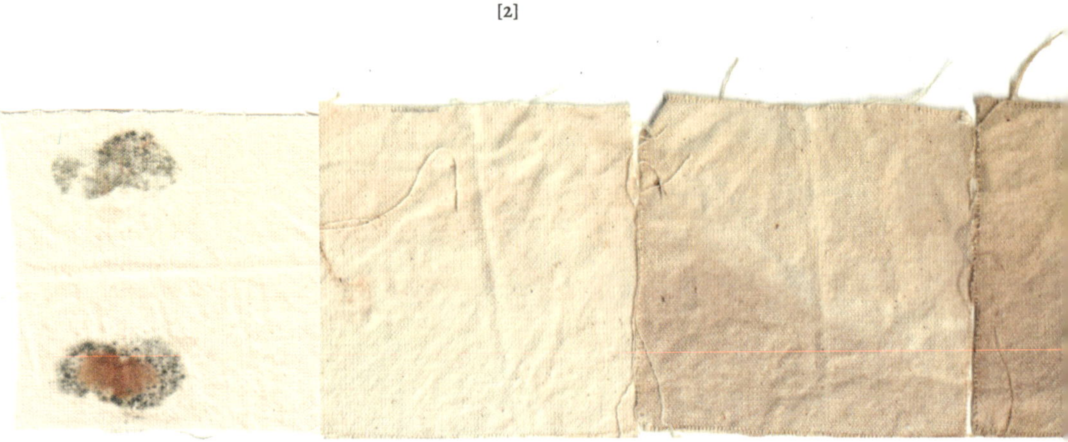

1. Cup of coffee	Coffee
2. Hand with cigarette	Tobacco
3. Tablecloth	Cotton / linen
4. Ash	Tobacco
5. Coffee pot	Coffee

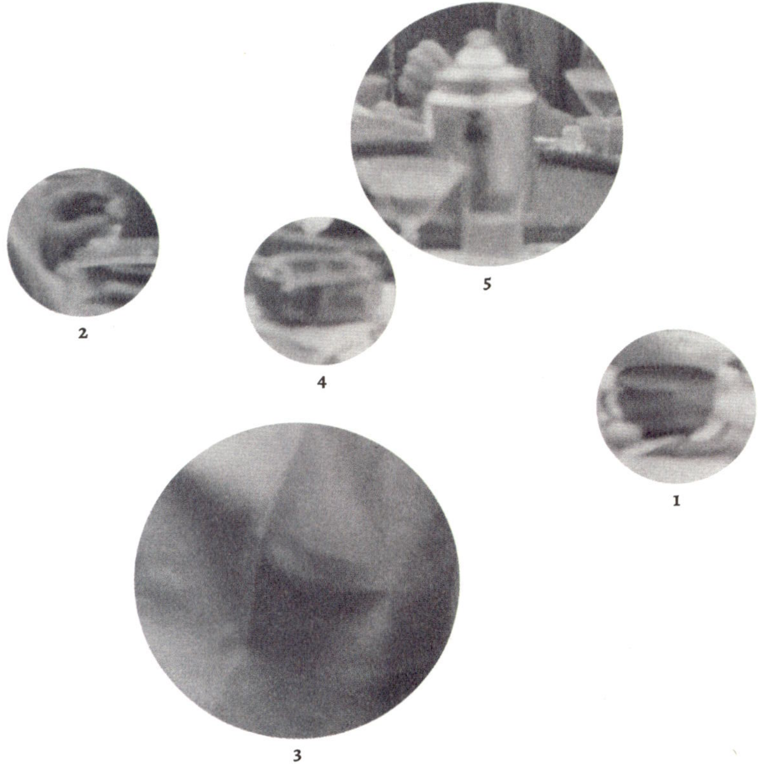

Textile Production Plant (2020)

ARTICULATING OR INTERMEDIATE

A family business that produces post-surgical girdles decided to build its new headquarters to increase the efficiency of its production and administration because it currently operates five premises in various areas. Given the product's complex sanitary conditions we needed to contemplate both the flow of inputs as well as the processes that organize the space. Considering this difficulty and the company's outlook over the next ten years, the factory has a skyscraper
[2] typology in order to concentrate, on the first third of a rectangular plan, the vertical circulation systems, thus freeing up the perimeters and façades on each side of the block. The five-story building, with a rectangular floor plan measuring 60 meters long and 30 meters
[1] wide, connects two busy industrial roads. The shorter façades receive strong sunlight in the morning and in the afternoon. The plot's depth gave us the idea of inserting two courtyards in the second (longitudinal) third of the plan, to provide cross-ventilation for the building's interior and an interior landscape of native vegetation that changes the atmosphere of the workplace. Understanding the project in the tradition of warehouses and factory buildings, we decided to use brick as a low-maintenance material that provides thermal insulation. On the north and south façades, the diagonally laid brickwork

[1]

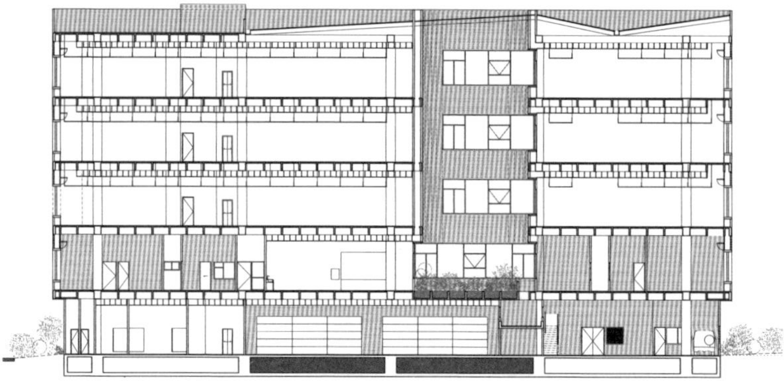

a.

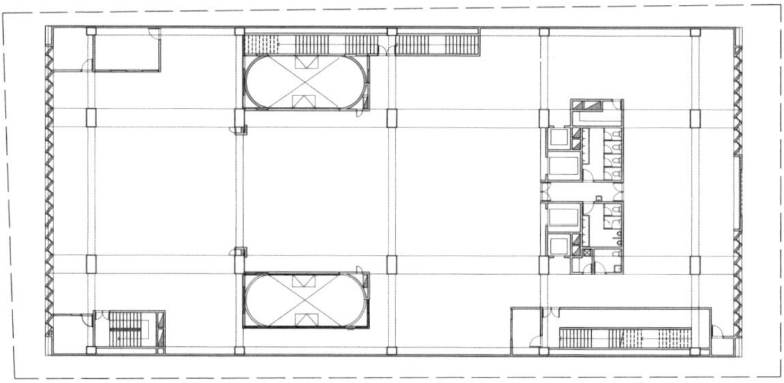

b.

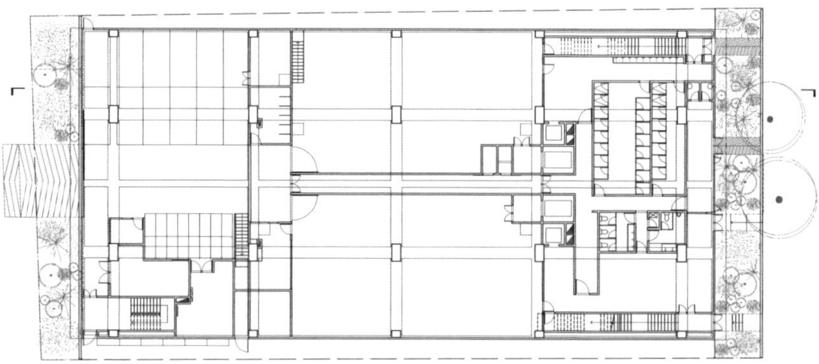

c.

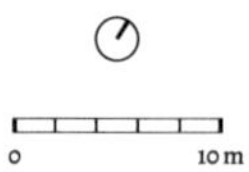

[2]

a. Section
b. Typical plan
c. Ground floor plan

creates a brise-soleil type saw-toothed system of panels and windows, which not only gives an industrial feel that fits in with the industrial context but also reduces noise and reduces solar gain without preventing the entry of natural light.

The building's design and choice of materials respond to the needs, awareness, and eagerness to certify the project as a low-energy and resource-efficient construction, earning it a LEED environmental certificate.

Pilares MX (2020)

In association with TO Arquitectura and +UdeB Arquitectos

ARTICULATING OR INTERMEDIATE

The Mexico City government announced an invitational competition to develop small community centers in various neighborhoods. The brief was to create specific programs depending on the demographics, needs, and vocation of the people in each of these neighborhoods. +UdeB Arquitectos (Colombia), TO Arquitectura (Mexico), and our own studio were each invited to design one of these centers. After discussions among the three studios, we decided that a collaborative approach was most sensible. Our primary concern was buildings' water usage given the lack of this precious resource in Mexico City. Therefore, our initial consideration for the three projects was to repeat a
[1] butterfly roof to harvest rainwater. Second, and in the understanding that we had to develop three projects, we sought to make the projects' structure and spatial qualities within the urban environment as something repeatable, requiring our projects to be considered as a system. According to these principles, we developed a spatial system where the structure is the form that defines and articulates the interior and exterior space, above all seeking easy access through urban connections as well as attracting visitors throughout the day. The structure combined pairs of slender panels of iron and wood, so that the space's permeability and definition were always connected to a thin membrane that was easy to read although with a diffuse interior space. Through this structural model we could provide the maximum flexibility to each space, anticipating changes in future uses and ensuring adaptability for various functionalities, as often happens in public buildings.

[1]

INBURSA

a.

b.

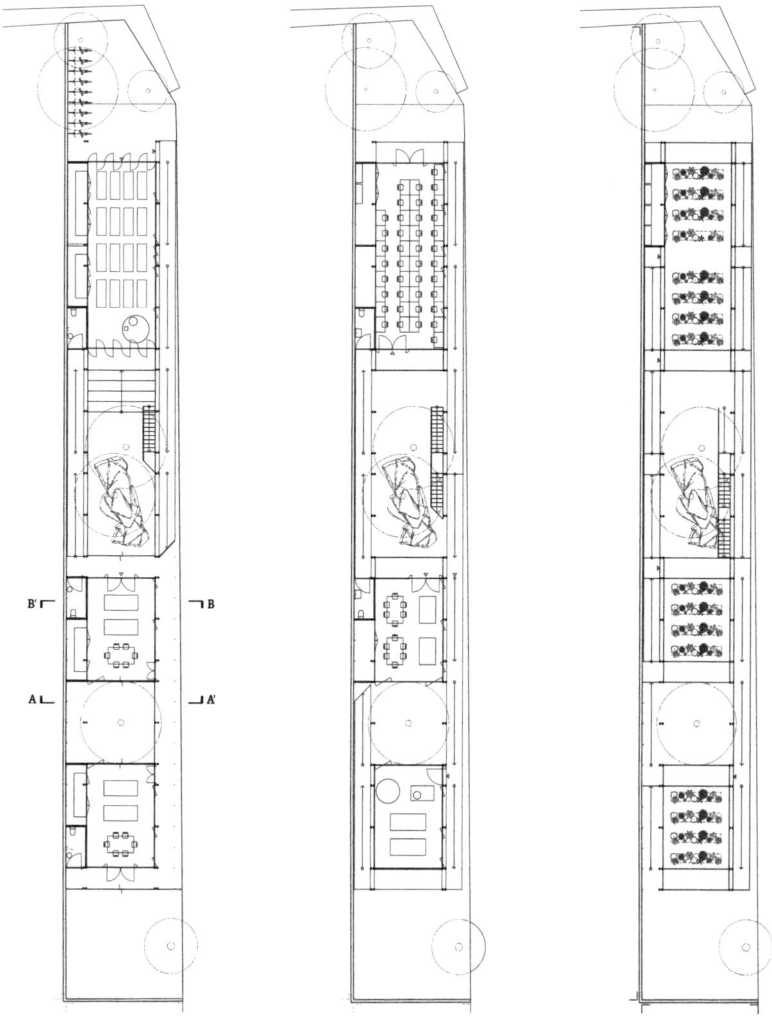

c.

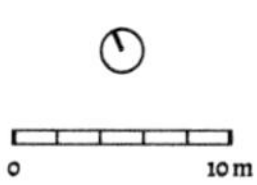

a. Section A–A′
b. Section B–B′
c. Ground floor plan, Levels 1 and 2

Epilogue

Camilo Restrepo Ochoa and Juliana Gallego Martínez

This book coincides with a set of ideas developed over the course of ten years' professional practice, thus concluding a period of strictly theoretical and critical introspection; the publication also accompanies the implementation of some of these material and spatial concepts through recently built projects and a wide range of conversations and collaborations with friends and colleagues.

The text and projects described focus on ideas and the commitment to a new understanding and practice of architecture, in territories where the eagerness to build and accumulate square meters of experience is considered the core purpose of this profession. We do not consider architecture solely as a purely commercial endeavor but something beneficial as a cultural instrument and a valuable resource for its content, rigor, and relevance.

An introspective approach with a capacity for self-criticism, deep reflections about our actions and ideas, and the temporary distancing from local architecture has led us to a certain ostracism that, from the perspective of this book's texts, has turned out to be incredibly productive. Apart from the COVID pandemic, a period of voluntary isolation gave us precious time to consolidate our ideas, and the opportunity to re-analyze and calmly reflect on projects built more than ten years ago. We refined a series of theories and conference transcriptions and compiled our various writings into a single but non-monolithic text.

As in any proposition, there are gaps that I hope we or others may open and close, following the discussions that this book has initiated and which we are very keen to hold. We accept that our positions are open to criticism. There is no alternative because it would mistake to live in an ideological straitjacket.

We hope that readers will experience the sensation of discovery and doubt. Our aim has also been to include more questions than answers and to offer some gentle illumination in this area of study already drenched in light by others, and that makes it possible to refer to other narratives.

After this effort, perhaps the moment has come to return to our immediate circle for a frank exchange of opinions, comments, and criticisms that this text will immediately instigate. We look forward to hearing and discussing the reactions of friends and colleagues—and of readers in general—to the book's ideas and projects. We also look forward to the response of those who have challenged us in our architectural work, with their questions and criticisms that are sometimes relevant and always welcome.

Although this book is slightly out of step with these times when readers are scarce, we passionately believe that without built projects, nothing can be proved, and without proof, evidence does not exist. Therefore, words scattered in the wind end up lost: they need material on which to stick in order to give them substance and traction.

The opportunities to approach the discussion from a different angle and to establish new perspectives through texts and built projects are those we can use to build something that patiently connects thought and deed. This approach hopes to secure the long-term future of our built work. Without physical proofs, we believe that architectural ideas are worthless. Ideas need to be tested, however flawed the outcome.

From this perspective, we are still only halfway toward our destination. So far, we are equipped with ideas, demonstrating some of them in buildings (with varying degrees of success) confident that we are participating in a broader-ranging conversation. In this way, we are keen to influence other people's ideas, and vice versa, through the teaching of architecture, writing, and building projects.

We hope that this may be the first of many of our studio's publications, which may reflect our (built and unbuilt) ideas, our critical gaze on architecture and on the shifting world around us. We hope that architecture may be the instrument to continue expanding and enriching our lives, helping us to continue adding friends in every discipline, of every age, wherever they live, and with whom we can hold conversations that lead to questions; friends who hopefully will help us learn about architecture and the world, but, above all, who teach us to enjoy what we do, both in the theory and practice of architecture.

Credits

AGENdA agencia de arquitectura
Juliana Gallego Martínez, Legal and Administrative Director
Camilo Restrepo Ochoa, Design Director

Current team 2022
Tatiana Colorado Mejía
Mariana Mejía Arango
Juan Camilo Ramírez Ortiz
David Soberón Restrepo

Collaborators in projects included in this publication
Julián Salazar, Paulina Vargas, Amalia Ramírez, Jorge Gómez, Juliana Ramírez, Felipe Walter, Manon Mollard, Erica Martínez, Flavio Medeiros, Leo Klis, Santiago Cadavid, Lina Gil, Catalina Patiño, Viviana Peña, Jorge Buitrago, Helen Winter, Camilo Toro, Hugo Restrepo, Hugo Herrera, Alejandro Restrepo Lalinde, Juan José Arbeláez.

Biographies

Camilo Restrepo Ochoa

Medellín, Colombia. 1974

Graduated as an architect from the Universidad Pontificia Bolivariana en Medellín (1997). Master's degree from the Universidad Politécnica de Catalunya, through the Metropolis program, and from the Centro de Cultura Contemporánea de Barcelona (2004–2005).

Design Critic at Harvard University's Graduate School of Design from 2013 to 2016, and from 2020 to date.

In 2022, guest editor of Japan's *a+u* magazine for a special "Colombia" issue, published in March that same year.

Nominated for the Mies Crown Hall Architecture Prize 2022 for the Gabriel García Márquez Public Primary School in association with J. Paul Restrepo, for the Shrine of our Lord of Tula, and for El Higuerón Community Center, in association with Dellekamp Schleich.

In 2020, *Domus* Magazine selected AGENdA as one of the world's top-fifty creative and influential studios in its list 50BEST.

Cemex Award 2021 for the best project in Mexico in the Social Value category, Shrine of our Lord of Tula (Jojutla, Morelos), in partnership with Dellekamp Schleich; the same project came second in the competition run by Fondazione Frate Sol (Italy) for the best church built in the world in the 2016–2020 period.

Frequent contributor to *Arquine* magazine (Mexico), *PLOT* (Argentina), and *NESS* (United States). Curator of *El trópico, los matices del asombro*, an exhibition held in Medellín, Colombia in 2021, organized by La Rambla reunión de artistas. Academic director of Ciudad Abierta, Festival of Architecture and Urbanism (Medellín, Colombia) in 2010.

Work and texts published in specialist magazines such as *Domus*, *2G*, *Abitare*, *a+u*, *Architectural Record*, *Arquitectura Viva*, *Summa*, ARQ.

Guest lecturer at Harvard Graduate School of Design, Columbia University, University of Virginia, McGill University, University of Buffalo, University of Chicago, Universidad Torcuato di Tella, Escola da Ciudade, BSA Basel, Centro, and invited professor at the Universidad

Torcuato di Tella in Buenos Aires, UCAL in Lima, Syracuse University in Syracuse, Universidad de la República in Montevideo, and professor at the Instituto de Arquitectura Avanzada de Cataluyna (IAAC) in Barcelona.

His works have been exhibited at the Chicago Biennial 2017 *Make New History*; LIGA DF, Mexico City, 2017; MAK Center Casa Schindler, Los Angeles, 2019; and at the Galería Albarran Bourdais, Madrid, 2021.

Mark Lee is Chair of the Department of Architecture and Professor in Practice at GSD. He is also a principal and founding partner of the Los Angeles-based architecture firm Johnston Marklee. Since its establishment in 1998, Johnston Marklee has been recognized nationally and internationally with over thirty major awards. A book on the work of the firm, entitled *House is a House is a House is A House is a House*, was published by Birkhauser in 2016. This followed a monograph on the firm's work, published in 2014 by 2G.

Mark has taught at the Harvard Graduate School of Design, Princeton University, the University of California, Los Angeles, the Technical University of Berlin, and ETH Zurich. He has held the Cullinan Chair at Rice University and the Frank Gehry International Chair at the University of Toronto.

The firm's work is in the permanent collections of the Museum of Modern Art in New York, the Art Institute of Chicago, the Menil Collection, the San Francisco Museum of Modern Art, the Carnegie Museum of Art, and the Architecture Museum of TU Munich.

Together with partner Sharon Johnston, Mark Lee was the Artistic Director for the 2017 Chicago Architecture Biennial.

Special Acknowledgments

To our current team of architects, financial administrators and accountants, for their commitment and professionalism, but above all for their human qualities, for always being ready to learn, to listen to our views, and to help put into practice our architectural ideas and approaches.

To Cementos Argos, in particular Tomás Restrepo Pérez, Juan Enrique Navarro, and Rodrigo Quintero, for promoting a culture of architecture and for believing in its transformative power, and for supporting this book, which would not have been possible without their trust and support.

To Miquel Adrià and Andrea Griborio from Arquine, for encouraging us to develop a book after many years of publishing silence and for trusting in this kamikaze project. Without their feedback, guidance, and leadership, we would not have embarked on the adventure of publishing an almost entirely text-filled book in this era of the image. To Brenda Soto, for coordinating the publication process, and to David Kimura and Gabriela Varela for their impeccable and exceptional graphic design for the book. And to the entire Arquine family for making this book happen.

To Mark Lee, for his generosity and commitment by agreeing to contribute a text, and for his support at Harvard University's Graduate School of Design by inviting me to be Design Critic (2020–2021).

We also owe a debt of gratitude to our associates on various projects: JPR Arquitectos, Plan:B Arquitectos, Derek Dellekamp, Jachen Schleich, Carlos Facio and José Amozurrutia of TO Arquitectura, +UdeB Arquitectos, Ricardo Vásquez of Estudio Transversal, and Carlos Zedillo for his enormous generosity in opening the doors for our projects in Mexico. Also, to Ignacio Mallol of Mallol Arquitectos in Panama.

To our clients, for their trust in allowing us to introduce notions of Tropical architecture and specific ambiguity into their lives.

To Johana Bojanini, for her support and work in the impeccable, precise, and stunning graphic and textile design work for the LIGA DF and MiesUnderstandings projects.

To Camilo Echeverri, for his attentive eye and power of observation that reveals aspects that help us discover new things about our work, and for his involvement, along with Camilo Echavarría, through an insightful and artistic gaze in generously collaborating on the MiesUnderstandings project for the Chicago Biennial of 2017, *Make New History*.

Our special thanks also to Sandra Pérez-Nieto, Cristóbal Palma, Federico Cairoli, and Rafael Gamo, for their extraordinary photography of our work.

Author's Acknowledgments

This book would never have gotten off the ground without Juliana Gallego Martínez's patience and support. Her eye for detail and generosity were essential in encouraging me to write and redirect my ideas. I also thank her for reviewing the text several times, and for managing the publication process.

I could not omit to mention all those with whom I have regularly held conversations in recent years, and without whose points of view these ideas could never have emerged: Felipe Mesa, Miguel Mesa, and, in particular, Felipe Uribe de Bedout—my neighbor who received my visits, resolved my doubts and read new versions, and whose perspectives brought many of my ideas to fruition.

My thanks also to Iñaki Ábalos, Ricardo Bak Gordon, Salman Craig, Emanuel Christ, Christoph Gantenbein, Simon Frommenwiler, Kersten Geers, Simon Hartmann, Wonne Ickx, Sharon Johnston, Janet Kuo, Mark Lee, Eric Lapierre, Sergio López Piñeiros, Carles Muro, Rahul Mehrotra, Paul Nakazawa, Florencia Rodríguez, Renata Sentkiewicz, and David Van Severen for so many conversations, exchanges, and learning experiences, but above all for generously opening the doors into their worlds without expecting anything in return.

This book is dedicated from the depth of my heart and with infinite gratitude to my family. To my father, J. Paul Restrepo Santa María, the best, most generous, and understanding partner you could imagine; thank you for showing me the way of architecture. To my mother, Jacqueline Ochoa Uribe, for clearly showing the virtue of patience; to my sister, Carolina Restrepo Ochoa, for helping me to understand life's processes and to believe in ideas different to one's own.

And finally—again—to my wife, Juliana Gallego Martínez, for enduring a relationship and an existence obsessively mediated by architecture, and for gracefully and willingly accompanying me on this adventure.

Images Credits

Camilo Echeverri: pp. 175, 199–201.
Cristóbal Palma: pp. 185, 192, 193, 196–197.
Federico Cairoli: pp. 251–253, 256–260, 262–263.
Florilegius / Alamy Foto de stock: p. 136.
J. Russell & Sons, Postal "Crystal Palace. The Grand Nave" (1910): p. 60.
Jaime Navarro: pp. 348–352, 354, 355.
Jean Pierre Crousse: p. 119.
Josep Lluis Sert Collection. Courtesy of France Loeb Library. Harvard University Graduate School of Design: p. 73.
Luis Gallardo: pp. 281, 282, 284, 285, 288–289.
Rafael Gamo: pp. 309, 311–315, 318–319, 321–323.
Reprography of the drawing "Caribbean Hut" in Gottfried Semper, *Four Elements of Architecture* (1851): p. 66.
Reprography of the illustration "Outline of Botanical Geography, The Distribution of Plants in a Perpendicular Direction" in Alexander Keith Johnston, *The Physical Atlas of Natural Phenomena: Reduced from the Edition in Imperial Folio for the Use of Colleges, Academies and Families* (1850): p. 65.
Reprography of the allegorical engraving of the Vitruvian Primitive Hut (Charles Eisen) in Marc-Antoine Laugier, *Essai sur l'architecture* (1755): p. 58.
Sandra Pereznieto: pp. 317, 324–327.
Sergio Gómez: pp. 163, 167, 170–171.
Staatliche Museen zu Berlin, Neue Nationalgalerie / David von Becker: p. 74.
Taiyo Watanabe: pp. 338–339.
The Josef and Anni Albers Foundation / Artists Rights Society (ARS), New York / VG Bild-Kunst / SOMAAP, Mexico City, 2022: p. 114.

On Specific Ambiguity Through the Idea of Tropical Space or the Reasoned Practice of Transitional Forms

First edition, 2022
ISBN 978-607-9489-92-2

Ámsterdam 163 A
Colonia Hipódromo, 06100
Ciudad de México
arquine.com

www.arquine.com

Directors and editors
Miquel Adrià, Andrea Griborio

Editorial director
Brenda Soto Suárez

Editorial assistant
Ana Luz Valencia

Translation
Quentin Pope

Design
Gabriela Varela + David Kimura

Prepress
Emilio Breton

AGENdA AGENCIA de ARQUITECTURA — TALENTO CREA COLOMBIA CREA — ARGOS

On Specific Ambiguity was printed and bound in August 2022
by ShenZhen TianHong Printing Co., Ltd., in China. It was
set in typefaces of the Alegreya and Atlas Grotesk families and printed
on 80 gsm Enso Classic paper. The print run was 1,250 copies.